MUSICAL LANGUAGES

For information about permission to reproduce selections from this book, write to
Permissions, W. W. Norton & Company, Inc., 500 Fifth Avenue, New York, NY 10110.

The text of this book is composed in 11/13 Fairfield LH Light
with the display set in Felix Titling MT at 65% horizontal scale
Desktop composition by Gina Webster
Manufacturing by The Maple-Vail Book Manufacturing Group
Book design by Margaret M. Wagner

Library of Congress Cataloging-in-Publication Data
Swain, Joseph Peter.
Muscial languages / Joseph P. Swain.
p.   cm.
Includes bibliographical references (p.   ) and index.
ISBN 0-393-04079-8
1. Music and language. I. Title.
ML3849.S83   1997
780'.04—DC20   96–38351
CIP

W. W. Norton & Company, Inc., 500 Fifth Avenue, New York, N.Y. 10110
http://www.wwnorton.com

W. W. Norton & Company Ltd., 10 Coptic Street, London WC1A 1PU

1 2 3 4 5 6 7 8 9 0

MUSICAL LANGUAGES

JOSEPH P. SWAIN

W · W · NORTON & COMPANY

NEW YORK   LONDON

FOR JOEY, GREGORY, CINDY,

AND THEIR MOTHER

CONTENTS

PREFACE

"How is music like language, and so what if it is?" is a succinct if some-what truculent way of summarizing the content of this book. To elaborate a little more generously, it is a book that shows how deeply all we have learned about spoken language from modern linguistics and cognitive psychology can explain our experience of music, and thereby seeks to revive and renovate the analogy of music and language, to make the ubiquitous expression "musical language" seem fresh, precise, intellectually respectable, and useful for the critical writing in which it most often appears.

Musical Languages was originally imagined to be the opening chapter or section of another book about the nature of musical style; now it must be a prolegomenon to that future project. The points of comparison between music and speech grew to be too many for a single chapter, for I have tried to develop the analogy for as many of the essential qualities of language as seemed appropriate: phonology, syntax, semantics, pragmatics, metaphor, learning languages, how languages evolve, and how they are communal, among other things. This breadth, I believe, is one thing that distinguishes this treatment of the analogy from some famous predecessors, in particular Deryck Cooke's *The Language of Music* and Leonard Bernstein's *The Unanswered Question*. Such breadth practically guarantees a certain cursory quality to the enterprise, since each of these topics, as linguists know, is huge in itself. So there is no intention here of giving the final word on musical syntax or musical pragmatics, to say nothing of semantics, but many of these linguistic approaches have never been applied to music before, and I hope that readers will find the convergence of various kinds of comparisons compelling.

Writing on such a broad topic means that certain fundamentals have to be explained from time to time, for the reader who already knows the difference between a phone and a phoneme may not know the difference between just and equal-tempered tuning, and vice versa. On such occasions I ask the reader's indulgence. Important terms and concepts are explicated as they appear, and there is a glossary for quick review. Otherwise I have tried hard to supply all the essential knowledge that readers will require. The exception is familiarity with standard common-practice harmony, whose ramifications are too complex to introduce here beyond the outline of Roman numeral analysis in the Appendix. However, the arguments and examples where this familiarity is prerequisite are few, and even in those cases I believe the main points can be clearly understood, if perhaps not all the evidence for them.

I hope the readership will be as broad as the topic: musicians, music historians, and theorists, of course, but also people interested in language, perception, cognition, meaning, and poetry. Yet above all I have written the book for music lovers, those who enjoy reading about music in the hope of enlightening their appreciation of it.

I thank with deep gratitude a number of those music lovers at Colgate University who freely gave their time by reading parts of the book that concerned their own areas of expertise: Peter Balakian of English, Jerome Balmuth of Philosophy, Alexander Nakhimovsky of Computer Science, and my friends Joscelyn Godwin and Dexter Morrill in Music and Adger Williams, linguist. I also thank most gratefully the Research Council of Colgate University, whose grant of a Senior Faculty Leave in 1995 greatly expedited the completion of the book; Michael Ochs, music editor at Norton, whose quick interest gave me encouragement; and the editors of *Music Analysis*, *The Musical Quarterly*, and *The Journal of Aesthetics and Art Criticism*, who allowed me to use substantial portions of my published articles in revised form. Extraordinary thanks I owe to my good friend Dan Brown, sometime Cornell musicologist, now poet and Systems Engineer at IBM, who read all the chapters and whose telling comments and questions initiated important revisions at many points.

JOSEPH P. SWAIN
HAMILTON, NEW YORK
JANUARY 1997

MUSICAL LANGUAGES

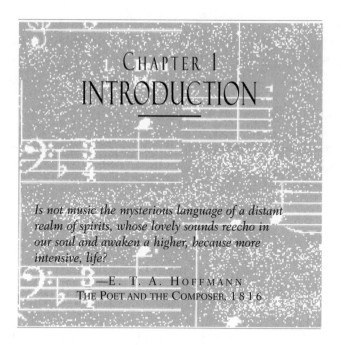

CHAPTER 1
INTRODUCTION

Is not music the mysterious language of a distant realm of spirits, whose lovely sounds reecho in our soul and awaken a higher, because more intensive, life?

—E. T. A. HOFFMANN
THE POET AND THE COMPOSER, 1816

Hoffmann asked this question at a moment in history when the image of music as a kind of extraordinary language had reached a peak of sympathy. The intimate association of music and language, chiefly in the form of poetry turned to song, had been recognized, of course, since the ancient days. For the Greeks the very word *mousike* connoted not merely pretty concatenations of tone but all poetic and imaginative uses of language. Renaissance thinkers argued over the proper relationship between words and music in vocal pieces, and these polemics satisfied the most pressing aesthetic questions as long as vocal music continued to hold the artistic high ground it had known for centuries as the only serious kind of music making. But by the eighteenth century, when the concerto, sonata, keyboard suite, and, eventually, symphony and quartet had successfully challenged the preeminent status of vocal music, these abstract genres found aesthetic justification in the idea that music itself was a kind of human language, first in Charles Batteux in 1746, who described it as a language of the heart, and then later in Rousseau, who believed that music began as a chant signifying both thought and feeling, a unified expression that only later broke apart into normal speech and instrumental music.[1] Instrumental music was a special rhetoric that, like all rhetoric, persuaded and compelled its hearers. Hoffmann's question is itself rhetorical because it only asks what most took for granted.

After Hoffmann came harder times for music as a "language of the heart" or of anything else. Eminent critics and aestheticians, such as Eduard Hanslick and Susanne Langer, and finally composers, such as Stravinsky, and many a modern serialist right down to the present have dismissed the analogy: music has no definite meaning as words have, it is incapable of translation, and besides, composition is about the manipulation of abstract sonic relationships, much better off without the baggage of meaning and convention that so weighs down spoken language. The most explicit attempts to invigorate the analogy—by Deryck Cooke, who offered a semantic profile of Western music in *The Language of Music*, and, most improbably, by Leonard Bernstein, who applied Chomsky's generative grammar to musical analysis in his Norton lectures at Harvard—were scorned so often and so pointedly that their contribution ended up providing only more fodder for the cannons of the opposition.[2] The skeptics seemed so right at a time when almost all theoretical and critical writing about music concerned itself with "structure," brushing aside the ancient problems of expression and communication as either insoluble or unworthy. After all, that tones are free from worldly associations is the triumph of musical art, allowing its composers the greatest creative powers of imagination and design. Why corrupt such a beauteous thing with the messiness of natural language?

But an idea that proved compelling for so long, even when cast as a metaphor, is hard to kill off, and like some phoenix risen from ashes, the idea of music as language has been revived, revitalized by new sources of insight. Among these are a new generation of composers who admit "expression" to be among the powers of music; the musical semiotics of Jean-Jacques Nattiez; and, above all, the growing mountain of evidence from the cognitive scientists that suggests fundamental affinities between the very cognition of music and language. The idea is back, indeed, and there is some doubt as to whether it was ever really gone, for its traces can be seen everywhere in musical discourse from the most casual to the most revered. Perhaps concepts such as cadence, meter, and period have enough technical precision in them to justify their complete translation into musical terminology from the rhetorical, but such terms as "phrase," "theme," "rhythm," and many others are surely so foggy that they can be useful only as live metaphors of language, metaphors indispensable to any musical discussion. The more general metaphor of musical language is ubiquitous, and yet the depth of its meaning is virtually unplumbed. Then there is "musical syntax," an explicit analog with modern linguistics, finding a highly respected, though ill-defined, theoretical standing in the most learned circles.

Yes, the idea was there all along, barely concealed beneath the surface of abstract theorizing. Since musicians had been for so long entranced by "structure," it was perhaps only natural that formal theories of linguistic syntax were the first to be adapted in the 1970s and 1980s. Then the theory of signs, semiotics, promised to create a new "science" of musical meaning. But late twentieth-century advances in language and music perception have outdone anything else to make a renewed analogy of music and language really worthwhile, allowing more and better comparisons that yield more and better insights into the nature of both. For that is the desired end. Whatever the specific causes, the idea of music as language has returned to favor because the analogy is too persuasive, too rich in comparisons and images to do without if we want to talk about music and its experience in depth and detail.

Comparisons and images are indeed the main point here, for the argument is unabashedly analogical, and they are the stuff of it. I am not out to prove that music is in fact a language, or even a special kind of language. Rather, the analogical argument sets out to show as many essential similarities as possible in order to make reasonable, plausible, and even compelling judgments about music based on the facts of linguistic experience. There will always come a point at which an analogy will "break down," as the saying goes, no matter how clever or insightful. If it didn't, then it wouldn't be an analogy at all but an identity. What matters is not whether it breaks down but where. What are the depth and nature of the essential similarities of music and language? And the essential dissimilarities, too, should not be forgotten or ignored, for analogy instructs by finding difference as well as sameness. Seeing where music and language part company can be just as important to the understanding of each, individually, as knowing how they act alike. As for the explanatory power of models and metaphors, only the most straitjacketed of formalists would deny it. After all, the natural sciences, so often held up as the *ne plus ultra* of modern intellectual inquiry, use them all the time, and not just to talk down to the poor, muddled public but as actual components of theories. Why? Simply because they can work so well. If fruitful, the analogical inquiry can have abundant and practical benefits for musicians, too: new premises for theory, new illustrations of musical effect, new ways for the critic to convey with exactness the elusive, if not ineffable, thing called musical experience.

The kinds of comparisons to be promoted in this book can be glimpsed in a short analysis of the very sound materials—the "phonologies"—of music and language. Here is where the analogy begins. While all the arts can lay claim to certain properties of expression and symbol, and therefore meaning, only music is made of the same medium as speech: the ephemeral sound sequence, here one moment and gone the next, present thereafter only in imperfect memory. "The findings of acoustics," writes Joscelyn Godwin, "compel one to admit the surprising fact that every time one hears language, whether sung or spoken, one is unconsciously perceiving an intricate melody of high harmonics." Indeed it is true that the physical aspects of sound that enable us to distinguish the consonants and vowels—frequency formants, onset transients, energy shifts over time—are the same ones that distinguish the instruments.[3] But the similarity goes much deeper than that, of course, since there are many sound sequences in the world that are neither music nor language in any but a metaphorical sense. Music and language are sequences made up of discrete, ordered parts, hierarchies of sounds: syllables, words, phrases, and sentences or notes, chords, measures, phrases, tunes, and so on up. They have structure, built from basic units in a fashion so logical that comprehending and learning them comes as second nature. Yet the similarity goes deeper still, for this well-worn image of discrete units and logical orderings is, for both music and speech, a mirage.

The spectrographs below and on the facing page offer snapshots of the physical world of music and speech.[4] The neat chemistry of linguistic and musical atoms combining into higher compounds is scarcely to be found.

SPECTROGRAPHS OF MUSIC AND SPEECH

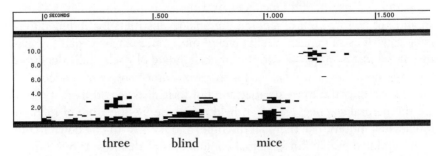

three   blind   mice

This graph shows the acoustic output of the author pronouncing "three blind mice" at normal speed. The relatively high energies of the vowels can be clearly discerned in the three columns (notice, though, that the two /i/ sounds are not acoustically identical), but the consonants generally blur into one another because of co-articulation (see main text, below). The [s] fricative of "mice" can be observed in the little cloud to the right at 10 khz.

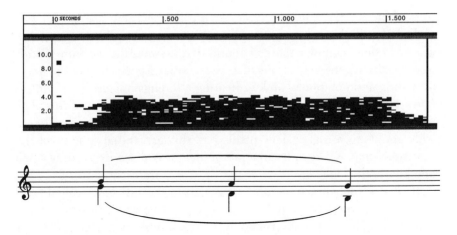

This graph shows the acoustic output of Adger Williams, linguist, and the author playing a two-part version of "Three Blind Mice" on violin and viola at approximately the same speed as that of the spoken version. The scale is the same as in the first graph. Most of the energy is concentrated in the lower frequencies below 4 khz.

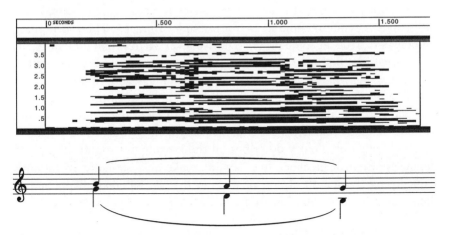

When the scale of the previous graph is enlarged, as it is here, the harmonics of the pitches, and to some extent of the three chords, become discernible, but the picture is still far more complex than our intuition of three two-note chords of one beat each.

Speech sounds and notes are indistinct, syllables and notes run into one another like watercolors. And yet, how real are these concepts, how strange and difficult it would be to talk about music or speech without these "things" that supposedly constitute them! There are in fact two realms of reality for music and speech, the acoustic and the perceptual. The incredibly complex mass of sound that assaults the eardrum distills into the simple, discrete atoms that we so faithfully reflect in our systems of writing and notation. Think of hearing a foreigner speak, how continuous the speech seems, how impossible it is to isolate single words. The experience of hearing a foreign music is much the same; we aren't sure what counts as a "note." The distillation, this perceptual analysis of the acoustic signal, is a cognitive operation that occurs effortlessly only when one knows the language.

It occurs, though, with a ruthless, cut-and-dried efficiency called categorical perception.[5] At some level, linguistic perception is blissfully oblivious to all the fine gradations and even acoustic blending that might, for example, occur between the low vowels [æ] as in "fat" and [ɑ] as in "father."* Despite the general awareness of Southern drawls and Midwestern twangs, when our hearing encounters the rapid onslaught of speech, all low vowels are instantly "categorized" as [æ] or [ɑ], and despite the subtle pitch inflections that singers and violinists might use to color their melodies, despite the gross differences in instrumental color, notes in melodic cognition come in as, for example, E♭ or E♮. There is nothing in between. True, at some other cognitive level we hear bad intonation, as some might be bothered by drawls and twangs, but that occurs by virtue of recognizing what a "good" instance of a pitch category should be.

Phonologists have recognized this distinction between the acoustic and the perceptual reality for a long time and refer to it as the phonetic/phonemic distinction. Phonetics describes all linguistic sounds in an objective manner, while phonology describes all the meaningful sounds of a given language. English speakers, for example, make no systematic distinctions concerning the length of consonants, so that if somebody happened to linger over the [m] sound in summer, the meaning of the sentence

Summer is coming.

would suffer no change. If an Italian speaker, however, were to do the same to the sentence

Saremo a casa stasera. We will be home this evening.

it might well be understood this way:

* Bracketed symbols are those of the International Phonetic Alphabet.

Saremmo a casa stasera. We would be home this evening.

The difference between the future and conditional tenses for first-person plural verbs in Italian is made by the length of the [m].[6] So phonologists say that English may have several phonetic versions of [m], several *phones* of [m], but only one *phoneme* /m/, whereas Italian has two phonemes, short /m/ and long /m/. To put the shoe on the other foot, consider that Japanese has only one consonant somewhere between the English pair [r] and [l], which is why, when native Japanese speakers learn English, they make a lot of errors confounding those sounds. Until they train themselves, they simply don't hear any difference.

The same phenomenon can occur when classically trained musicians begin to listen critically to jazz. Certain notes sound out of tune to them, because the classical tradition makes hard categorical distinctions for every half-step division of the octave, so that F is always distinct from F♯. In blues traditions, though, these two acoustic points may be melded into a single "blue" note. It is not that jazz musicians play or sing out of tune; rather, they simply have a different phonemic inventory, as the phonologists would say, a different concept of what counts as a proper note. Serial composers, using Arnold Schoenberg's method of composing with twelve equivalent tones, have yet a different view, since for them the functional meaning of each tone within the octave is absolute. There is no distinction between F and E♯. But now consider Example 1.1 from Beethoven. This is one of the truly magical moments of this concerto, where the solo violin, having achieved and sustained the dissonant F, the seventh of a V⁷ chord in C major, after a big virtuosic flourish, full of tension, mysteriously resolves it *upward* to F♯ while the bass sinks to

Example 1.1. Beethoven, Violin Concerto, I. mm. 295–299.

another F♯ four octaves below. The gesture makes sense only when the listener realizes retrospectively that Beethoven has reinterpreted the F♮ as an E♯, a factor in an augmented sixth chord that wants to rise, sharpening a conflict of F♮ and F♯ that Beethoven has established from the beginning of the movement.[7] But that means there is a cognitive difference between E♯ and F♮; otherwise, "reinterpretation" would make no sense.

What, then, are the units of music and speech? The tempting response—notes and phonemes—puts the acoustic and perceptual realities against each other in a curious tug of war. The acoustic reality would indicate higher-level units, such as syllables or melodic-harmonic fragments. After all, English speakers can easily process thirty phonetic segments per second in listening to normal speech,[8] and a thick orchestral passage could present that many notes. But that is far more than we find in any other kind of auditory perception, enough to produce a low hum, if indeed those were individual acoustic events. The perceptual reality would prefer lower-level units, since some constituent parts of notes and phonemes are easily perceptible. Musical notes have at least two independent constituents, pitch and duration, to say nothing of metric stress, or more subtle factors such as the power spectrum of formants that color the pitch, the acoustic shape or "envelope," the kind of attack, and the length of decay. Phonemes, too, have constituent "features." The phoneme /p/ is a bilabial, unvoiced, stop consonant, while /b/ is a bilabial, *voiced*, stop consonant. Hearing the voicing makes the difference.

But as the grain gets finer and features become more precise and plentiful, some essential similarities seem to disappear. Clarinet notes are surely distinct, both perceptually and acoustically, from violin notes, but then how can we claim that they ever play the same "notes" together, as in Mozart's Clarinet Concerto? What about octave equivalents? If all possible atomic constituents were taken to be absolutely distinctive, then Western music would have thousands of notes in its inventory, a picture far more complex than intuition about our musical "system" suggests. Speech, too, has acoustic equivalents of octaves and instrumental colors in music, for every individual speaker has a unique voiceprint and accent, but these are routinely dismissed as inessential noise in favor of some overwhelming likeness of language. Here the attitude toward music is quite different. Listeners can "overlook" the difference in color between clarinet and violin to equate, on some level, the sounds they are making, but it is never dismissed. On the contrary, such differences are highly prized. Lately, phonologists have become interested in higher-level sound qualities such as stress and intonation. These aspects, long familiar to musicians, of course, complicate the phonetic picture and force phonologists to use multilevel models of various features, much as music theorists have done in referring to metric structure, pitch structure, and so on.[9] Thus, the theoretical image of both musical and speech phonologies approaches that of the spectrographs, an image that reveals various components related in such complex and multilevel ways that the impression is one of continuity, not discreteness. Curiously, that image does not do away with the psychological and practical value of the things, the discrete notes and phonemes and their most obvious constituents.

It is also curious that, despite the potential for a wealth of sounds, individual natural languages and musical traditions restrict themselves to a relatively small number of sounds. Since the work of Roman Jakobson, linguists have classified these sounds as sets of binary oppositions in various dimensions: voiced or unvoiced, lips round or not round, tongue high or not high, and so on.[10] There are enough dimensions to make hundreds of different sounds, yet individual languages have inventories far smaller. English is content with about forty. Musical languages, too, have inventories, but they are largely scalar, not binary. Along the dimensions of pitch and duration, certain values become distinct. The inventory for Mozart has twelve pitches per octave, out of at least a hundred that could be perceived, and about five basic durational values in strict proportions, but Josquin has eight pitches per octave and rarely more than four durations. Completely banned from all languages are laughs, whistles, and other vocal products that are simply deemed to be nonlinguistic.[11] The world of music, too, despite the great efforts of John Cage and other postwar composers to open up the inventory, refuses to consider "musical" very many sounds that are not tones.

Classical phonologists and certain schools of abstract music theory have seized upon sound units—phonemes and pitch classes, generally—as logical primitives, sounds without meaning, arbitrary, upon which complete syntactic and semantic systems may be devised. In other words, the sounds of French have no meaning or value in isolation, and neither do the notes of the Dorian mode. Only when they are combined into the systems we call French and Dorian music do they acquire meaning and function. There is without doubt an attractive neatness about this conception, but, alas, it cannot account for certain surprising facts.

Acoustic spectrophotography of speech has clearly shown that the production of any phoneme is affected by those that precede and follow. This is why there is no simple correspondence between the marks on a spectrograph and its constituent sounds. While the word "have" contains the phoneme /v/ in most cases, in the following sentence

I have to go now.

particularly when spoken rapidly, /v/ is realized as its voiceless cousin [f]. So, in comic strips and other less exalted writing the rogue spelling "hafta" usually appears. The conversion occurs because the vocal tract is getting ready to pronounce /t/ in the next word, which is a voiceless consonant. If the voicing does not "turn off," /t/ will come out [d], and usually the voicing cuts out prematurely to ensure that this does not happen. This extremely common phenomenon, called co-articulation, does not impair listener comprehension in the slightest, but it does imply that sound items cannot operate in a completely primitive manner, from the ground up, since this systematic deformation takes nothing away from the meaning of the utterance. Indeed, it is not even noticed.

Any instrumentalist knows that this kind of distortion is endemic in musical art. Every instrument has its spots, from the "break" in the clarinet to the string crossing of a violin to the shift of the whole hand on the keyboard, that introduce deformities or inconsistencies in the sound production. But here is a significant difference between musical and linguistic phonology. Speakers are largely unaware of the effects of co-articulation and, since comprehension goes on unaffected, do nothing to control it, whereas musicians spend countless hours practicing to eliminate its deforming effects. The breaks, crossings, and shifts, which are physical consequences of the instrument just as co-articulation is a physical consequence of the mouth, are made to disappear.

In addition, it is not true that isolated sounds are absolutely bereft of meaning, as good primitives should be. If the instrumental color of a musical note is part of its phonology—it is hard to see how it could not be—then meaning must be part of it too. Who would deny that a saxophone note has immediate connotations of one distinct sort and an organ note an entirely different sort? Countless choices in orchestration rest on such connotations, from the string instruments that represent angels in Baroque oratorios, to the trumpet that stands for Siegmund's sword in Wagner's *Ring*, right on down to the bassoon quartet that plays the theme music for a television show about a humorous curmudgeon of a British barrister. The obvious parallel in speech is selective intonation and stress, pure sound qualities that stand utterly independent of a language's lexicon and syntax, which apparently follow systematic rules that phonologists are just beginning to understand. More surprising is the occasional influence of phonemes themselves on words, the things that are supposed to be arbitrary, completely free to take on assigned meaning. Consider the following list:

slack	slave	sloppy	slum
slag	slay	sloth	slump
slam	sleazy	slouch	slur
slander	sleet	slovenly	slurp
slap	slick	slow	slush
slash	slip	sludge	slut
slattern	slobber	slug	sly
slaughter	slogan	sluggish	

Although there are exceptions such as "sleep" and "slumber," the English consonant cluster *sl* seems to be characteristic of pejorative words. The sounds in a word sometimes affect meaning after all. That is why advertisers on Madison Avenue are paid well to "design" new product names, and indeed, semanticist David Cruse remarks that "a new breakfast food marketed under the brand name of *slub* would stand little chance of success."[12] Shakespeare might well agree, since his line "Slubber not business for my sake, Bassanio"[13] is a warning against doing business in a hasty or slipshod manner. The cluster *gl*, as in "gleam," "glow," "glitter," "glimmer," has the opposite effect.

Mere conventions are these trumpets and *sl* sounds? Probably so, but not being "naturally" meaningful diminishes their power not a bit. Such conventions preclude even isolated sounds from primitive status, and that is the issue.

Co-articulation and meaningful phonetic combinations such as *sl* hint that a characteristic found pervading other aspects of language invades its most fundamental sounds as well: the influence of context, the linguistic environment, or what the psychologists call top-down processing. Perhaps the blow most crushing to the appealing but illusory model of language comprehension from the bottom up, from simple sounds to syntactic sentences, was the discovery of phonemic restoration. Experimenters substituted noise for the /s/ in a recording of this sentence:

> The state governors met with their respective legi*latures convening in the capital city.

Not only did listeners claim to have heard the /s/, but they could not locate the one phoneme they were told was missing. In the following drill:

It was found that the *eel was on the axle.
                                                    shoe.
                                                    orange.
                                                    table.

listeners heard "wheel," "heel," "peel," and "meal" in order to complete the sentence in the most sensible way.[14] Phonologists speak of "grammatical conditioning"—modification of a word stem in accordance with its function in a sentence, as in the choices between "knives" and "knife's" or "wives" and "wife's."[15] In music, again, it seems all important to experience the entire sound, which is why we will tolerate noise in the background of a conversation but not a concert; even so, there are illusions that are reminiscent of these phonological effects. Chords with factors missing retain all their harmonic function if the preceding context is set up carefully, as in the Beethoven example, and what is commoner than the kind of imitation shown in Example 1.2? As usual in a fugue, the imitation of the subject is not precisely strict, and yet the answer is

Example 1.2. J. S. Bach, Fugue in B minor, Well-Tempered Clavier I, mm. 1–5.

routinely taken as a faithful copy of the subject. As in "legi*latures," the deformation goes by unnoticed, and, if asked, most listeners would be hard pressed to identify where it occurred. In music as well as in speech, listeners understand what they hear, but they also hear what they understand.

Even though this tour of the phonological correspondences of music and language has been brief, it has already uncovered the three most important leitmotifs that will characterize this exploration of the analogy between music and language. The first of these marks what is perhaps the most decisive and consistent break in the analogy: music's preference for sound over meaning compared with speech's preference for meaning over sound. When communicating with the spoken word, listeners will take as a matter of working conditions all manner of background interference, competing conversations, inconsistencies of pronunciation, and, to a point, syntactical errors, as long as the message gets through. On the other hand, most music lovers would prefer not to listen to music at all if they must contend with even mild background noise; listening to two pieces at once is out of the question, and what might be called "syntactical" errors are tolerated only with forced smiles in amateur performances and not at all in professional ones. Most of a performer's energy is devoted not to the communication of some musical "message," whatever that might mean, but to the perfection of the sonic medium itself: accuracy, intonation, ensemble, and quality of tone are what consume rehearsal time. Still, these are but characteristic priorities of speech and music, not irreconcilable destinies.[16] Most musicians will admit that the "meaning" of what they compose, perform, and hear, however imprecise, is not only important but an essential aspect of the art. And we do from time to time admire not only what a speaker has to say but the way it is said, and fluency, intonation, tone, even regional accents have aesthetic qualities.

These sounds, whether phonemic or tonal, are never understood as isolated events that are strung together to make speech and music. Rather, every sound is heard in a contextual background, so that the listener takes an active and essential role not only in figuring out the grammatical function of the sound but in the very identification of the sound. This is the second leitmotif: the pervasive and uneliminable role of context in perception. "Context" in this broad sense covers useful information from the sound's environment, such as its source (a colleague or a stranger on the telephone, the cello or the violin section), its social circumstance (the workplace or the train station, a jazz club or a child's recital), and any visual cues that help in identification (movement of the lips, motion of the violin bow). It also covers all the knowledge—grammatical, semantic, episodic—that a listener brings to bear on the interpretation of acoustic signals. Finally, it covers the contextual relations of the signals themselves, how the sounds affect one another both physically and cognitively. These context relations produce perceptual "circles," feedback loops that psychologists divide into "bottom-up" and "top-down" paths. The curious instance of "legi*latures" showed how preceding information formed a context that determined the comprehension of *, an acoustic signal, even though that context itself was made up of acoustics signals (see figure below). It appears to be a logical paradox that listeners interpret incoming sounds in part with information brought by those sounds themselves, but we are not dealing with logic, rather perception. Context is an irreducible part of that perception.

MODEL OF PERCEPTUAL FEEDBACK

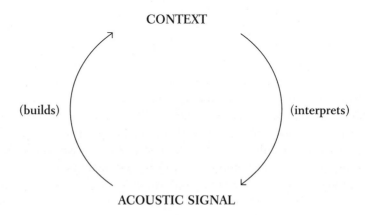

CONTEXT

(builds)   (interprets)

ACOUSTIC SIGNAL

That the "higher" levels of context are always interfering with the "lower" levels of phenomenal perception means that all attempts to separate cleanly the various linguistic and musical provinces of study are doomed. The stance of classical phonology was that the laws governing sound relations in a language are independent of the laws governing syntax, on the next level up, and certainly independent from those of semantics, up in the linguistic penthouse. But the *sl* group clearly carries meaning in English, along with its rules of combination, so that the semantic power has crashed through the floor of syntax right down to the sounds themselves.[17] Perhaps it is an unsuspected benefit of the entire analogy of music and language that cooperation among the various interests of sound, structure, and meaning will be enforced, for we shall see time and again that the linkages among these general aspects are strong. This is the third leitmotif.

But however powerful and insightful such linkages might be, there is no getting around the fact that linguistics is built on the central topics of phonology, syntax, and semantics. If a powerful and insightful analogy between music and language is to be constructed, it must begin with these elements.

The most useful correspondences between music and language in phonology have been surveyed here. In the following two chapters we will take up the fundamental matters of musical syntax and musical semantics.[18] Context, having already made its appearance, will continue to be an important character in those discussions—so important, in fact, that I have included a summarizing retrospective, especially since "contextual studies" has become a buzzword of recent criticism and critical theory. Contextual perception in music and language, and some speculation about its significance for music theory, are the main concerns of chapter 4. At this point in the analogy we can afford to explore other aspects of language and their usefulness for music. A special kind of language called poetry might afford the closest analogy in many ways, particularly in the construction and meaning of metaphor—a suggestion made in chapter 5. I then introduce the notion of artificial languages as a consideration in the problem of twentieth-century musical aesthetics (chapter 6) and consider the evolution of languages, a perennially fascinating topic in music even if it has taken a back seat in linguistics (chapter 7). Finally, I will summarize these accumulated ideas comparing music and language and attempt to crystallize the metaphorical term "musical language" (chapter 8). We will see that musical language is judged to be distinct from musical style, with which it is often confused and employed synonymously. Indeed, the concept of musical language provides a foundation for a theory of musical style still to come.

The evidence, assumptions, ideas, and conclusions throughout the book rely very much on the notion of perception. The point of view taken, most of the time, is that of the listener, whether music or speech is at issue. Only what the listener can perceive is capable of effect. [19]

The defense of this perspective is a complicated affair,[20] but let us clear away two common misconceptions right away. I do not take "the listener" to be any particular "ideal" or "perfect" listener as chemists theorize upon an ideal gas. The particular qualities and capabilities of a listener are part of the context of listening, so crucial to the end effect. But a theory is interested in explaining not every individual's experience but the significant shared experience, shared among the members of a musical or linguistic community. Naturally, communities and listeners vary, according to times and places and tastes, from the novice to the expert, but the intersubjective agreement among their members is within the reach of a general statement, and it remains only to specify which community is doing the listening.

Mistrust of "perception" arises, too, when musicians interpret that word much more narrowly than I intend here. "Perception" is too often taken to be limited to the immediate, reflexive kind, thus excluding all kinds of reflection, score study, and other modes of "long-term listening" that might be practiced by performers and composers. That is by no means the whole picture of perception. Surely other kinds that cause one to say "I've never heard it that way before" are legitimate perceptions if only because they bring about a new state of awareness. If music and language perception is broadly conceived as any kind of cognitive "awareness" of stimuli, their relations, and their effects, then there is no reason to exclude perceptions that result from repeated listening or extended study, or, indeed, the perceptions of speakers, performers, and composers—who are really specialized kinds of listeners. A perception gained after twenty seconds, or twenty hearings, or twenty years of composing, is still a perception.

CHAPTER 2
MUSICAL SYNTAX

How can someone detect mistakes in performance even when hearing a piece for the first time? This "wrong note" phenomenon is indeed remarkable. For one thing, it needn't require a superb musician; often enough, not a musician at all. For another, it is a highly variable phenomenon. Wrong notes seem most glaring in Bach and Mozart, which is perhaps why performers regard them as among the most treacherous of assignments. They are harder to hear in thickly scored Romantic music, and in serious music of the twentieth century most wrong notes escape undetected, even by trained musicians. One might be tempted to think, therefore, that hearing mistakes is just a matter of acoustic consonance and dissonance. As everyone knows, Mozart's music, the picture of grace, controls dissonance to a high degree whereas modern music is awash with it, and so picking out which dissonances are the wrong ones becomes an impossible task. But the situation is certainly more complicated than a simple judgment of acoustic consonance, for there are many, many moments in Mozart and Bach when the most extreme dissonance sounds absolutely right, where a more consonant sonority would be the mistake.[1] Then again, even in that transparent music the situation is not always black and white. Some errors stand out like sore thumbs, others merely raise a questioning eyebrow, still others get away unapprehended. What, then, allows listeners to make such a variety of precise and complex judgments without the experience of hearing the music even once before?

The linguistic concept that begins to address the wrong note phenomenon is syntax.

Of all concepts borrowed from linguistics for thinking and writing about music, syntax has enjoyed the most prominence, particularly in theoretical writing of the late twentieth century. Indeed, while in general the analogy of music and language has taken a beating, the unabashed use of "syntax" as a technical term has only increased steadily.[2] First put to extensive use by Hugo Riemann in his book *Musikalische Syntaxis* of 1877, a description of chord progression in Western music, the term now embraces almost any kind of abstracted relationship among musical phenomena in a composition, and one finds it in a wide variety of sophisticated musicology.

Most of the time, "syntax" retains the general sense of relations that hold between items such as syllables and words in the sound stream, and it is this sense that is presented in encyclopedias and introductions to linguistics.[3] Here the connotations of "musical syntax" are not much more specific than those implied by its original Greek meaning: *syntaxis*, "arrangement." In such cases, "musical syntax" alludes to low-level or local relationships such as hold between notes and chords and phrases, and it is probably preferred to the more traditional "musical structure" only because that term often connotes large organizations in a way that syntax does not.

The popularity of the concept in theoretical writing is not hard to understand. The primary issue for music theory since about 1950 has been the issue of "structure."[4] Since linguistic syntax involves the idea of relations among sound items that are spoken, and since "relations" is fundamentally tied into notions of structure, the link is quite natural. Both language and music appear to create structures in a real-time stream of sound. In fact, when Noam Chomsky's generative grammar seemed to have elevated exactly that part of linguistics into a "science" in the late 1950s, just at the time when both logical positivism and serial composition with the twelve tones were reaching their high-water marks, the adoption of "syntax" by musicians was probably inevitable. But when we adopt "musical syntax," are we getting anything more than a modish synonym for "musical structure"? What does the concept of musical syntax really imply?

WHAT IS SYNTAX?

Modern linguistics, having made the notion of syntax attractive to musicians, is now divided on exactly what the idea should entail. In the hands of generative grammar, syntax, as an independent system within a language, is a formalism that can describe all the well-formed sentences of that language, analogous to an equation such as $ax + by = c$, which can produce all possible straight lines. Chomsky's idea of a finite number of rules able to generate the infinite variety and number of sentences, many of which are utterly original, remains powerful and attractive to musicians. Serial composers took the notion of syntax as a completely independent system to heart, so that "languages of the musical and visual arts" could be free "from the constraints of conventional norms and syntactical and lexical formation and association."[5] It governs Fred Lerdahl and Ray Jackendoff's important *A Generative Theory of Tonal Music*, which describes the syntax of traditional art music of the eighteenth and nineteenth centuries. The generative system of rules provides an explanation of the wrong note phenomenon: listeners intuitively sense a violation of the rules, the "grammar" of the music, in the same way they can spot a grammatical error in a sentence they had never heard spoken before.

Functional linguists, on the other hand, think that a syntax independent of all other aspects of language is an inadequate conception. Language is more than a mathematical generator. "Language is viewed as a system of human communication, rather than as an infinite set of structural descriptions of sentences."[6] This conception of syntax retains the idea of generative syntactic rules as part of a person's linguistic competence but contends that they can be bent by the immediate context of a real conversation. Knowing how to interpret syntax according to the speaker's intention and tone of voice, the listener's relationship to the speaker, and other "extralinguistic" matters is just as much a part of someone's linguistic competence, and indeed completes it. An analogous notion of musical syntax underscores the importance of extramusical reference, emotional content, expression, social usage, genre, historical origin, and other semantic aspects that seem so crucial to deep musical appreciation, even if they are not the whole story.

So, musical syntax is a concept that could explain a great deal. The generative idea provides for compositional constraints that listeners can hear and appreciate—otherwise there would be no sense of wrong note—at the same time that it guarantees limitless freedom in the number and variety of pieces that can be realized within those constraints. Functionality, for its part, takes into account the real world of music, the contextual aspects of performance, use, and interpretation.

But neither conception of syntax, generative or functional, translates neatly into musical terms—not, at least, in a way that retains its powerful linguistic features without bringing in a lot of unwanted hangers-on. "It is no easy matter to define grammar such that it is sufficiently general to cover all those phenomena that are clearly grammatical while not engulfing everything that has any systematic properties at all."[7] Bringing over the generative concept of syntax as an infinite set of sentences, for example, means that the term "sentence" must be generalized somehow, since music has no sentences. But if we expand "sentence" to mean any kind of "relationships" or even "well-formed" relationships, according to some set of rules, then suddenly the world is full of syntax. Does a traffic light have syntax, for example? How about the signals of a basketball referee? They do convey messages, after all. Perhaps chess has syntax, since it has a set of rules that characterize a virtually infinite set of well-formed games. A baseball game, a social occasion, dance? "At what point do we limit our definition of syntax, and what will this limit buy us?" as Curtis Roads asks, is a difficult question indeed.[8]

WHAT IS SYNTAX FOR, ANYWAY?

Linguists have pretty much taken syntax as a fact of life, a condition of all natural languages. But why should this be? What does syntax do for languages that is so essential? Does music do something analogous?

As a thought experiment, imagine a natural language without syntax, a language with only sound items, say phonemes, combining into lexical items, or words. What would such a language be like? First of all, it would have a tremendous burden of vocabulary, for there would have to be a different lexical item not only for all the objects, states, actions, and other semantic features we need to express but also for each category of usage. A different word for "house" as subject, "house" as object, "house" as prepositional object, a different word for "speak" for each grammatical person, for each voice, and for each mood would be required, just to take two examples, two words that would turn into dozens. And each of these words would have to be essentially different, sharing no more relationship than membership in the language, and certainly nothing like a common root as in Latin declensions, since any such connection would be a form of syntax.[9] Second, a language without syntax would have no ordered patterns in its utterances. Function words such as "a," "of," "to," all those articles and conjunctions that telegraph the linguistic pattern, have to go. So the speaking order of the enormous vocabulary is random. The consequence? A tremendous information load for the listener trying to grapple with incoming speech.

There are some systems of communication, such as the traffic light and the signals of the basketball official, that have such characteristics, and they have no syntax. When the official calls a foul, he might make three signals: one to identify the number of the guilty player, one to show the type of foul, and one to indicate how many shots. Each signal is unique and their order of presentation affects their meaning not in the slightest. But note how limited this finite language is: the number of possible messages is perhaps something on the order of two hundred, a trifle in comparison to the expressive power of any natural language.[10] Poverty of information is the exorbitant price of a communication system without syntax.

Syntax controls the flow of information in two ways. According to the everyday sense of information as "communicated knowledge," syntax allows a manageable amount of required vocabulary, remembered in the form of lexical networks, in which the items have both semantic and syntactic relations with one another, rather than an impossible list of discrete items having only a semantic dimension. The price here is precision of meaning: words have multiple meanings and multiple roles in the syntax. (Just think of all the meanings and grammatical uses of "running," to take one example: noun, verb, and modifier.) In the more technical sense of information as calculated probability, syntax crucially reduces the randomness of elements in the incoming sound stream. Function words having little or no meaning by themselves indicate what sort of word follows. Isn't this one real purpose of gender agreement in languages, as when the utterance "la" immediately rules out half of all French and Italian nouns? Isn't this why we strain to understand the foreigner whose English syntax is fractured? Syntactic rules heavily constrain the order of items in general, organizing words into phrases or perceptual "chunks" that can be further ordered in a hierarchical system.[11] Even the aesthetics of poetry recognizes the necessity of controlling information: "For if Landor was right in thinking that images in a poem must be 'spaced', then if the poet abandons the spacing he can get by syntax, he has to find some other means. Eliot and Pound find typography. . . ."[12]

So information control is obvious. The monster lexicon of the thought experiment, however, shows upon reflection a more subtle contribution, too, for the experiment not only inflated the number of words but changed what words would have to do, changed the very nature of the lexical item. Consider the following simple sentences:

The boy hit the ball.

The ball hit the boy.

The sentences contain the same content words—"boy," "hit," and "ball"—and yet, of course, the difference between the two means rather a lot to the boy. The only way to account for the difference in meaning is in the syntax: in this case, the word order. Our vocabulary words don't have to contain meaning about all the *relationships* they might entertain with other words, as they would have in the thought experiment. Some of that information is left to syntax to express. If the semantic aspects of content words express things, actions, and states in the world,[13] the syntactic relations among those words convey the relations among those things, actions, and states. Syntax expresses relationships among lexical items that mirror relationships in the world.

Consider some slightly more complicated examples.

Susan changed the tire on Phil's car.

The tire on Phil's car was changed by Susan.

Here we have two sentences whose "main" meaning is the same, and it is the achievement of generative grammar to show that the "deep" syntax is the same for both, thus mirroring the sameness of meaning. But it is also true that the change of surface syntax inevitably brings about a change in emphasis, which changes the relationships among Susan, Phil, and all the rest and therefore the meaning, however slightly. The first sentence is the more neutral in intention, the simplest statement of fact. The second would be called for only in a particular context, perhaps to emphasize to the listener that it was not Phil who changed the tire. If syntax is inextricably tied to relationships "out there," then it is inextricably tied to meaning. The slightest change in the syntax, however superficial, changes something in the meaning, however small.

Psychologist Roger Brown suggests that children's perceptions of relationships in the world and their mastery of syntax are concomitant events, perhaps different facets of the same thing:

What makes us think, when the Stage I child produces two or three words in succession, that he intends to express certain relations between or operations upon ideas? Why should we not suppose that he is simply naming in temporal succession various aspects of a situation as these aspects attract his notice, without meaning to relate them in any particular way at all? . . . The most important reason for thinking the child intends relations is the fact that his words are produced in a particular order and that order is almost always appropriate to the relation that is suggested by the non-linguistic setting.[14]

And Donald Davie, in his study of the syntax of poetry, that most imaginative use of language, maintains the indissolubility of syntax and semantic relations: "the fact remains that in reading poetry we do feel some words or some arrangements of words to partake of the nature of the things they stand for, in a way that other words and arrangements of words do not."[15]

MUSICAL SYNTAX

Once it is understood that linguistic syntax has two basic functions—to control information load and to mediate expressed relationships—imagining an analog for music, and only for music, becomes a bit easier. For it is abundantly clear that a primary purpose of musical organizations, from meter and scales through phrase patterns to high-level forms, is to control and order the flow of information streaming to the ears in real time. To this end, the very phonology of music constrains the nature of musical sounds categorically in almost all musical languages so that there is no difficulty in discriminating one sound from another. There is no time for ambiguity; the mind must make instant judgments between A and A♭, a quarter note and an eighth note. So, just as natural languages exist by restricting admissible sounds to a small number of phonemes out of a very large number that the vocal tract could make, each articulated and made discrete by binary oppositions, so do musical languages limit the pitches to a small number within the octave out of the hundreds available. Rhythmic values too are traditionally restricted to certain ratios of duration. As Nelson Goodman and Fred Lerdahl have pointed out, it is the categorical perception of discrete sounds that makes syntax possible.[16]

That these discrete sounds are organized into hierarchies is of course the most famous postulate of modern music theory. Hierarchical organizations—systems of levels—are persuasive models for music because they provide a ready mechanism to control information flow, and so cooperate with syntax. Research has shown that humans can effectively perceive only about three or four abstract items presented in real time.[17] That is, the short-term memory for items with no intrinsic relations among them—a sequence of bingo numbers, for example—begins to fail when their number exceeds four. The information in a musical phrase, however, obviously exceeds this limit as a matter of routine without our experiencing the slightest trouble. Someone listening to a richly scored nineteenth-century symphony may process upwards of twenty-five notes per second, because those notes are organized into hierarchies of motives and chords, which in turn become metric groups and phrases, and so on. Syntax is the agent of these organizations because it specifies how the motives and chords might be composed. Discovering or, indeed, creating a musical syntax guarantees nothing in the way of music's value or even perceptibility—that requires an external criterion—but it does guarantee the possibility of comprehension, at least.

In both music and language, syntax seems to be most powerful at the same levels of structure. At the bottom, the level of notes and durations, the innate gestalt tendencies probably exercise as much influence on perception, if not more, as any rule of syntax, but the ascent through the hierarchy shows its organizing power increasing enormously. At the phrase level of structure, musical syntax is working hard, reducing the randomness, extracting patterns of melody and harmony, thus allowing listeners to process the phrase. At higher levels, however, the rule of three or four reasserts its authority in the prevalence of three-part forms or in schemes of organization based on repetition, which can sustain less tightly ordered patterns. Linguistic syntax, too, seems most powerful and explicit within the sentence and clause. The rules of conversation and discourse are extremely fluid if they exist at all.[18]

These essential syntactic elements—finite discrete events bound by rules in hierarchical organizations—eliminate the pretenders to syntax. Sports and social occasions may certainly have rules, often explicit ones, but there are no basic discrete elements underlying them. The essences of baseball are characterized by a continuous flow of infinite variety: no two curve balls are the same in the way that two $B\flat$s are the same. Chess, which does have discrete elements in its pieces and well-defined moves, has no hierarchical system. There are the moves within the match and that is all.[19] Music, whose elemental notes and beats give rise to motives and meters, eventually to phrases and compositions, is left to stand with language as a mode of perception that is authentically syntactic.

CONTEXT

Limiting the flow of information just enough so that the listener keeps abreast without robbing language of its infinite flexibility depends on one more feature of syntax: context. It is true that nonsyntactic communications depend on some contextual background, which is why a traffic light loses its effect everywhere except at an intersection, but true syntax creates its own ever-changing context out of its own elements, which then affects how the syntax itself functions. In natural language, for example, we suppose that words come with syntactic tags, that "car" is a noun, "run" is a verb and always will be. But for many, perhaps most, common words these tags are hardly exclusive. What is the syntactic function of "running"? Even more elaborate utterances, such as "running after the ball into the street," are ambiguous in the absence of sufficient context:

> Running after the ball into the street can be dangerous.
> (*noun phrase*)
>
> Running after the ball into the street, the little boy forgot everything his mother said. (*noun modifier*)
>
> Running after the ball into the street, he was! (*verb*)

The syntactic function of "running" is determined not by any particular word form it happens to have but by its immediate environment in the sentence. Indeed, the environment determines whether grammatical forms are even correct:

> *I were a rich man years ago.
>
> If I were a rich man . . .

Context is what elevates American Sign Language above the rank of a simple code to that of an authentic language, because its individual signs change meaning and function according to the context in which they are made.[20] How similar is this to the situation in music, where the function of phenomena are so influenced by what surrounds them, where every rule of composition seems to have exceptions justified by context.[21]

And how does this affect information? It turns out that when a syntax is sensitive to its context, both the environment it creates and that in

---

*The asterisk indicates either an ungrammatical sentence or an unconventional syntactic form.

which it occurs, it is a much more efficient control of information than is one whose rules are absolutely independent:

> . . . context-sensitive redundancy is not as expensive as context-free redundancy. It can be increased by a reasonable amount without cramping the message source too severely. . . . It permits greater variety, while at the same time controls errors. English is higher in context-sensitive than context-free redundancy, which accounts for the rich variety of the language, coupled with its excellent readability, even when distorted by misprints and mistakes.[22]

Indeed, compare English with an artificial computer language. The statements of BASIC are reasonably context free but are severely limited in application and cannot tolerate a single error. And beyond information theory itself lies a mountain of psychological and psycholinguistic evidence showing that top-down processing is indispensable when listeners deal with even the most mundane linguistic and musical information.[23]

So, music can organize and control its sound stream in ways that are quite the same as those built into natural language syntax, but what can music offer to match that other essential feature of linguistic syntax, the mediation of expressed relationships? After all, many have argued that music has no definite semantic aspect at all, and few would try to argue that, outside the most exceptional circumstances, music could handle anything like specific relationships among states, actions, and things of the world.[24] But if musical syntax cannot express relationships in the world, what relationships can it express?

SYNTAX AND TENSION

Leonard B. Meyer has written that "in order for syntax to exist . . . successive stimuli must be related to one another in such a way that specific criteria for mobility and closure are established."[25] Fred Lerdahl likewise hints that "stability conditions," which seem to have no parallel in language grammars, are intimately connected with musical syntax.[26] Sarah Fuller is more explicit: "The power of the directed progression lies in its syntax of tendency followed by resolution."[27] Syntax in music is more than a system that controls information by organizing pitches and durations. As it mediates expressed relationships in natural languages, syntax mediates the relation of tension and resolution in musical languages.[28]

Consider some of the primary features of syntax in a motet of Josquin (Ex. 2.1), for example. The five melodies are restricted to just seven pitch classes of the A mode. Each one moves conservatively; there are no melodic intervals greater than a perfect fifth within the phrase, and only a single minor sixth (altus, mm. 51–52) and perfect octave (quintus, m. 54) between phrases. There are but three rhythmic values, with the

Example 2.1. Josquin, Miserere mei, Deus, *conclusion to secunda pars. ("Free me from bloodguilt, God, my salvation, and my tongue shall exult in your justice. Have mercy on me, O God.")*

smallest limited to turns and runs beginning off the half-note beat. There are no syncopations within the quarter. Intervals within chords are consonant, with dissonance allowed only in well-defined circumstances. On the other hand, there is little syntax in the order of the chords. It is hard to demonstrate on harmonic grounds alone the choice of C-E-G to begin the last phrase. On the other hand, there is an essential syntax of texture: the *pars* of the motet must end with all five voices, and Josquin builds up to this requisite ending in his wonted fashion. Beginning with imitative pairs (mm. 49–52), he allows just enough overlap, four beats, to hint at the fuller texture to come before tapering back to three voices, then, briefly, two (mm. 52–56). Then the four are allowed to make a full, climactic phrase that ends with a weak-beat cadence (mm. 56–59) before all five finish this motet section. Josquin cannot activate any of these elements of syntax without affecting tension and resolution in the composition. Every melodic interval, every tone combination, every duration contributes. Explaining the sense of climax in measures 58–59 is impossible without calling on syntax. And it is likewise impossible to apprehend the syntax in the Bach excerpt in Example 2.2 without sensing its own intrinsic tension and resolution at the same time.

The definition of texture here is hazier, allowing the interlocking thirds in the opening bass gesture to count as two voices moving in parallel. On the other hand, harmonic progression is much more precisely syntactic than in the Josquin, so that the cadential progression measures 30–31, itself highly predictable, virtually determines the one in measure 46. The tension and resolution in this passage depend more on harmonic progression and meter than on the variety of rhythmic durations and texture.

Such a precise harmonic syntax frees up the syntax of melody. All

Example 2.2. J. S. Bach, Goldberg Variations, No. 16, mm. 29–47.

kinds of notes outside the prevailing key are allowed, and there are successive semitones (m. 31), a tritone leap (m. 41), and a double leap (m. 43), impossible in Josquin's language. All these are justified by the context of harmonic progression that they help to create. The trade-offs in Bach's syntax and Josquin's, made between harmonic and melodic progression, reflect what normally happens in linguistic evolution: "Languages have an internal rationale for what is going to change and in what way. As the case system went out of Latin, for example, Latin started to impose a fixed word order, and these changes went inexorably together, because there must be a way of giving information about structure, and if cases no longer do so, then the order of the words in the sentence must take on that task."[29] Fixed word order became responsible for the mediation of expressed relationships that was once the duty of case. Similarly, the principal source of tension and resolution passes from melody and duration in Josquin to functional harmony and meter in Bach.

The hypothesis that syntax mediates tension and its corollary—that if there is no sense of tension and resolution then there is no sense of syntax—do not entail that all tension is syntactic in origin. Tension can certainly come from something as simple as a crescendo, for example, or from an accelerando, and clearly these things, having no discrete elements, are not intrinsically syntactic. But although such continuous tensions are important to some musical languages, Leonard Meyer is right in naming them "secondary,"[30] since entire musical styles, such as Josquin's high Renaissance polyphony, have gotten along very nicely without them. They contribute to some kinds of music but are not prerequisite, as is syntax, for music to exist. Neither are motivic and thematic derivation, use of canon and imitation, ostinato bass, nor other high-level formal organizations. The imitation of Bach's subject in the bass by the soprano in the next measure (mm. 31ff.) creates no tension or resolution by virtue of the fact that it is an imitation. Neither does the cantus firmus organization of Josquin's motet. Such devices might occasionally create expectations about their future course that may generate tension of a sort, but the fact of their being there creates none. They are rather more within the purview of composer's choice, artistic tradition, or what might be generally termed "focusing" a musical language.[31]

So, how does syntax create these qualities of tension and resolution in music? Some kinds of tension and resolution trace back ultimately to sources in nature. Eric Clarke writes, "The environment, and in particular the human speech environment, continually floods our auditory systems with the properties of the harmonic series (and has done for millennia), and it would be strange indeed if such a pervasive influence had not left its mark on our musical cultures—analogous to an architectural tradition that did not reflect the influence of gravity."[32] Helmholtz's effort to determine the entire harmonic system of Western music from the overtone series has been debunked time and again, but it is no contradiction, or any betrayal of culture, to hold that the physical properties of tone can influence the choices a culture makes, no more than it would be to point out that the physiology of the vocal tract limits the available phonemes for language. This is the sensible position of Fred Lerdahl when he shows that the choice of pitches within an octave more often than not derives from small integer frequency ratios, since "resultant intervals provide a broad and graduated palette of sensory consonance and dissonance. Sensory consonance and dissonance can in turn form the basis for musical consonance and dissonance, where in a general sense consonance is equivalent to stability and dissonance to instability."[33] The tension of voice leading, too, may owe its different effects to the physical effort required to make larger and smaller intervals when departing from a central tonic.[34]

Probably, though, most specific kinds of tension and resolution come from cultural associations, learned by listeners along with the syntax itself. Syntactic procedures, endlessly repeated, teach the kinds of tension and resolution associated with them. And, as with syntax in language, most of this learning focuses on the lower levels of structure, where syntax is strongest. The musical phrase is the locus of the most salient effects of tension and resolution. Even a neophyte, for example, would probably sense some resolution when Josquin brings four voices, all but the cantus firmus, together to close on the final syllable of the phrase in measure 58. For the first time, no quarter-note rhythm interrupts the long duration. The pancultural gestalt law of proximity would be enough for the listener to make the discrimination. The Bach passage makes the same effect around measures 30–31 and the downbeats of measures 32 and 36, where brief cessations of the motor sixteenths show even the newcomer that these are relative points of rest. Certain "absolute values," innate in the human mind, however basic, build and teach the more subtle and cultural aspects of syntax.

Tension and resolution, then, are essential effects of syntax. Conceptually separate from syntax's function of information reduction, tension and resolution yet emanate from syntax as inevitably as linguistic syntax must express some conceived relationship among the things that we speak in every utterance.

KINDS OF TENSION AND RESOLUTION

The unity of syntax and musical tension has a rather important consequence: that the difference in musical languages, say between Josquin's and Bach's, are heard not only in their means of organization, their hierarchical structuring, but in the tensions and resolutions they create. To recognize that the two passages are different because one comes from a motet composed of an overlapping, imitative texture that creates various levels, while the keyboard variation creates levels by virtue of its functional harmony within the form of a French overture, is to imply at the same time that they will make different effects on the listener not just through their dissimilar structures but because their different syntaxes produce different tensions.

Different . . . in degree, certainly, but what if tension and resolution are musical qualities that usually differ in *kind* as well as degree when they come from different sources? Music analysis usually explains the great variety of musical effect in a composition by collecting and evaluating the tensions and resolutions at the various levels of the hierarchy. The E-minor cadence in the Bach (mm. 30–31), for example, resolves the low-level tension of the immediate progression while articulating a higher-level tension owing to the distance of E minor from the home tonic, G major. The change to eighth notes contributes to the resolution of the local cadence, and its clarity bolsters the sense of harmonic distance at large. The penultimate B-major triad comprises various tensions deriving from the function of the triad within the local key (V), its root position, its third-beat position, its eighth-note length, its soprano leading tone, and so on. All these things contribute to the particular character of that penultimate chord and the effect of the cadence itself.

But is the resulting tension really a sum, or rather a compound? Is tension like heat, that can be related to a common measure, or more like a color or chemical make-up? The critical difference is that in measuring the amount of heat in a room, we can soon disregard the individual sources because heat is heat, no matter where it comes from, and compare that sum to the measurement of another room, but woe to dieters who disregard the sources of their total calorie intake. For the body, the source of the calorie matters a great deal, and the property that allows the name "calorie" to all is too basic to be of use here. If tension is like a calorie, it means that the tension of disparate moments in a composition cannot be precisely compared on a scale.[35] As tempting as it might be to calculate that the tension of the B-major chord is "higher" than that of the D-major chord in the parallel spot of measure 46, on account of its distance from the home key, it could be that its tension is simply different in character, as a calorie from fat is different from a calorie from sugar.

Some straight facts of musical tension point the way to the compound model, not the sum. Some sources, for example, produce tension in rather discrete and constant amounts, like quanta, whereas others are more continuously variable. Of the quantized kind, meter and texture come to mind. Every third beat in the Bach passage seems to reproduce exactly the same tension in the same amount, and when Josquin is operating with only two voices, the resolution of the texture required is precisely quantifiable, at least in the sense of what needs to be done. But what of the tension in the subdominant functioning harmonies of say, measures 29 and 30 leading into the cadence? There is tension, yes, but precisely how it changes from chord to chord, even whether it rises or falls, is much less easy to say.

Some kinds of tension move to resolutions instantly while others require time. In the Bach passage, where the sense of meter is strong, the tension of the beat changes instantaneously from one amount to another when the beat changes. It might be pictured as in the diagram below. There are no gradations of metric tension, no gradual buildups or declines. In a similar manner, when Josquin brings in the fifth voice in measure 59, the tension of the incomplete texture drops to nothing immediately. But harmony and melody seem to act much less like a switch. Because pitch sequences cannot be severed from durations, the listener

GRAPH OF METRIC TENSIONS IN EXAMPLE 2.2.

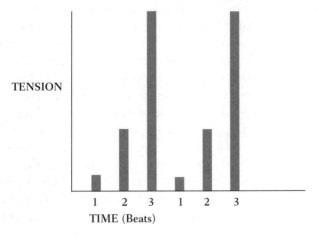

TENSION

1 2 3 1 2 3

TIME (Beats)

must wait some time, although not much, to perceive whether the tonic goal implied by a melodic course lasts long enough to make resolution. Thus, the difference in effect between the cadential E in measure 31 and the G in measure 36 in Example 2.2 (page 31). The second is "less" of a rhythmic resolution, because it is off and running again on the next eighth note. With harmony the effect is magnified. If measures 36 through 44 were erased so that measure 35 led right into the final cadence, the requirement of returning to the home key of G would have been technically fulfilled, and yet the end would be pitifully disappointing. The establishment of a G-major environment does not instantly resolve the tension of harmonic distance: it requires some time for the home key to attain commensurate structural status, during which the tension declines gradually.

Key relationships, too, suggest that, despite the infatuation with recursive levels in generative grammar and much hierarchical music theory, various structural levels may not be perceived alike.[36] The syntax of key relationships in Bach, for example, seems to differ markedly from the syntax of harmonic progressions. All the Goldberg Variations, since they are variations of a bass, follow the same progression of keys: G major–D major–E minor–G major (with V/IV embedded).[37] Now I-V-vi-I is not a typically conclusive harmonic progression when used in a phrase. There is no recursive syntax here.[38] Could it be that hypermeter, high-level melodies, prolongation, and the like, while sharing names and certain essential characteristics with their lower-level counterparts, are nevertheless different in kind? And the tensions they make, too, different in kind?

If these speculations have any truth to them, then musical tension and resolution are complex qualities, not simple measures. It may even be wrong to speak of elementary sources of tension as the most important. Consider how harmonic function and meter in Bach's syntax are bound together. The sense of tonic (I) or dominant (V) harmony depends not only on the vertical combination of pitches but on the chord's metric position. The resolution of a tonic is strongest when the chord occurs on the downbeat and nearly disappears on any other beat. The tension of a dominant, on the other hand, is bound to the ultimate beat of a metric group, the "upbeat." But this formulation makes it appear as if harmonic functions proceed from a sense of meter. That is not entirely true: the sense of meter proceeds from harmonic function at the same time. Sound a dominant seventh in isolation and it already sounds like an upbeat (remember the opening of Beethoven's First Symphony or Pizarro's march from *Fidelio*). Metric tension and harmonic tension feed

back on one another in a curious circular relationship that is characteristic of so many perceptual phenomena, in particular the perception of
language.[39] Such incommensurate complexities of tension and resolution
give to any particular musical event a unique stamp, features that are
essentially incomparable with others. This is not to deny equally essential similarities without which musical syntax could not exist but rather
to suggest that unique qualities, often beautiful ones, can easily be
understated in our efforts to generalize for the sake of theory.

Inspired composition, bringing together the precise amount *and kind*
of musical tension and resolution for the effects desired, all framed in
the proper syntax, is a triumph of musical coordination. Consider how
many different things must work together to make the climactic gesture
in the Josquin excerpt, in measures 56–58. First, there is Josquin's
patented false homophony that hides a canon, with the bass and cantus moving together to establish a simple parallel third (or tenth) texture by the third beat, joined by the altus making a strict canon at the
fifth with the bass, while the quintus, singing motivic variants, moves
homorhythmically with the altus. Next, there is the control of the
meter, which must be barely hinted at, on the one hand so as not to
break up the fragile forward motion, and on the other hand clear
enough to make the last two chords sound strong-weak, leaving enough
tension to elicit the last phrase. He does this by placing half notes on
beats 2 and 3 in measure 56, then gently establishing the downbeat by
actually violating the rule against similar fifth motion in having the bass
make a root-position chord on the first beat of 57 (the rule would have
preferred a C for the bass) and letting the quintus have the longest note
of the passage for the next downbeat, preceded by an emphatic anacru-
sis of three quarters. Finally, Josquin must design the note rhythm,
itself limited by metric considerations—nothing is really independent.
Here the strategy is an obvious acceleration just before the end of the
phrase, which then slows radically. But, again, it must be done in such
a way as to avoid breaking the essential continuity. The Renaissance
rule to avoid starting runs on the strong beat abets Josquin, but the
canon must be worked out so that the acceleration in all three voices
coincides with the peak of the cantus line, at which point the quintus
has already begun the deceleration process. Yes, a prodigious feat of
coordination, for all of these things are constrained by syntax. Indeed,
even as we sense the brilliance of imagination in the design of this
phrase, we realize that imagination alone is insufficient: the handling
of musical syntax requires technique.

SYNTAX AND TECHNIQUE

The drama theorist Eric Bentley once wrote, "The knowledge that an acrobatic trick is difficult is not irrelevant to the experience of watching it. On the contrary. We know it is easy for many creatures to fly up and down at great speed: the interest is only in seeing men and women do it, because it is not easy for them to do it."[40] Isn't this true to some extent for the arts? The constant, if unconscious, thought that not just anybody could bring off what is put before our eyes and ears is an essential part of the aesthetic effect. Appreciation comes best through hard knocks, in learning about how something artistic is done and the technique it requires, in order to acquire for ourselves just this kind of admiration. It may be obvious to the point of banality, but still worth remarking in this regard, that without the constraints of harmonic syntax a four-voice fugue is child's play. Perhaps that is why a good number of late nineteenth-century fugues give such an overstated, if not laborious, impression, since the harmonic syntax on which they are based is so lax that the sense of technical achievement is nearly gone.[41] Indeed, although one can cite a number of good reasons, perceptual, aesthetic, and otherwise, to justify the technique of imitation, one certain reason for its continued attraction since the fifteenth century is that it is an ambitious technique. Musical syntax, while it organizes structures and regulates essential tension, demands a coordination of its various aspects that must challenge the technique of a composer.

A key virtue of syntax in music is this unbreakable bond with a sense of virtuosity, not a showy virtuosity in particular but the kind that is demanded as the standard equipment of highly trained artists, that make them members of an exclusive musical community.[42] It is this aspect of musical composition that our modern structural theories have failed to capture, for, when looking at the various graphs, reductions, and diagrams, one is always left asking, "Why couldn't I compose something just like that?" Perhaps the reason they don't show why is that syntax is most powerful, and its challenge most acute, not in the big structural picture but in the details.

Listen one last time to two of the best moments in the two excerpts. The motet passage begins with an imitative pair construction so typical of Josquin's style. The perception of pairing comes from the timing of the imitative entrances. A single beat separates the first two (m. 49), then a hiatus of five more beats precedes the next entrance (m. 51). But Josquin allows exactly one beat of overlap among all four voices, a brief glimpse of the full sonority without the cantus firmus. When the original pair returns with the word "Deus," the overlap recurs, but marvelously extended. Altus and bass reenter with octave Fs, and then the quintus is allowed to depart from its strict imitation of the bass and slips from D to C (m. 52), revealing a luminous F-A-C sonority for the first time in this passage. Nor does the quintus exit; it reiterates "Deus, Deus" before uniting with altus and bass in a classic descent of parallel sixth chords. The cantus, too, is allowed to sing the extra words on the downbeat of 53, with the altus there, but at twice the speed, linking up with the bass. The major-triad sonority coupled with the rhythmic disposition of the four voices and their text set "Deus, Deus" positively ringing, an imploring outcry at the center of this penitential Psalm 51.

Equally marvelous, though so different in effect, is the propulsive drive to the last cadence in the Bach overture (mm. 40–47). No doubt the cadence itself is built on the same formula as the earlier one in E minor (mm. 29–31), and yet how much more brilliant and powerful is the one in G that ends it all. Some of this power is due to the return of the home key of the whole piece, but Bach will not rely on that rather abstract structure alone. More is due to Bach's handling of texture and rhythm. The E minor cadence is approached matter-of-factly, with the interlocking third motive in the bass harmonized by rather slow melodies in the top voices (m. 29). The G major is prepared to be brilliant by running the sixteenth notes in two voices at once, and at first this is only hinted at in alternating measures, so that in measure 39 one voice has them, in 40, two, in 41 one voice again, in 42 both, and then the missing alto voice joins in with them, completing the texture and ensuring that there will be no letup from then on.

But this device, while making perfect musical sense, is hardly a test of Bach's technique. It is rather the coordination of this textural manipulation with the syntax of harmonic rhythm, so crucial in Baroque music, that creates the sense of brilliance, a little *tour de force* inspiring Donald Tovey to call this variation "one of the most audacious experiments Bach ever made."[43]

Harmonic rhythm is one of the most complex sources of tension, bound as it is to three elements of pitch, note duration, and harmonic identity, itself a troublesome analytical problem. In this piece, the harmonic rhythm varies from one chord per measure to three, with many rather uncertain values in between. A measure like 29 is almost certainly one chord, since the interlocking thirds in the bass can easily be understood as passing voices. The next measure is clearly three, but that is the first measure so unequivocal in the piece. Some measures have a short-long pattern of two chords (m. 31). Then there are places like measures 33 and 34, where long notes becoming dissonant and then consonant again make the harmonic identity ambiguous. Is the third beat of 33 a collection of passing notes or a "real" chord? In this way, Bach sets a solid motor rhythm of eighths and sixteenths against a backdrop of an ongoing but fluctuating harmonic rhythm from the E-minor cadence up through measure 39.

In measure 39, a change. Bach has introduced a new variant of the running figures in the soprano. The counterpoint of this figure is so designed that, especially when combined with the interlocking third idea, it makes three distinct functional harmonies. For four measures there is a clear harmonic rhythm of three, a motion articulated forcefully by the borrowed dominants. Then, just as the alto voice enters to complete the texture, Bach slips again into the vaguer, slower harmonic motion (articulated by the long notes in soprano and alto, mm. 43–44). It is right here that the harmonic progression, having dallied in secondary keys that delayed the expected resolution, aims at the cadence with the strongest syntax (ii going to V), creating the greatest harmonic tension. Breaking the faster harmonic rhythm at this moment, while relentless sixteenths in two voices want to power it onward, tenses the music like the strain of an archer's bow. And doesn't this strain come from Bach's syntactic technique itself when we intuitively sense, from experience and from the burden on our faculties, that such counterpoint is more easily controlled by faster chord changes, not slower? So the faster must return. And so they do, in the cadence formula itself leading to the final tonic (m. 46). Textural completion, harmonic progression, motor rhythm, harmonic motion, all are satisfied in a single gesture, a stunning coordination of several resolutions.

How characteristic it is of music as an art that such audible details exhibit its most paramount techniques, techniques that, while essentially constrained by syntax, triumph over those constraints without the slightest violation to create music's most impressive effects!

Isn't natural language equally fussy in its details? The first steps in learning a foreign language syntax seem to accomplish so much: verb conjugations, tense, noun declension, agreement, and so forth. But soon one enters territory where no "big" laws seem to apply. Every masculine and neuter German plural noun has to be memorized individually. The same is true for gender in Romance languages, and then there are the dreaded idioms and prepositions (Why must Italians say "*in* televisione" instead of "*on* television," like everyone else?). These are the provinces of the "tiny" rules, conditions of syntax that evade generalization, and the failure to master them marks one as a foreigner just as quickly as a mistaken conjugation. In the same way we seem unable to specify completely the syntax of even the best-known musical languages. Why else do counterpoint teachers find themselves at a loss to explain why a "technically correct" exercise is flawed, or why a great composer will contravene one rule or another, given the proper context? Actually, the Italians have just the right phrase to analyze tiny syntactic flaws in speech: "non suona bene," "it doesn't sound very well." Sometimes it seems as if that is the most we can say.

Despite this fussiness, we are much more forgiving of syntactic errors in the performance of natural language than in music. Slips of the tongue, minor grammatical flaws, and lackadaisical pronunciation are taken as routine in the normal business of speech, but a single wrong note in the final running passages of the Bach might well ruin that variation. For in speech, after all, the primary goal is to communicate with others, and there is sufficient redundancy in the syntax to allow less than perfect performance. Small errors go by unnoticed as long as they do not interrupt the flow of information or make its reception difficult. Music, too, "communicates," at least in the sense of providing information, but because its syntax is tied to an immensely important aesthetic effect—tension and resolution—a mistake here seems like the vitiation of perfection, as glaring as a chip on the face of a fine marble statue. Language may approximate this state when it adds a virtuosic element in the form of supersyntactic conditions: meter, alliteration, and rhyme. These conditions, like a composer's choosing to write ostinato variations, raise the level of technical virtuosity by establishing criteria for sound to accompany meaning. For Robert Frost such challenges make serious poetry possible: "Writing free verse is like playing tennis with the net down."

SOME IMPLICATIONS OF MUSICAL SYNTAX

The power of any analogical argument stems from an unfortunately vague sense of aptness, some essential similarity between two things that invites other comparisons in the effort to make the better known reveal secrets of the lesser known. Thinking through the implications of the points of contact often brings in unforeseen, unbidden, and occasionally unwelcome insights demanding the same kind of faith that was put in the more salient likenesses. Where does the concept of musical syntax eventually get us?

It brings to the center of conceptual awareness aspects of music that are always in the center of musical awareness. Foremost of these is the notion that music, like language, is a physically continuous soundstream that competent listeners manage to break into interrelated bits—concepts—that are quickly organized into hierarchical patterns of some depth, all in real time. This truism must never be lost to sight, since it guarantees nothing less than music's comprehension, if it is to be considered syntactic. It demands an explanation of the range and limit of perception, an explanation that, as in the Bach example, can itself become a rationale for musical effect.

Comprehension by whom? Here comes an unbidden analog. No natural-language syntax exists for a solitary person. Every one comes with a linguistic community whose members produce and comprehend utterances according to rules known "tacitly" by them. In an analogous musical community, the exchange may indeed be lopsided, listeners outnumbering composers and performers, depending upon the particular community at hand, but there must be shared syntax for composers and listeners alike if the community is to be. This is the social dimension of music, present everywhere in the world. In this sense, syntax is not just in the musical artifacts, the pieces we hear and study, but is in the nature of an agreement between all members, producers and consumers, of the musical community. It belongs to competent listeners as much as to the composers and performers who enthrall them. Music that cannot attract, develop, and sustain this kind of bond can hardly claim to be syntactic in the way of natural language.

If perceptual control of this acoustic stream is the foundation of syntax, musical tension is certainly its artistic raison d'être. The fashioning of tension and resolution, in their marvelous multiplicity of quantity and kind, surely deserves a central place in music analysis and criticism. But there is no fashioning without technique, the essential property of syntax that constrains musical information for the sake of both comprehension and, indeed, the deep senses of beauty at the same time.

The concept of musical syntax therefore marshals the central concerns of listener comprehension, musical tension, syntactic technique and the idea of musical community into a single framework. Describing a musical syntax begins to have practical value, and even the recondite metaphor of musical language takes on an inchoate clarity. It is true that a complete specification of even one syntax will be elusive for the fore-

seeable future, if not forever, if only because of the pervasive influence
of immediate context, ironically one of the essences of syntax. The situation is similar in linguistics: context cannot be excluded from the interpretation of syntactic rules. Unless some "context generator" is
discovered—some finite set of rules that can describe all possible contexts—then the virtually infinite number of contexts will provide for a virtually infinite number of syntactic interpretations. But we know what
musical syntax requires—finite discrete elements, rules of combination,[44]
hierarchical organizations, tension and resolution, a comprehending
community—and even the preliminary and intuitive distinctions among
these go a long way toward making sense of the gulf that separates
Josquin from Bach, to say nothing of more distant relations.

CHAPTER 3
THE RANGE OF MUSICAL SEMANTICS

Musical semantics is a paradoxical matter.

On one hand, semantics seems at first blush to be the most compelling of all possible analogies between music and language, and it is not too much to say that the idea of music having meaning has driven the analogy throughout its long history more than any other single idea. After all, communicating meaning is the raison d'être of natural language. However fascinating are the phonetics, phonologies, and syntax of language, these are but necessary components that make possible the "sovereign" semantic function.[1] Music, too, is commonly taken to convey meaning of some kind. Widespread and consistent connotations of emotion, to take only the most popular association, have been found experimentally for decades, even in listeners as young as three years old.[2] Natural language inheres in the very fabric of music in songs and operas where listeners believe that there is some kind of semantic matching going on. Indeed, for many, such meanings account for most of their interest in music and for a good many of music's most edifying effects on them.

On the other hand, the analogy between musical meaning and linguistic meaning appears to break down in the slightest communal application. A good sentence commands the most precise understanding in a whole auditorium full of hearers, but passages of music elicit only the vaguest inarticulate impressions. The very same experiments that show listeners consistently matching the positive emotions with the major mode and the negative with the minor, for example, can bring such results only when the listeners are artificially forced to choose between starkly contrasting expressions such as "happy/sad." When a more varied palette is tested, agreement breaks down. Unlike any natural language, music resists translation. Just consider the disparities in the criticism or conversation that ventures to describe what a single piece means.[3] Even the most fundamental semantic functions of declaration, interrogation, negation, and command are absent, not to mention mood, tense, or more subtle qualities. A musical passage is neither true nor false, nor can it make any discernible propositions, except under the most constrained circumstances. It seems that Bertrand Russell's famous remark about a dog's barking—that it may be very eloquent but it cannot tell you that his parents were poor but honest—could very well describe the situation in music.

The ancient paradox of musical semantics is simply this: music seems full of meaning to ordinary and often extraordinary listeners, yet no community of listeners can agree among themselves with any precision that comes close to natural language about the nature of that meaning.[4] Agreement is essential for any useful meaning to exist, since communication among members of a linguistic community cannot do without it.[5] Can music therefore really mean anything? The answer at one end of the spectrum, that a musical passage contains no semantic value but the tautological one of referring to itself, traces back to the aesthetic theories of Edouard Hanslick in the nineteenth century (and Schumann reportedly replayed one of his piano pieces when asked about its meaning)[6] but has found greater champions in the twentieth. Stravinsky, despite his meteoric rise to world prominence via the stage, boldly proclaimed that "music is, by its very nature, essentially powerless to *express* anything at all, whether a feeling, an attitude of mind, a psychological mood, a phenomenon of nature, etc. . . . *Expression* has never been an inherent property of music."[7] The serialists, of course, have made self-reference into a compositional system of manifold layers and permutations so abstract that they are best characterized as pure relational ideas, not perceptible identities. The "science" of semiotics broadens the notion of self-reference to include not just the passage in question but an overall system of introverted signs: "The semiologist, like Hanslick, is more interested in the system of signification than the material signified; he sees systems as empty webs of relations, 'without positive terms.' "[8] In short, "relation" in the abstract, never referential, sense—the theorist's fixation on structure—comprises all the semantics of music.

Susanne Langer has taken these thinkers to task for the aesthetic import of their stance:

> They are suddenly faced with the dichotomy: *significant or meaningless.* And while they fiercely repudiate the proposition that music is a semantic, they cannot assert that it is meaningless. It is the problem, not the doctrine, that has infected them. Consequently they try to eat their cake and have it too, by a logical trick that is usually accepted only among mathematicians—by a statement which has the form of an answer to the question in hand, and really commits them to nothing. Musical form, they reply, is its own content; it means itself. This evasion was suggested by Hanslick when he said, "The theme of a musical composition is its essential content." He knew that this was an evasion; but his successors have found it harder and harder to resist the *question* of content, and the silly fiction of self-significance has been raised to the dignity of a doctrine.[9]

This is extreme, of course. A lot of good theory and fine criticism has demonstrated self-significance and self-reference to be resources much more powerful than any "silly fiction" could be, but it is certainly not the whole story either. Consider the practical consequences of the position.

Believers in pure self-reference must hold that the match of music and any extramusical addendum is arbitrary, including text setting, word painting, titles of pieces like *La Mer*, programs of symphonic poems like *Tod und Erklärung*, and the actions on stage that accompany the music of operas and ballets. Now, word painting might be dismissed as a compositional game, much like the encryption of anagrams into the cantus firmus of certain Renaissance masses and motets, intended only to gratify the composer's patron and his own amusement without affecting the listening experience in any kind of material way. And it is certainly true that certain vocal genres can bear the substitution of new and often very different texts without apparent harm: numberless church hymns come to mind, and the wholesale adaptation of secular music for sacred liturgies has been one of the recurrent complaints of church authority for at least five centuries. "The Star-Spangled Banner" was once a drinking song. In fact, the verses of every strophic song undergo this kind of manipulation. But the art of *contrafactum* (text replacement) has its limits. Would anyone agree that "For unto us a child is born," from Handel's *Messiah*, could be just as easily rendered by the music of its preceding number, "The people that walked in darkness"?

With opera, the prospects quickly become too onerous to bear. Pure self-reference must insist that all Wagnerian leitmotifs could be interchanged without harm, save that the abstract pitch relations are somehow maintained. The sword music could easily stand in for Siegmund and Sieglinde's staring in *Die Walküre*, and their original melody, a chromatic and lyrical line played by a solo cello at first, would do just fine for the sword. The recall of the opening chords of *Don Giovanni* at the statue's arrival is purely a structural event; it might as well have happened during the dinner scene while Leporello is choking on his stolen mouthful.

Sometimes one hears in response to such conundrums a line of reasoning that might be termed conventionalism and goes like this. There is nothing natural about listener associations between the darker emotions and the minor mode or between a dotted-rhythm trumpet figure and a sword. These associations are "merely conventional" aspects of our particular culture, popular myths maintained by the incognoscenti. They have no logical force. This charge is quite true, as it is true of virtually all words in any natural language. There is no logical relation between the acoustic utterance symbolized by "floor" and its referent in the world. It is merely a convention of English speakers that such a sound can refer to the thing we walk on. It is quite possible, then, that the relation between the fanfare and the sword has no more force than this—and no less.

But the position at the other end of the spectrum, that music certainly signifies something besides itself, cannot shake off the imprecision and vagueness that would defeat effective communication in any natural language. Peter Kivy's idea that music is "expressive of" different emotions based on both conventional associations and abstract facts of a piece is a striking theory of how a composition and an emotion might be connected,[10] if we could only agree on what that emotion was, but the thought of surveying even a knowledgeable crowd of listeners after the performance of a Mozart string quintet, say, or even a single passage from one, is enough to make one give up in despair. Langer and Leonard Meyer, believers in music's emotional content, can avoid this damning imprecision only by limiting the relationship to emotional life in general. Music never communicates anything so specific as Kivy has in mind but rather is a constantly moving picture of a single all-embracing Emotion.[11] This is reasonable but not of much help in criticizing or understanding a particular piece. It explains, in other words, why we care about music, but not why we care about some pieces a lot more than others, nor does it begin to handle the semantic matching that goes on in vocal music, or to justify other well-defined semantic boundaries, such as that between sacred and secular music in the Middle Ages and Renaissance.

SEMANTIC RANGE

A more practical analogy between natural-language semantics and musical semantics comes at the cost of abandoning two powerful preconceptions about the nature of meaning itself. First is the idea that meaning is entirely bound up with propositions or truth values, the predications characteristic of sentences. There is a long philosophical tradition of treating meaning in this way, and for good reason. Sentences are the primary tool of communication. Even in his book on *Lexical Semantics*, David Cruse writes that "We do not communicate with isolated words; words are not the bearers of messages; they do not, of themselves, 'make sense'; they cannot, taken singly, be true or false, beautiful, appropriate, paradoxical or original. A linguistic item must in general have at least the complexity of a simple sentence to show such properties."[12] Indeed, it is often fiendishly hard to define a word without using it in a sentence as a defining demonstration.[13] Generative linguists, starting with Chomsky, define language itself as the set of all sentences to be created by its use.

Music is occasionally capable of propositional meaning. When, in Wagner's *Die Walküre*, Siegmund recounts the story of how he lost his father in flight, it concludes with the passage shown in Example 3.1. The orchestral accompaniment following Siegmund's last note contains a proposition: "Siegmund's father is Wotan." The communication of this sentence, however, depends upon strict circumstances. The hearing of the leitmotif must accompany the understanding of Siegmund's text and perhaps the context of his singing it. The hearer, too, must know the symbolic import of the leitmotif, either from having heard *Das Rheingold*, where its meaning is established, or from simply being told about it. These circumstances are perhaps not really different in kind from those that attend the communication of any proposition in natural language, but the fact is that in music they are rarely so constrained. The Mozart string quintet passage cannot be filled up with meaning in this way. Faithfulness to propositional meaning cannot be prerequisite for musical semantics.[14]

Nor should it necessarily be prerequisite in semantics generally. A

Example 3.1. Wagner, Die Walküre, *Act I. ("I found a wolf's skin in the forest; empty it lay before me, my father I found not.")*

number of writers, while not challenging the preeminence of proposi-tions and predication in the communication of relations, logic, and oth-er complex forms of meaning, claim only that there are good bits of meaning without predication. "Referring-and-predicating is only one of the many socially constituted functions of language and not a privileged one at that."[15] Isolated lexical items—words—are full of a "presentation-al," symbolic meaning that need not depend on predication at all.[16] Might there be a useful analog for musical semantics in isolated words?

The explorations of Wye Jamieson Allanbrook, Kofi Agawu, and others into the symbolic use of musical "topics" in Viennese Classical music suggest that there is indeed a useful analog there. Topics are lexical items, "musical vocabulary," "configurations of notes and rhythms," each of which identifies a "particular expressive stance."[17] Agawu suggests that topics come in the form of compositional types such as minuets or com-positional "styles" such as "military and hunt music, fanfares, horn-calls, singing style, brilliant style, French overture, musette/pastorale, Turkish music, *Sturm und Drang*, sensibility or *Empfindsamkeit*, the strict or learned style, and fantasia."[18] Some have a striking consistency even over the centuries. The musical symbols for "storm" in Vivaldi's *Four Seasons*, in Beethoven's *Pastorale*, in Rossini's overture to *William Tell*, in Wagner's *Die Walküre*, and in Verdi's *Otello* all have very fast notes set in a minor key. Evidently, one cannot pronounce "storm" in music without those characteristics, and such consistency increases the topics' intelligibility. By reading these topics we may divine some semantic content of the composition that uses them.

A great deal of music makes all manner of references to fanfares, horn calls, and the rest, and so here is a source of meaning without predication. But these topics do not act like words, the lexical items of language. They lack what David Cruse calls the property of "discreteness."[19] In English, for example, "floor" is one word and "deck" another, and although there is similarity in the referents of the two words, there is no question about whether one is using one or the other in speech. But where does the horn call leave off and the fanfare begin? The two sounds blend into one another as the sounds "floor" and "deck" never could. Horn call and fanfare are not discrete, and they lack the power of articulation that discreteness confers.

And how do we modern listeners learn them? In natural language most words are learned through experience, by being shown in a context what they mean and when they are appropriate, and Allanbrook argues that topics would be "tacitly shared by the eighteenth-century audience" that heard them in Mozart operas.[20] But today we cannot experience the horn call or minuet in context; we must be told about them, told what they once meant. It is like trying out dictionary vocabulary of a new language in a live situation: the cheap English-German phrasebook may translate "letter" as *Buchstabe* (a letter of the alphabet), but asking the postman for one will guarantee only a bemused expression. The experience of seeing *Buchstabe* in action is missing, and that can be crucial. Of course, the dictionary meaning is always a start that one can build on, and perhaps topics can acquire the same layers of experiential meaning for listeners after instruction by the book.

But the rather vague quality of most of these topics seems to leave them defenseless against Suzanne Langer's charge, by which she dismisses the possibility of a fruitful analogy between language and music: "The analogy between music and language breaks down if we carry it beyond the mere semantic function in general, which they are supposed to share. Logically, music has not the characteristic properties of language—separable terms with fixed connotations, and syntactical rules for deriving complex connotations without any loss to the constituent elements."[21] The charge is devastating only if we accept Langer's premise that words in natural language do indeed have fixed "connotations" or meaning. This is the second preconception that must be abandoned in order to arrive at a practical analogy.[22]

Once during a discussion of music and meaning, I asked a class of college freshmen to list the various possible meanings of the word "floor." In a very short time they came up with something like the following list:

1. part of the building that one walks on
2. the level of a building: "seventh floor"
3. a bottom surface: "ocean floor"
4. a minimum value: "salary floor"
5. to astonish: "he was floored by the announcement"
6. to accelerate a car as fast as possible

A good dictionary will list several more that the students missed, such as "holding the floor" in a deliberative body.

Here, then, is a single common English word that has over a half dozen distinct meanings. The meaning of "floor" is fixed only when it is used in a particular context; in the abstract it has a great deal of semantic elasticity.[23] This elasticity is what prevents perfect synonymy between words in a language, at least in the sense of infallible substitutions. For if two words seem synonymous because they can be exchanged in one context

He was astonished by the news.

He was floored by the news.

others come to mind where they cannot:

The astonished queen nevertheless smiled gracefully.

*The floored queen nevertheless smiled gracefully.

English speakers can use "floor" with semantic precision because the context acts as an essential ingredient in its active meaning, the ingredient that philosophers of language have tried to capture in their notions of "intentional meaning" and "connotation." This is why observation of usage, not dictionary reading, is the preferred mode of learning vocabulary in one's native language. No one learns all the possible meanings of "floor" at a single hearing, and it is highly doubtful that one could master them all by studying the dictionary. It is only after experiencing the various usages of the word in many different contexts that anything like total command of the word is won. In the real life of language use, word meaning is a combination of abstract sense and the nuts and bolts of context.

Is it possible that the various meanings of "floor" actually betoken different lexical items: "floor"1, "floor"2, . . . "floor"n, which just happen to have the same sound symbol? After all, many homonymous pairs in English such as "sole" and "soul" have nothing more in common than a coincidence of phonetics. Yet to take that kind of strategy in order to eliminate context from any role in word meaning ignores the most obvious fact that the various meanings of "floor" all have a core concept in common, quite unlike the situation of "sole" and "soul." Why should "floor" sometimes mean "to astonish?" Because one is supposed to fall, hyperbolically speaking, to the floor with the shock of surprise. Accelerating a car rapidly means pushing the gas pedal to the bottom. The core concept of "the thing one walks on" is never far from even the most fanciful meanings of "floor," always lurking in the background of linguistic competence, often as a dead metaphor. Thinking of them all as unrelated would give up this essential semantic connection, which psycholinguists think highly valuable in the network organization of long-term memory.

And it would not even save the idea of fixed meaning for words. Consider such technical terms as "chromosome" or "tonicize," or such proper names as "Beethoven." If any words are to have fixed meanings, it should be these. But do they?

> Chromosomes are the bearers of genetic material.

> The chromosomes of the frog's egg cells were damaged by the radiation.

> A Renaissance composer can tonicize a modal degree other than the final by constructing a suspension cadence upon it.

> As the hierarchical properties of harmonic syntax were clarified, composers like Beethoven could tonicize whole periods of music with greater confidence in the stability of the overall sense of key.

> Beethoven composed his first piano concerto after 1795.
> The piano music of Beethoven is generally beyond the reach of the amateur.

Clearly the referents of "chromosomes" are not the same in the first pair of sentences, since the first refers to all chromosomes everywhere and the second points to a chosen few. The same is true, although with distinctions difficult to qualify, of the last pair, since the concept "Beethoven" in the context of 1795 does not contain the same attributes, such as deafness, that an overall concept of "Beethoven" might contain. The technical verb "tonicize" seems to retain the greatest sameness of meaning over different contexts, but even here the broad connotations, what the word brings to mind, are not precisely identical. No knowledgeable student of Renaissance music would ever take "tonicize" to apply to a "period." Now there is no question that in these words there is less elasticity of meaning, less dependence on context, than in more common ones such as "floor," but if these extreme cases still show signs of semantic movement, then Langer's presumption of fixed word meanings for language in general is not such an obstacle. "There seems little doubt that such variation is the rule rather than the exception: the meaning of any word form is in some sense different in every distinct context in which it occurs."[24] The range of this meaning may be broad, it may be narrow, but that a range of meaning exists for most every word is sure.

SEMANTIC RANGE AND MUSIC

The meaning of a word is both elastic and definite. There are limits beyond which the word's connotation may not be stretched. No one can know which meaning of "floor" will be activated until the word is uttered in a context, but everyone can be sure that it will not have anything to do with orthography, to take one of infinitely many possibilities, so that the phrase "misspelled floor" will surely be semantically deviant, or nonsense.[25] For every legitimate usage of "floor"—and there may be infinitely many—there are many nonsensical ones. Its meaning is variable but bounded.

The semantic range of "floor" may be conceived of as a space with definite boundaries, like a sphere, made up of infinitely many points within and infinitely many others out of bounds. The core or prototypical meaning is at its center, and the context acts like a window that indicates which of all its meanings is active in any given use. Meaning arises by the interaction of this semantic range and a context (see diagram next page). A version of this idea seems to have been first articulated in Mary Haas's

REPRESENTATION OF THE SEMANTIC RANGE OF "FLOOR."

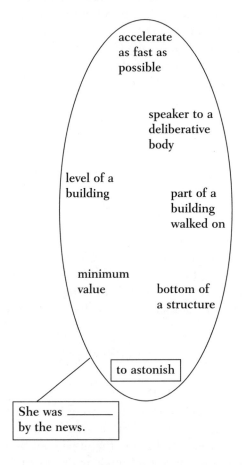

"Semantic Value," and some form of it has found a place in modern lexical semantics.[26] Here again is the feedback or circular relationship that applies to the two ingredients, making semantic range resemble so much perceptual theory that must account for the contextually oriented "top-down" perceptions as well as stimulus-oriented "bottom-up" perceptions. The context selects the active meaning out of many possible ones in the range, but at the same time the range restricts the possible appropriate contexts that can act as window. Thus is avoided the deconstructionist semantic swamp where no bearings are sure and no limits are known. Buildings, the ocean, numerical limits, surprises, and driving cars are contexts that could activate the semantic range of "floor." Spelling is not. "Misspelled floor" is still nonsense.[27]

A passage of music could have a semantic range that is essentially the same as that of any word in a language, only much broader in its scope; sharing the same kind of elasticity but of much greater degree than is typical in language. That explains the data showing that listeners might agree about which of only two contrasting adjectives to apply to a musical passage even though they cannot agree about the precise meaning of any isolated passage. Choosing whether the French overture in Bach's Goldberg Variations connotes "sublime confidence" or "deep despair" is easy, because the semantic fields of those expressions are so completely "separate." One seems coincident with the music and the other far from it. Choosing between "sublime confidence" and "easy triumph" would not likely yield any such consensus; both might belong within the passage's broad semantic field, though one might well be closer to its center than the other.

This concept of musical semantics entails all of the traditional formulations of meaning—reference and sense, connotation and denotation, indexicality, iconic and symbolic traits—as well as the newer idea that an essential part of linguistic meaning is its syntactic function,[28] but it does not mean that these aspects must be part of every musical passage. Context and semantic range comprehended together determine the meaning specific to every case. It may be tantalizingly vague or unmistakably precise, as when the appropriate window just small enough to admit a narrow beam of meaning can yield the precision of meaning found in language. Language itself provides just such a window.

WORDS AND MUSIC

The music of a successful vocal piece is not a translation of its text and is nothing like the translation between two natural languages. Rather, the music seems to contain the meaning of its text as one of infinitely many meanings in its semantic range. The text, acting as a context window on that range, and—crucially important—deemed appropriate for that range, selects and activates the one that coincides with the meaning of the text itself. We have a semantic match between words and music.

There is nothing in the tune of "Hark! the Herald Angels Sing" that necessarily connotes angels, kings, Christianity, or any of its symbols, as there is nothing in Handel's great chorus "For unto us" in *Messiah*. But the fanfarelike melody and processional rhythm of the former, the quick tempo and fleeting rhythms of the latter, and the major modes of both include those connotations as possible or appropriate. To put it most mildly, they are not unapt. These texts, as highly defined contexts, activate those potential meanings out of vast semantic ranges of those pieces. Unapt would be to set "For unto us" to the music that Handel wrote for the movement "The people that walked in darkness." The combination of B minor, slow tempo, slow harmonic rhythm, and insistent dissonances has a vast semantic range too, but not so vast as to be appropriate for the text of "For unto us."

Is the union of words and music then no more profound than "appropriate"? Alas, many times it is not, as perhaps in "Hark! the Herald" and many other well-loved songs. But profundity is not ruled out, either. When in Handel's chorus the words "the mighty God" come round for the last time and the composer asks his sopranos to sing a high G on the word "God," coincident with the most climactic harmonic articulation of the piece, there is, for that moment, a closer unity of text and music than there is for the work as a whole (Ex. 3.2). But again, the gesture is not a translation of "God," and the interpretations of its meaning could run from "the power of God" to "the majesty of God" and beyond. Handel's profundity here is in the economy of gesture, in the number of imaginings fused onto a single moment.

Hanslick countered any thinking along these lines with the apparent mismatch of "Che farò senza Euridice?" from Gluck, and many simpler

Example 3.2. Handel, Messiah, *"For unto us."*

pieces such as "God Rest Ye Merry" come to mind too. Hanslick points out that the major mode and flowing rhythm of the aria's melody can in no wise be taken as a faithful expression of the despairing text.[29] In the carol, the Dorian mode seems equally unapt for "comfort and joy." Hanslick's criticism suffers from construing the semantic range of Gluck's music too narrowly. He may not believe that the traditional "sighing" figure in the melody has any relevance for his own century, but there it is, and criticizing Gluck for failing to express his text universally is different from claiming that all such expression is impossible. The use of the major mode for mournful texts is hardly outlandish in Gluck's time, for Handel does it frequently; think of his great elegy in *Saul*, or "Priva son," the almost unbearably moving aria that Cornelia sings upon the death of her husband in *Giulio Cesare*, or even "He was despised" from *Messiah*. In the case of "God Rest Ye Merry" we hear, not a mismatch, but a different musical language, with a different semantic system. Its proper interpretation is a matter of retraining, as it is when we hear English soundalikes in a foreign tongue: "Chow" is no longer a down-home invitation to dinner when heard in Italy. The meaning of the sound token has changed, modified, as always, by its immediate context.

The circularity of the relationship between semantic range and context is actually more thorough than we supposed. Surely Handel's dramatic gesture at the close of "For unto us" is more than simply appropriate, even superbly appropriate, for "God." For the music interprets that expression, too, and gives us a fleeting image of a certain kind of God out of all the ones we could imagine. In this sense, it is the music that is the context window on the range of the *natural-language item* "God." Lest this seem to make the whole notion of semantic range too bizarre, consider that the same thing happens regularly in speech.

> It seemed that the floor of the house would not be taken up and removed after all.
>
> It seemed that the floor of the House would not be taken by the Speaker after all.

It is natural to think that in these sentences it is the end of each one that acts as the crucial context, specifying which meaning of "floor" will be active. That is true. But it is also true that the items "speaker," "house," removed," in fact, *all* the other sound items in the sentences also have semantic ranges that must be specified before comprehension occurs. So, "floor" acts as context for them and is acted on by them. There are circles of meaning in language and circles of meaning in music.

Many lovers of Handel know that the chorus "For unto us" has an alter ego as an Italian duet dated July 3, 1741, just a few weeks before he began work on *Messiah*. In this persona the music bears an Italian text whose title is "No, di voi non vuò fidarmi" ("No, I do not wish to trust in you")—a contrafactum, in other words. Now there are good contrafacta and bad, and the difference is mostly this. When a different set of words is applied to music and the fit seems apt, it means that the new text provides a context that is still appropriate and whose meaning is well within the semantic range of the original music, which, as we have seen, is generally far more vast than that of individual words, never mind an integrated text. The new text locates its window at a different "place" within that range. When the adaptation is poor, then the meaning of the new text cannot activate anything within the great range of the music; it does not make a suitable context. Actually, Edward Dent wrote that "*Messiah* incorporates some of Handel's own chamber duets, the melodies of which were more suitably illustrative of their original Italian words than of the sentences of Scripture to which he adapted them."[30] So, Dent believes that the Italian texts create a more readily understandable context for a semantic match than does Scripture. That many who know only the chorus would find it hard to agree with Dent merely underscores the importance of learning meaning, even musical meaning, through experience. There is nothing like a first impression.

LEITMOTIFS

The analogy of leitmotifs as lexical items—musical "words"—is particularly inviting, because listeners learn them in much the same way they learn words in a language, that is, by observing them against a clearly defined context.[31] Wagner introduces his leitmotifs with explicit stage actions that make their various meanings clear from the outset, so listeners learn them through association as easily as they might learn commands of a foreign language by watching the actions of children following their parents. Unlike text matching, the appropriateness of the context is to be measured in the action on stage, not necessarily in what is being sung.

Of course, if leitmotifs were truly wordlike, there would be no standard for appropriateness at all. A key property of words that is often cited to account for the precise and expressive power of language is that words are arbitrary symbols.[32] Speakers of English agree to let the sound token "floor" symbolize the parts of buildings that we walk on, but there is no logical necessity or advantage in "floor." It could have any one of countless sounds the human vocal apparatus can produce, and the arbitrary nature of this agreement is the source of language's power to represent virtually anything, because there are no "natural" constraints on what its words may stand for. Are leitmotifs arbitrary, too?

The leitmotif that Siegmund uses to question Brünnhilde after learning he is to die might come close to pure arbitrariness (Ex. 3.3). Aside from the fact that its rising melody mirrors the rising intonation used for interrogation in nearly all the world's languages, there seems to be nothing about this particular melody, this particular rhythm and harmony, that suggests questioning. On the other hand, the sword motive is definitely traceable to preexisting cultural topics. The use of a trumpet to introduce the motive and its dotted rhythm based on a tonic arpeggio combine to make a recognizable military symbol appropriate for the weapon. It is far from arbitrary, and therefore, to say the least, arbitrariness in the design and usage of leitmotifs is a matter of degree. But then, upon further reflection, might not the same be said of words? If "floor" and "god" are basically arbitrary symbols, then compounds such as "floorboard" and

Example 3.3. Wagner, Die Walküre, Act II. ("Who are you, tell me, who appears to me so lovely and stern?")

derivatives such as "flooring" and "godlike" are certainly not. They are based on precursors in much the same way as is the sword motive. Indeed, it would be highly inefficient for a language to consist entirely of basic words when the meanings of compounds and derivatives are more often than not immediately clear. They multiply the expressive power of a small base vocabulary.

In any case, the semantic principle of leitmotifs is the same as that of text matching. The dramatic context is the window that selects the meaning of a leitmotif out of that melody's entire semantic range, and, as before, that range ensures that the action on stage is appropriate for that motive. It is not that an arpeggio played by a trumpet must mean "sword" but rather that it can mean it. Once the meaning of the motive is established—meaning that the semantic range of that melody has been narrowed down to something like that of a common word—it can be used for dramaturgy by elaborating or further specifying that meaning by more immediate contexts (Ex. 3.4). Here the original "question motive" has been translated into the major mode. This transformation, though great, does not affect the identity of the motive, much as a stress or change of intonation leaves unaffected a word's root meaning while changing its immediate meaning. That this kind of modification is so much more frequent and palpable in music may say more about the kinds of meaning music is suited for than any great difference in musical and linguistic usage. The immediate con-

Example 3.4. Wagner, Die Walküre, *Act II ("Shall a woman gladly greet me in Valhalla?")*

SIEGMUND

zart

Grüsst mich in Wal - hall froh ei - ne Frau?

pp

text of Siegmund's new question leaves no doubt about the significance of the major mode: he shifts the object of his questioning from himself to the sleeping Sieglinde. As he suddenly realizes what Brünnhilde's message means, he is overcome by an onrush of deep and tender feeling, carried by the change of mode, to be amplified moments later into the passionate sixth question that asks for Sieglinde with a directness he can no longer restrain, an emotional outburst that can only be surpassed in intensity by the recall of the love motive that follows close on.

WORD PAINTING AND PICTURE PAINTING

In an introductory music class I once demonstrated the word painting that occurs in Handel's "Every valley shall be exalted" by showing a list of excerpted words to be "painted" and then tracing the melodic contour of each as it was heard (see diagram below). The response was uproarious laughter. It's not too surprising, really; even experienced listeners smile when they catch a bit of clever word painting here and there.

Word painting and picture painting are instances of authentic translations into music, fairly defined passage-to-word semantic equivalents in the same sense that "opus" and "work" are equivalents in different languages. The difference is that the Latin and English items are arbi-

WORD PAINTING IN HANDEL, "EVERY VALLEY."

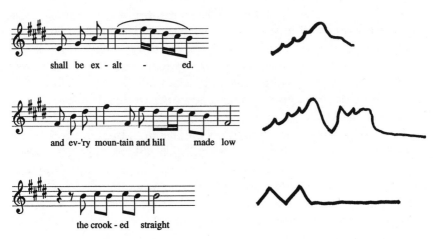

trary in nature, while the musical equivalents in Handel for "mountain" and "low" are iconic symbols in Charles Peirce's sense of having some essential similarity in their physical makeup that allows the translation from words to music. It is notoriously difficult to specify exactly the nature of this similarity, as anyone who has considered the similarity of a stick figure and its referent has found, and some thinkers agree with Umberto Eco that it is entirely cultural,[33] but obviously it is sufficiently powerful to achieve widespread agreement within a musical community. Hanslick goes so far as to insist that it is the principle expressive power of music:

> We are forever being solemnly reassured, when the question of "tone-painting" arises, that music cannot by itself in any way portray phenomena which lie outside its own domain, excepting only the feelings which are produced in us by music. However, it is exactly the other way around. Music can aspire to imitate only the external phenomenon, never the specific feeling it produces. The fall of snowflakes, the flutter of birds, the rising of the sun—these I can paint musically only by analogy, by producing audible impressions dynamically related to them. [34]

Why, then, the laughter?

The English words that come closest to being iconic symbols, words such as "boom," "crash," "squeal," "meow," "howl"—sound words all, apparently—are a tiny fraction of one's active vocabulary and hardly the most distinguished or respected items in the lexicon. It is as if there were some universal sense that, while English permits these few deviants, as a whole it is not supposed to convey meaning through icons, and those words that do are mostly childish. The same must be true of music. Wagner has shown how the semantic range of a motive may be narrowed to the precision of a sentential proposition, but the reference is hardly ever iconic. Music is not supposed to act that way, and when it does, we react as we do to any play acting. Here is music, the quintessentially abstract art, pretending to copy something solid in the world. Word painting is a kind of semantic clowning.

Why, then, do so many composers indulge in it, from the great madrigalists who seem to have made it an indispensable part of their art down to composers of the present day? There can be so many examples of absolutely beautiful word painting in a single work, the B-minor Mass of Bach, just to take one outstanding example, that it seems a shame to dismiss the whole business as compositional shenanigans. On the other

hand, no composition survives in the repertory by virtue of its word painting alone, and therein is the clue. The best examples are loved only in
conjunction with more fundamental musical effects. Word painting is an
appendage to the basic business of musical syntax and the conveyance of
deeper kinds of meaning contained within the normal semantic range of
that syntax. As an appendage, word painting acts as an additional constraint on the art of composition, a challenge to the composer's ingenu-
ity and technique, the appreciation of which is crucial for the listener's
sense of the syntax.[35] It becomes audible almost in spite of the things normally listened for. "See! I can do all these tricks and still make a beautiful aria," the music seems to say. So the most virtuosic word painting in
a facile composition will still seem facile, the mountains and valleys of
Handel one can take or leave, and the chromatic descent of the chorus
for "et sepultus est" at the end of Bach's "Crucifixus" may yet be ravishing. In the last case, the descent that translates "sepultus est" is so inex-
tricable a part of the composer's idea—here entailing an unexpected
change of key—that it overcomes any instinct to laugh at it and elicits
wonder and admiration instead. That same instinct in comic circumstances can actually amplify rather than blunt the expression that is
desired. When Leporello lists all the kinds of women that attract Don
Giovanni, the music mincing with "la picina" and rising to a most clichéd
climax with "la grande maestosa," all set against the most courtly topic of
minuet, the overdrawn translations make a perfect complement to Leporello's own buffoonery.

"ABSOLUTE" MUSIC

Musical semantics that are precise, in that most listeners within a
community agree on the content, are possible when the context is
highly defined, usually a text of some sort where a match with the
music is intended. In the case of instrumental music, or even with certain vocal traditions such as plainsong where there seems to be no
semantic match with the accompanying words, there is much less definition in the context surrounding the music. The semantic range created by a passage of notes is left virtually unencumbered, and
interpretation is given free rein. Thus, Alfred Einstein comments on
the opening of Mozart's C-major Quintet, K. 515 (Ex. 3.5): "The first
of these [quintets] is to be compared only with the Quartet in the

Example 3.5. Mozart, String Quintet, K. 515, mm. 1–21.

same key [K. 465, "Dissonant"] except that its beginning is not striving or yearning, like the Allegro of the Quartet, but proud and regal and pregnant with fate."[36] Einstein actually quotes the first five measures to illustrate this remark. Another critic from Einstein's generation, John Burk, writes quite differently: "The Allegro in the first of the great quintets begins with an ascending arpeggio by the cello, the first violin completing the phrase to repeated chords of restless eighth notes, a pattern of melodic top and bottom and accompaniment in between."[37] This comment is easily modernized by organizing the cello motive and the violin motive on a time-line chart and referring to them as "signs."

There is nothing illogical in either remark, as long as their import can be conceived to lie somewhere in the semantic range of Mozart's quintet opening. Burk does little more than translate the musical notation into the English terminology of musical syntax. Interpretation is minimal, but agreement within the community that understands the terminology should be nearly unanimous. Einstein will find unanimity only in the rather tepid response allowing that his interpretation is possible, that is, within the range. On the other hand, he offers new information, a novel hearing. Too bad it can't elicit more confidence.

In natural language, meaning and structure, semantics and syntax, are inextricably intertwined. Although one aspect may dominate the other in certain circumstances, there is nothing of one without some of the other, and one cannot be changed without affecting the other.[38] The quoted remarks seem strained because complete isolation of syntax in Burk and of semantics in Einstein is what they attempt. Now, of course, it is not quite fair to excerpt their writing so meanly. Burk's next sentence, in fact, moves toward a commonsense middle ground: "The thematic triad invites constant and unequivocal modulation." Here syntax is allied to function: there is a syntactic effect that can be interpreted within the music's context.[39] A theoretical premise yields an explanation, not just a description, of what is happening.

Consider one more recent comment on the work:

> The opening of the C major Quintet K. 515 . . . inevitably recalls the first measure of Haydn's op. 33 no. 3, the *Bird*: there is the same mounting phrase in the cello, the same inner accompanying motion, the same placing of the first violin. Yet Haydn's nervous rhythm is avoided; in place of his independent six-measure phrases—the motion broken abruptly between them—Mozart has a linked series of five-measure

phrases with absolutely uninterrupted continuity. In other words, a larger period is imposed on Haydn's system of phrasing: the twenty measures of the first paragraph are divided into 5, 5, 5, 4 plus 1 (the last being a measure of rest—even Haydn's remarkable use of silence in op. 33 no. 3 is turned to account here, but in a grander sense in the context of the larger period). The irregular phrase-length helps to assure the feeling of continuity, and the symmetrical arrangement gives it balance. The transition from the third to the fourth phrase of the paragraph is imperceptible; it is almost impossible to say where the new phrase begins as the violin and cello overlap: while the violin finishes the echo of the first phrases, the cello enters . . . on a new harmony, a dissonance that is given poignance and even sweetness in a spacing that covers four octaves. The symmetrical articulation dissolves at the end, and the measure of rest is all the more dramatic.[40]

With Charles Rosen there is interpretation aplenty, but, as in Burk, almost all of it is tied to the syntactic facts of the passage. This is a wise course, because in order for syntax to exist there must be a community of listeners who understand it, so the critic who begins there can rely on some intersubjective agreement about what is happening. But analysis from syntax can never suspend the rights and privileges of interpretation, because describing the effects, the functions of syntax, as Rosen does here, means applying some notions, if not a theory, about syntax within a particular context. The conditions are the same as interpreting the meaning of a word, and, indeed, interpreting the "functional semantics" of music means choosing from a semantic range. The meaning of a syntactic event, like Mozart's spacing, or the five-bar phrasing, or the rest measure, is what the syntax creates, what effect on the understanding community of listeners it has, among other things. We are therefore far beyond the claims of pure self-reference, that these things mean only themselves. But no event does the same thing, or has the same effect, in every situation. A five-bar phrase has a range of effects, to be interpreted according to the context. Interpretation is inevitable if anything worthwhile is to be said at all.

In the end, therefore, Rosen's commentary is the same in kind as Einstein's but different in degree. By pinning his interpretation on syntax, Rosen narrows the range of interpretation to a point where disagreements are restrained. There might well be many who would complain that "sweetness" is not the right way to describe Mozart's dissonant chord of measure 15, but there would be far fewer to disagree that it is important to the passage, and none that it is dissonant. It is an interpretation of fine but significant details. In skipping over the syntactic details, Einstein must hope that his readers are imagining the same ones as he does in the way that he does. That is not an altogether unreasonable hope—it is not hard to imagine that "yearning" and "regal," respectively, reflect the consistent dissonant strong beats that open K. 465 versus the consonant fanfarelike triad of the quintet—but it is risky. If he hits the mark, though, within the interested musical community, he will have communicated much with a few words.

That is one argument for interpretation beyond, or without, syntax: concision, the insight that hits hard and fast. Another is the sincere desire to supplement the effects of syntactic meaning with other kinds, and, in view of much critical tradition and recent psychology, the importance of these other kinds is hard to deny. Even the ardent abstractionist Hanslick admits that "terms drawn from the vocabulary of our emotional life" are tools that "we cannot do without,"[41] and the semantic range of instrumental music seems to accommodate such connotations with ease and furnish the best cases for the arguments of Susanne Langer and Peter Kivy, who see in it an essential, indexical link with emotions. But emotions are hardly the whole of it. When Rosen compares the quintet opening with the beginning of a Haydn quartet in the same key, he makes a historical point that, however interesting, may not affect anyone's perceptions of the music in the least, but he also invites listeners to consider the quintet opening as an homage to Haydn, Mozart's friend and artistic champion. That is an idea, laden with emotional overtones but not intrinsic emotion, that can become part of the experience of hearing the piece. Such things are surely pointed out often enough in other more obvious instances, such as Mozart's use of Handel in the Requiem, or Brahms's quotation of Beethoven in the finale to his First Symphony.[42] It is silly to dismiss such sensitivities as merely personal, especially if they are common enough to be intersubjective, but it is also silly to claim that the homage paid is the passage's meaning.[43] It is a potential meaning, accessible and useful for some listeners in the community. It is no analytical demonstration, still less a proof, but rather an invitation to a mode of listening that might be enriching. Rosen has through this comment expanded the semantic range of the quintet by illuminating a hitherto unsuspected region. Perhaps that is what good interpretative criticism generally does.

WHAT DOES IT ALL MEAN?

The utterances of both music and language have varying degrees of semantic potential, a potential that is limited by the same principle: the strength and clarity of the context in which any utterance occurs. The semantic range of a sentence, its potential to carry distinct meanings, is comparatively small, because its component parts define its context very well. The window cannot move very much; all those words limit its degrees of freedom. Each one of those words, however, when isolated, has a far greater range of meaning. A passage of instrumental music like the Mozart quintet has a semantic range far greater still. But the semantic difference between this quintet and a sentence from natural language is therefore a difference in degree, not in kind. Given the proper context, any musical passage may have a semantic content that comes quite close to the precision of a sentence, as so many opera composers have shown us.

Context, obviously, is the key element. Certain passages, particularly from instrumental music, to be sure, are best criticized in terms of internal reference and syntactic effect, the kind of criticism characterized by motivic and thematic analysis, conformant relationships, and axiomatic theories. At the other extreme, discussion of opera, or indeed the very composition of opera, becomes absurd if music has no capacity for more stringent semantic content. It is the context of the passage that shapes the kind of meaning it may have. As many contexts as can be imagined, so many are the potential meanings.

In music, the potential can remain just so. Certain pieces, certain kinds of music, and even entire traditions such as liturgical plainsong and Baroque fugal writing may simply refuse to activate that potential, refuse to circumscribe the context any more than absolutely necessary for its performance. For such traditions, any semantic activation beyond the "functional semantics" of syntactic effect is an inessential aspect, even a hindrance to the musical effects they wish to create. That may be why the meaning of a passage or a piece, while an important aspect of its character and identity, is hardly ever the single overwhelming factor in its success. For it is a relatively easy matter to compose topics and create general semantic effects, so easy, in fact, that seventeenth- and eighteenth-century theorists compiled charts and tables of musical figures, very much like a bilingual dictionary, so the young composers would have no trouble saying exactly what they wanted to say in their music. It may be quite true that the semantic content may be very important to the listening experience of a piece that has survived in the repertory, but it is rarely responsible for that survival. It is more like word painting, another kind of compositional constraint, something to be admired in the context of all the other things a composer has to control. That it is a potential and not a fact of music makes it sensible to interpret the referential topics of certain classical works and the programs of tone poems of the nineteenth century and yet impossible to imagine doing anything similar for a Bach fugue without embarrassment. The general context of the fugue is so ill defined, even regarding instrumentation, that there is nothing to justify any specific focus within its semantic range.

Even though traditions such as fugue writing may have only the vaguest of contexts, that does not mean that there can be no interpreting this music, or even that all interpretation of it must be idiosyncratic. There is always syntax, and syntax will always have effects for the community that understands it. A rare delight for an ensemble in rehearsal comes when someone makes the kind of error that changes the syntax without wrecking it: say the violist plays E♭ instead of E♮ in the opening of Mozart's C-major Quintet, instantly transforming the fanfare from a "regal" major to a "perverse" minor. Everybody laughs (unless they are in performance), because it is a musical pun: the syntax works but the effect, its meaning, is wrong. These effects—tensions and resolutions above all, but also tempos, textures, modes, and a myriad of other musical details—make up a "functional semantics" that founds any interpretation, even of passages of word painting and musical dramaturgy that seem to leave syntax far behind. Every word in a natural language has its "functional" semantic side to it, its syntactic job in addition to its symbolic meaning; it is less salient only because the semantics of words is so much more precise than that of musical "passages," so attention is commanded by their symbolic import, what they say about the world. The broader, less precise semantic range of musical gestures requires that interpretation stem from syntactic effect in a way that is unnecessary in language. How a composition creates effects in listeners is the beginning of meaning.[44]

So the paradox is true, after all. All too often listeners cannot agree on the symbolic import of a piece of music simply because the context does not permit it. The same could happen in language; very often it does. At the same time, something is always conveyed to an understanding musical community, and when circumstances permit, the message can be precise enough to translate into natural language. But such precision is hardly the point of music outside those circumstances, and if there is a "sovereign" semantic of music, it resides in musical effects on which all meaning depends.

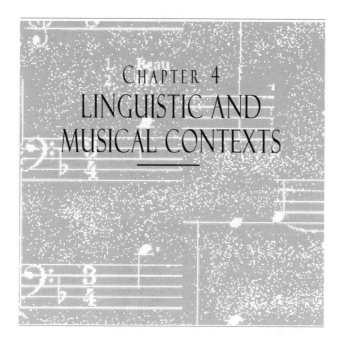

CHAPTER 4
LINGUISTIC AND MUSICAL CONTEXTS

Is it any surprise that the notion of context seems all but indispensable in the preceding development of musical phonology, syntax, and semantics? In these days when context is buzzing about every academic discipline, no phenomenon is self-evident anymore; everything demands a background. But the most urgent contexts in music and language perception are not historicisms, that is, *reflections* on percepts, facts, words, ideas, theories and—in the extreme—even entire disciplines. Instead, they are part of everyone's everyday intuitions, *reflexes* that are immediate, subconscious, and fluent.

Surely this facility is nothing more than an example of the part-whole dynamic made famous by the gestalt psychologists. In a general sense it surely is, of course, but in music and language the assembly of parts into wholes is quite extraordinary. The perception of music and the perception of speech are real-time operations that process countless items of information with superb accuracy at high speed,[1] and it is this speed that links the two most essentially; that, and a kind of constant review of the present, a continual reconsideration of percepts just heard, in raw form, along with others precisely imagined yet to come. The perception of music and speech is incomparably dynamic.

This contextual dynamic operates at every level of musical and linguistic perception:

Wife: Will you be getting out of work late again today?
Husband: Do you need the car?
Wife: I have to go to that parents' meeting at the school at six.[2]

In the phonology of language, the identification of any single elemental sound comes about with the identification of others in virtually parallel transmission. "The signal is *context dependent*—the acoustic wave for any speech unit changes because of the surrounding speech units. At any single moment, the signal will have information concerning successive sounds, because of their overlap."[3] That is why the wife will use the phone [f] instead of [v] when she says "have to": the anticipated unvoiced phoneme /t/ transforms the preceding, normally voiced /v/ into its unvoiced counterpart [f]. Pronouncing them "normally" means slowing down and speaking with rather artificial deliberation. No physical dimension seems constant: the length of time it takes for the voice to begin the vowel following a /v/ or /f/ is critical for the hearer to distinguish these phonemes, and yet the categorical boundary varies according to the rate of articulation even in *individual speakers*.[4] Musical performance, which prizes the consistency of sound, would appear to insist on an absolute phonology, but in fact the habitual "adjustment" of pitches away from equal temperament that has always been suspected of singers, string and wind players—anyone whose pitches are not pre-tuned—has been found in the psychologist's laboratory.[5] D♯ is not the same physical event as E♭, and even notated E♭s will vary according to the situation.

Does the husband hear "parents" as a plural noun, singular possessive, or adjective? That the least probable usage, adjective, is the answer here shows how pervasive is the role of context in the understanding of syntax. The case in music is the same: one of the earliest and most important lessons every student of harmony learns is that a chord's function is never simply the product of its construction alone but of its presentation and surroundings. Milton Babbitt has remarked that so fundamental a harmonic property as "consonance and dissonance are context dependent tonal concepts; it is impossible to assert that an interval is consonant aurally, since it always can be notated as dissonant, and this notation reflects a possible context."[6] Thus, syntactic context is given a logical basis. It is given an empirical one from innumerable sources; the simple perception of tonal center, the key of a piece, arises as much from the order of pitch presentation as from the content of the pitch set: "the same group of tones that elicits nearly unanimous identifications of one key can be temporally reordered such that it evokes strong concurrence in the identification of a second key."[7] The dependence of syntax on context is part and parcel of one of its essential functions. We saw in chapter 2 how context-sensitive grammars are the best ones for controlling information without limiting unduly the semantic power of a language.

That semantic power comes from the precise identification of lexical items—which "school" is the wife talking about: nursery, elementary, university, Mannerist, or maybe one of fish?—and this occurs when a word's semantic range is suitably narrowed by the context. Researchers in cognition, philosophy of science, and musical aesthetics find similar things happening with the perception and memory for categories, the use of scientific terms, and the phenomenological perception of musical events.[8]

MUSICAL PRAGMATICS?

So, already we have phonological contexts, syntactic contexts, and semantic contexts—all are essential if a language is to work. There is yet another kind. When linguists observe how language is used in actual situations, they extend the semantic context beyond the interactions of words with one another to the interactions of words with the environment of conversation and discourse. This is known as pragmatics. It links language with the world.

The conversation above, for example, seems perfectly normal, completely comprehensible, and yet is actually rather strange when the semantics of it are taken at face value. The husband not only avoids answering his wife's question, he does not even reply with a statement but rather returns with a question that has nothing to do with getting out of work. At least the wife answers him with a declarative sentence, but, again, one that is completely off the subject.

Such a reading is obtuse, of course, because the context of the situation has been deliberately forgotten. Only when this context is brought back—a big context of American social practices, including work, education, marital relations—as a set of necessary assumptions does the series of non sequiturs make sense. Then, it makes more than good sense; it makes for a very efficient exchange, where the obvious is better left unstated, better because to state it would only waste time.

In their book *Relevance: Communication and Cognition*, Dan Sperber and Deirdre Wilson provide a commonsense framework for the use of context in this way. The principle is simply this: the speaker can safely assume that the hearer listens with the assumptions available from the immediate social context, from the linguistic context, and from the much greater context of cultural background and personal history, and searches for the greatest possible relevance of the utterances coming from the speaker. So, the husband, surmising that his wife does not want to know when his workday ends for information's sake, tries to find another reason. His question is a test to see whether his guess was correct. Her reply is in effect a confirmation and a justification of her need to use the car at the same time. Very efficient, very reasonable.

Such assumptions, guesses, inferences, and deductions depend on precise semantic relations between the utterance and the real world, relations that can be quite subtle indeed. The reason the wife does not begin by saying outright "I need the car this afternoon" might depend on a host of tacit understandings between the couple, personal assumptions and beliefs, and social conventions about making requests. Can music have a similarly pragmatic dimension and link up with the world?

Consider the opening of the Beethoven Violin Concerto (Ex. 4.1).

Example 4.1. Beethoven, Violin Concerto, I, mm. 1–13.

Inference is most conscious when the normal meaning does not fit the situation. When the woman asks, "Will you be getting out of work late again today?" the context, in her hearer's judgment, does not justify the literal meaning of the question, so he infers another meaning. In the concerto, the opening bar requires an inference of sorts, because it is unharmonized, so that the function of the pitch is ambiguous, and because it is played on the timpani, perhaps the most audacious choice before 1808 for presenting the first motive of a symphonic work. The first puzzle is solved immediately in the second bar when the most likely inference that the opening Ds are tonic notes proves correct. When this motive returns in measures 10 and 12, played by three different string groups on an unharmonized D♯, the need for inference returns more urgently. The tonal context is clear now; what can the D♯ be doing there? In the first instance it moves to a leading tone as part of a V⁷ chord. Is the note really then a Neapolitan E♭, belying Beethoven's own notation? In the second instance it rises to G while the first violins add the ninth factor B over the dominant again. Was it then a strange kind of V of ii, a temporary leading tone, D♯—Beethoven can spell after all—which then resolves irregularly? And why should violins try to play like drums?

This kind of observation has stimulated a good deal of fine criticism in the past half-century or so, particularly on the works of the Classical repertory. The piece presents a syntactic ambiguity, a puzzle, a problem, which the composer works through in the course of the composition. Beethoven, in fact, writes passages in his concerto that seem to exploit both the E♭ and D♯ interpretations of the pitch, perhaps exploiting at the same time, in a pragmatic sort of way, the listener's willingness, even desire, to find some relevant solution to the puzzle (Ex. 4.2). Here the D♯, at the top of a diminished seventh, acts like a leading tone to E, but the syntax is not unequivocal, for this particular diminished seventh is commonly used as an altered subdominant (B♯-D♯-F♯-A) that moves to an

Example 4.2. Beethoven, Violin Concerto, I, mm. 64–73.

inversion of V, which is in fact its goal here, though not the most common one of V⁶. Then, on the third, most emphatic presentation, when the diminished chord does resolve to ii⁶ (m. 71), the D♯ has withdrawn into the middle of the texture, so that its syntax is occluded. Later (Ex. 4.3), in the most mysterious and dramatic shift in the development, the harmony changes from a root tonic in the key of E-flat major (mm. 342–343) to what can only be a V⁶ in D (m. 344), with the E♭ in the bass moving to C♯, as happened in measure 11 of the opening. How beautifully the link with the beginning is underscored by the return of the

Example 4.3. Beethoven, Violin Concerto, I, mm. 343–345.

drumbeats on the opening motive, till now barely hinted at by horns and bassoons, now amplified by trumpets. Again, the unusual syntax reveals the supposed Neapolitan function only in retrospect.

The problem for the analogy of musical pragmatics so far is that the person listening to the concerto is making inferences about syntax, not semantics. The context that interprets the D#/E♭ is not connected to the real world but rather seems contained within the world of the composition. But why should the violins act like drums?

THE CIRCLES OF PERCEPTION

If we suspend judgment for the moment on the propriety of musical pragmatics, the essential first lesson about musical and linguistic contexts is that they are inherent in every level of linguistic and musical perception, from the phonological on up, and inherent in that reflexive way that is part of an effortless and fluent comprehension. The second lesson is that context affects perceptions not just within a level, so that the syntax of "parents" will inform the syntax of "meeting," but also across levels, so that the meaning of one word will inform the syntax, even the phonology of the sounds to come: hearing "I" ensures that /haf/ is understood as "have" and not "half." Often, the pragmatic situation is so pointed that it overrules the ear. This exchange actually occurred:

> Undergraduate (from Brooklyn, New York): I would like to take that new course "The Philosophy of Nature."
>
> Advisor: Really! Why are you interested in that?
>
> Undergraduate (puzzled): Well . . . it's just interesting.
>
> Advisor: I ask only because Nietzsche is rather advanced if you haven't had philosophy before. Do you know any Nietzsche?

Such influence is the rule, not the exception.

It is not a tidy situation. Logic would have it that natural languages were built like computer languages, with atomic particles of discrete identities and unique interpretations connecting into units in a pre-scribed and unvarying order according to type, resulting in sentences of similarly unique interpretations. In BASIC, the string PRINT "BEETHOVEN" means only one thing, forever. Natural languages, alas, must contend with human perception and experience, and logic is too often left in the dust. Syntax is indeed responsible for ordering the strings that produce meaningful sentences, but we have seen that the semantic realm circles back upon the syntactic, so that "meeting" makes "parents" a noun modifier. We have seen that not one detail of syntax can be changed without affecting the meaning. We might hope that phonemes at least are too atomic to have anything to do with meaning, but we have seen how English words beginning with *sl* are biased toward the pejorative[9] and how the mention of "philosophy" can transform "nature" into "Nietzsche."

For composers these practical realities are unavoidable, for they cannot write a single note without deciding what instrument will play it, and that single phonological decision already biases the semantic range of whatever follows. Try to imagine for a moment the Violin Concerto beginning with any other instrument. The register is crucial here, because it allows the motive to act as a harmonic root when the melody sounds above it (m. 2). String bass or cello? Too comic, if they are to have a staccato effect, as Beethoven obviously wishes when he carefully uses eighth notes and rests in the violin version (m. 11). French horn? Possibly, but the register there is not very grateful. Bassoon, the clown of the orchestra? What the timpani opening means is not easy to specify, like most things in music having broad semantic range, but it clearly communicates the seriousness, even portentousness, of the composition about to be heard, the longest first movement of any violin concerto of its age, and the greatest one of any age.

The conclusion is difficult to escape: the melodic idea is not to be abstracted so easily into pitches and durations, because an important part of its meaning is bound to the practical world of phonology, what plays it. Phonology and semantics are bound together in a mutual context. And since musical semantics depends so much on the kind and level of musical tension, how can semantics be insulated from syntax, which produces and controls that tension? Audition researcher Stephen Handel, writing about rhythm in speech and music, writes that "meanings cannot arise without intensities or durations, without rhythms or textures, and so on. In circular fashion, intensity, pitch, duration, rhythm, and so on are perceived within the structure provided by the meaning. The parts and wholes coalesce into one percept; it is not that the whole determines the parts as the Gestalt psychologists argue. Allport, pointing out that the whole at one level may be a part at a different level, has termed this the inside-outside problem."[10]

BOTTOM-UP, TOP-DOWN, AND FORMALISM

The "circular fashion"—"loops" in David Lewin's phenomenological view, "reciprocals" in Gjerdingen's schemas[11]—captures in one picture the cognitive scientist's distinction between "bottom-up" and "top-down" perception; the former names the mechanisms that process sensory data coming in through our ears and eyes into usable information and concepts, and the latter accounts for the contextual effects of concepts and knowledge upon the selection and processing of sensory data. The circle image is apt because part of the context acting upon new sounds consists of sounds just processed. Thus arises the paradox of sounds forming the context that regulates their own perception. The top-down process has at least two dimensions: one operating on a single perceptual level, say syntax, but forward in time, as a kind of anticipation based on what has just been heard; the second operating among levels, backward in time as well as forward, so that semantic and phonological factors can revise syntactic judgments already made. The circle implies in its bottom-up, top-down tandem that perception and subsequent understanding in the manner of concept formation, mental computation, and so on are irreducible to one-way causes and effects.

The circle idea has its critics. "You can't help hearing an utterance of a sentence (in a language you know) as an utterance of a sentence," writes Jerry Fodor in an influential book called *The Modularity of Mind*.[12] He argues that human cognition is best characterized by certain specific faculties, such as a language faculty, which are insulated in their most basic operations from conscious thinking, thus accounting for their speed and fluency.[13] Such insulation would block much of the top-down interpretation of incoming sensory information. It could not, however, do without any, for how else would one know which faculty to begin using? Fodor's parenthesis "in a language you know" already implies a role for background knowledge, if only to decide whether the acoustic sequence bombarding the ear is English or not.

The acute problem is explaining how contextual listening can retrace its steps when music and speech go only forward in time. The answer appears to be that the "psychological present" can last as long as five seconds, which is a very long time on the scale of music and speech perception.[14] During this period raw acoustic information can be held up, subject to evaluation not only in the context of background knowledge but also in the context of sounds that immediately follow.[15] How many of us, while concentrating on some unrelated task or even an ongoing conversation, have had the "echoic" experience of letting someone else's remark—"He was fired last week"—fly by unnoticed until some alarm in the working memory brings it to consciousness in its original form?

Here the circle can close. A working memory[16] that can reevaluate the phonology, syntax, and semantics of sounds helps to explain the results of psycholinguistic experiments showing that many meanings of a spoken word are briefly entertained.[17] This is but a glimpse into the first stages of evaluation. It is the broad sense of context, working with the sound, that forms the "final" percept.[18] Long practice with familiar patterns allows a hierarchical "chunking" to come into play well within the time allowed, so that there can be contextual exchanges among perceptual levels and highly efficient processing. "This is true for the average language user and for the trained musician. In extremely overlearned and overpracticed domains it may be quite difficult to switch attention to the acoustic details, but it is obviously possible."[19]

The absolutely pervasive role of context in perception has been resisted, because it makes formal theories of language and music much trickier to design. Context is infinitely variable and infinitely particular. No one has proposed a context generator akin to Chomsky's generative grammars.

Eugene Narmour's ingenious and rigorous theory of melody, the implication-realization model, is a calculus of melody designed by formal rules. He postulates first that "the theoretical constants invoked herein"—including hypotheses of melodic similarity, difference, process, reversal, and the inferences we make from them—"are context free and thus apply to all styles of melody."[20] Unable to ignore the contextual aspect, however, he provides that "ultimately, the model coordinates the constants of process and reversal with certain empirical, top-down psychological theories of episodic memory, schemata, and representativeness."[21] And so it does; the analytical diagrams are marked with some symbols denoting the theoretical constants and with some denoting various "influences" such as "intraopus style" (what has already happened in the piece), "extraopus style" (what the listener should know about how this kind of music works), and "harmony." The credibility of this formal system, then, depends upon the relative weight of each contributor. If context is a bit player, having little say against the brute forces of the theoretical constants, then all is well. But what if context generally competes on a par, or, yes, outweighs the natural laws? Then all the formalism, and all the effort its use requires, yields at best a rough approximation to the truth, which in the end must be evaluated in the old way, by critical judgment.

Isn't this similar to the situation of classical physics, the inspiration for so much formalist theory? Physics provides beautifully simple and true laws of force and motion. The trouble is that when engineers apply these beautiful laws in bridge building or airplane design, they have to go out and take on-site measurements of wind stress, ground support, and other contextual factors, messy things that appear only as little constants in the formulas. In practical situations, in real-world contexts, such little constants demand testing in every new circumstance. There is no context-free formula for friction. This is to say nothing of multivariable, chaotic systems when even the classical formulas cannot predict the emergent properties that arise out of weather patterns and such. In physical science it is the generality that is interesting; in music, a most practical art, it is more often the details of the specific situation that are compelling. Did not our perusal of musical syntax show as much?

If we cannot formulate context, do we then abandon all hope of objectivity in music analysis and criticism? What arbitrates the phonological, syntactic, semantic, and pragmatic practices of music and language?

MUSICAL COMMUNITIES

How do we explain why things are wrong in speech? Not very rationally.

Where is the logic that requires a Briton to say "at home," a German to use a different preposition with "zu Hause," and a Parisian to use no preposition at all in "chez moi"? A European tourist, visiting America on schoolhouse English, might say to his host after a long morning of sightseeing: "I have hunger" a literal translation of his native idiom. What is wrong with that? It is a matter not so much of lost meaning but of form unacceptable to the English-speaking community, unacceptable in the sense that no English speaker would use it. There is no rationality that will explain why European communities "have hunger" while English-speaking communities "are hungry," except for the convention of a linguistic community. Proper pronunciation, proper grammar, right use in semantics are all in the nature of a tacit agreement among the speakers of a language. "It isn't said that way." The passive voice hides the omnipotence of this communal pact. The particulars of the agreement take many years to learn and can be extremely fine in their detail, but

the resulting conformity assures the easy processing, the linguistic fluency that is second nature to native speakers and really quite necessary
if we are to exploit human language to its fullest powers. Until fluency
is achieved, the mental strain required to meet the community on its
own terms leaves one too exhausted to do much beyond the minimum
with language, as anyone immersed in a foreign language knows all too
well.

Listeners who share perceptions of music make a community in the
same way.[22] The judgment that the Beethoven Violin Concerto begins in
D major is a judgment ratified by the community of listeners who know
Beethoven's musical language and who, by the way, are the ones most
interested in such judgments. It is of course possible that a change in
some context for that piece—a different harmony in the second measure,
say—might alter that judgment or make it ambiguous, but those new perceptions would be equally subject to the ultimate judgment of the musical community. Any critical or analytical statement, ranging from
whether a wrong note has been played to whether a piece is poorly conceived, is responsible to an interested community in this way. The community is the arbitrator and the source of objectivity for criticism.

Music theory speaks about the nature of these shared perceptions that
define a community. Its generalizations point out the commonalities of
the perceptions, usually holding the particulars of context at bay for as
long as possible with escape clauses in the manner of *ceteris paribus*, "all
things being equal." So we can write that "a tonic chord in a strong metric position is perceived stable" as one particular of the community of the
European classical musical language, unless, of course, a particular context overrides this general perception. Charles Rosen gives a compelling
example from Beethoven:

> It is, in fact, with this fundamental triad [I] that Beethoven attains his
> most remarkable and characteristic effects. At one point in the G major
> Piano Concerto [see Ex. 4.4], he achieves the seemingly impossible with
> it and turns this most consonant of chords (into which all dissonance must
> be, by definition, resolved by the end of the piece) itself into a dissonance.
> In the following measures, almost by rhythmic means alone and without
> modulating from G major, the tonic chord of G major in root position
> clearly requires a resolution into the dominant.[23]

Rosen's observation takes both the linguistic rule and the overriding context into account. Critical judgments are in fact judgments about musical languages in a particular context, and the power and veracity of the

Example 4.4. Beethoven, Piano Concerto, Op. 58, I, mm. 23–28.

judgments are measured by the degree to which the critics's community ratifies them. Does Rosen's judgment persuade us, both as to its truth and as to its significance for the matter at hand? In this sense the critic's opinion, like the context it must judge, is not unbounded, and one opinion is never as good as another.

The notion of musical community has an empirical side, then, in that it appeals to a kind of statistical data, the response of the community members regarding conventions and their relation to the immediate context—a kind of intersubjectivity that is not monolithic but cannot be ignored. Reading this data is much more complicated than estimating carbon-14 atoms, because all community members are not all alike, and indeed, they have decisively different roles within that community.[24] The response of a Heifetz or a Perlman to the opening of the Beethoven Violin Concerto carries a lot more weight than most. On the other hand, a musical community does not rule out the existence of musical absolutes or universals, since history has made it clear that certain responses to music and musical compositions have been elicited time and again from ever changing communities. These absolute aesthetic values may be ineffable or undiscoverable, but critics try, somehow, to grasp something of their essence in analysis, to strike a chord in the community that their writing seeks to enlighten.

One certain aspect of a musical community: it is part of the real world. Can composition say the same?

GENRE, THE PRAGMATIC CONTEXT

The genre of a composition, whether it be symphony, sonata, or song, has not been a matter of concern in theoretical analysis of the last half-century. Indeed, it is often impossible to tell by looking at an analytical graph what kind of piece the work under analysis is, or was. The reason is quite simple: genre appeared to have little to do with syntax, which has been the main concern of analysis during this period. The bare fact of the matter is, however, that there must be some relation between the genre of a piece and the pitch relations that go into it, if only because transcription is so often unsatisfactory. Who wants to hear "Eroica" played by an organ, by a wind band, by anything but a symphony orchestra?

By supplying listeners with a set of cognitive premises that can be used to interpret the sounds to come, genre becomes one of the most important choices a composer makes at the outset of the work.[25] Genre presents a defining context. At its base are the technical limitations, banal, perhaps, but no less essential circumstances that define what is commonplace and what is difficult, since each genre, no less than each instrument, has its idiomatic strengths and weaknesses. Then there are the social and functional aspects, cultural associations about what a piece should be doing and where it belongs and how its sound fulfills those requirements. Such contextual considerations of the genre, particularly the technical ones, can engage the notes written by the composer, and then we have a logical relation between genre and the syntactic and semantic aspects of the composer's musical language. Simply put, there should be a match between the musical ideas, themes, motives, and so on and the kind of piece that presents them.

Anyone who has visited the great Basilica of St. Mark's in Venice and spent just a little time studying the wealth of mosaic decoration has experienced the practical import of this matching in visual terms. Here the great Byzantine works of the twelfth and thirteenth centuries are seen side by side with sixteenth-century "restorations" carried out by some of Venice's master painters of the Renaissance (see figure facing page). After seeing them it is easy to believe that not even a Michelangelo could produce a good mosaic. The little *tessere*, so right for medieval abstraction, preclude the precise detail that the brushstroke can create for the ideals of Renaissance realism, and the gold background connotes a medieval symbolism that finds no answer in the design. A Renaissance mosaic is almost a contradiction in terms.

MAFFEO DA VERONA, DISCESA LIMBO (1627), ST. MARK'S BASILICA, VENICE

It is similarly difficult to imagine a truly Mendelssohnian madrigal, and only the vitality of choral societies maintains nineteenth-century sacred works characterized by much of the same vulgarity we find in the mosaics of St. Mark's—the Sanctus of Verdi's *Requiem*, with its vaudevillian ending, comes to mind. But this is to dwell on the exceptional mismatches to illustrate the principle; on the other side of this coin is the multitude of truly idiomatic compositions that exploit the characteristics of their genres in alliance with the syntax and semantics of the composition.

A truly idiomatic composition is one that takes fullest advantage of the genre context to shape its syntactic and semantic material, its melodies, harmonies, and rhythms. The material for a late sixteenth-century madrigal is so different from that of a motet as to qualify as a different language altogether. Their communities could accept and understand radical chromaticism, violent rhythmic articulations, weird leaps in voice leading, and unexpected dissonances in the settings of their love poems but not for their sacred texts, which demanded a much more conservative, traditional idiom. For a composer to use such devices in a motet would only antagonize the community and disqualify the composition, but to hold to the traditional language when writing a madrigal in 1590 would baffle the singers as some kind of inept understatement. More subtle are the distinctions, say, between the thematic material of Haydn's quartets and that of his symphonies, but the briefest imagining of one transformed into the other reveals how real those distinctions are. Now there is a middle ground, where a composition neither exploits nor contradicts the context of its genre. The contrapuntal studies of J. S. Bach are perhaps the greatest examples of this inspired neutrality.

Is that why Bach transcribes so well, compared to other composers? Transcription is a practical, mysterious problem, and yet some telling facts about it are reasonably clear. Bach's music, particularly the fugues but also many dance movements, have been transcribed for other instruments ranging from guitar to symphony orchestra with scarcely any damage. Early madrigals and Parisian chansons were regularly adapted for other media, and there was a tradition, now discreetly forgotten, of Lieder transcription in the nineteenth century. But then, the later, dramatic madrigals of Monteverdi, say, fail of transcription, and the attempts to fit Beethoven's late quartets and *Hammerklavier* Sonata to orchestral forces are generally condemned, as are some of the composer's own attempts to repackage certain pieces—the Violin Concerto and the Grosse Fuge especially—to squeeze a little more money out of them. At the extreme, the transfer of chant to instruments is practically unimaginable, and using violins and clarinets in place of the vocal parts in operas is laughable.

In the Monteverdi, the match of text and music is so finely detailed that each is contextually beneficial for the other. The sudden pauses and chromatic shifts become nonsensical in an instrumental medium, where the missing semantic range of the text no longer justifies its aberrant musical context. Earlier madrigalists such as Verdelot and Arcadelt were content with much broader strokes, general reflections of the sense of their poems, general enough to translate to an instrumental form whose syntax was still intelligible without any textual gloss. The situation of the *Hammerklavier* is analogous. The music of the melodies, harmonies, and rhythms feeds off its pianistic context in an essential way that a fugue of Bach does not. The Bach triumphs with the abstract relations of pitch and duration alone, whereas these things in Beethoven take meaning from their immediate instrumental context. "The opening of the *Hammerklavier*, which sounds so feeble and ineffective in any orchestral transcription, is gigantic on the piano."[26] In short, the tighter the circular relation between genre and syntax of a musical composition's arrangement, the less likely a transcription will succeed. Chant is a peculiar example of this phenomenon. Although it has little in the way of semantic matching between music and text, its much more generic connotations of a cappella sound and "church music" must exclude any instrumental arrangement, excepting, in highly defined circumstances, the organ.

The linking of these generic connotations with the syntax of the work makes music pragmatic in the linguistic sense.

Remember what happens in the pragmatics of language. When the wife asks her husband about quitting time, the utterance presents him with a range of possible meanings. He uses the context of the situation, everything he knows that might possibly bear on this asking, and seeks the maximum relevance—why should she ask about quitting time?—to infer the precise meaning of her sentence. The speaker, for her part, can depend on his good faith to seek the true motive for her asking, beyond any literal interpretation. Semantic range has been linked with the real-world context.

The difference in musical pragmatics is that the "real-world context" is the genre, and the link is not usually with the semantics of the music, although it can be, but with its syntax. The genre constructs a situation that, like a conversation, limits what can be reasonably said. Listeners expect that these idiomatic bounds not be traversed, except in extraordinary circumstances, and in turn composers can expect good faith on the part of their musical community, a willingness to find the best interpretation. In this way the community is an active participant in constructing the experience. As in a good conversation, good listening demands that kind of responsibility.

Beethoven depends on that willingness to infer a syntactic function for the odd D♯s played by the violins in the opening measures of the Violin Concerto. There is no question that the unison of measure 10 captures the listener's attention irresistibly. The opening motive, so plain in rhythm, has nevertheless been made riveting by its timpani persona, and now very early on it is turned into a puzzle in at least two ways: in its syntactic inflection to D♯ (or E♭?) and in its new orchestration. The violins, in one sense, make a caricature of the motive, but in this Beethoven makes a virtue of necessity. Eighteenth-century timpani simply could not play the raised tonic degree—a phonological limit to the language—so to present the motive on D♯ without changing its character, Beethoven makes the violins act like drums, changing the motive's notation to make sure that they do. But that only draws more attention to the anomalous syntax of the motive, specifically in a way that links the ambiguous D♯ function with the sound of the timpani itself.

As we have seen, some of the key moments in the first movement interpret in diverse yet inconclusive ways the syntactic meaning of that pitch. How remarkable it is that the violin soloist is allowed to play the timpani motive only once in the exposition and once in the recapitulation but in both instances becomes an interpreter of that question (Ex. 4.5). That the principal violin itself plays the motive on D♯ and resolves

Example 4.5. Beethoven, Violin Concerto, I, mm. 438–442

it upward pushes the leading tone hearing, but the important thing about these two moments is that they bring the concerto genre into the puzzle. Somehow the essence of what a concerto is should be integral to its solution.

The Neapolitan hearing is favored at points very close to the solution, if that indeed is the proper concept for what happens at the conclusion of the rondo finale. The first hint comes in the extraordinary passage just before the cadenza, where the home key of D major is dramatized by a series of cadential gestures (Ex. 4.6). The passage is like the previous example in that Beethoven's use of the E♭ creates the correct impression, this time of the familiar Neapolitan syntax, but an impression that is bothered, ever so slightly, by certain idiosyncrasies: the Neapolitan chord

Example 4.6. Beethoven, Violin Concerto, III, mm. 248–253.

as a seventh, with the new factor in the bass, followed by a second inversion, then in root position, but never its conventional arrangement as a Neapolitan sixth; then its "resolution" as a real dominant seventh onto, of all harmonies, an A-flat minor triad, a chord that has no harmonic function whatsoever in the key of D major. At this point the pragmatics of the concerto form come into explicit conflict with the gesture, since the very articulation of the home key required by the classical rondo and by Beethoven's own style is called into question. The low-level syntax here, a typical dominant to tonic in A-flat minor, can only be understood as such if the high-level syntaxes are forgotten. But this moment of disorientation is quickly rescued by the reinterpretation of the E♭, carefully maintained as the top pitch in the soloist's arpeggio, as a D♯ (and the C♭ as a B, moving to A, the A♭ as a G♯, moving to F♯—the voice leading is impeccable) in a conventional V of ii harmony that starts to finish off the cadence. How quickly these reinterpretations occur. That speed, in fact, makes it easy for listeners to keep up with them, for the six critical beats take about 4 seconds, and the cross-comparisons can be made nicely while the sounds are still ringing in our mind's ear.

This passage concentrates in a few measures the solution of the puzzle, namely, a progression in which both interpretations of the mysterious violin drum note are both valid and indispensable. What is so astonishing, after this elegance, is the confidence that Beethoven shows in this syntactic artifice, for now, after the cadenza, at a point where nothing but D-major cadences should articulate a formal resolution, he expands on this idea with a freedom that can only come from absolute conviction in its rightness (Ex. 4.7).

Example 4.7. Beethoven, Violin Concerto, III, mm. 288–308.

The modulation device here, the chromatic reinterpretation of a diminished seventh, is familiar enough in Beethoven, but never in this concerto has the composer moved from his home key so quickly, so directly to the remoteness of A-flat major. Its exotic relation with D major is plain to the ear and of no little import for the effect of these pages, but why A flat? So many reasons apply, really, that the imagination behind the sheer amount of technical coordination is, quite simply, stunning. A flat is the one key neither on the sharp side nor the flat side of D, the home key, so it need not commit to an interpretation of the violin drum note as an E♭ or D♯. It is biased toward the former because the soloist changes the upper note of the supertonic trill from F♯ to F♮ (m. 289), so the mode is changed from D major to D minor before the crucial reinterpretation of the G from seventh factor to leading tone that will get us to A-flat major. But the trill change ties in to so many contrasts of F♮ and F♯ that Beethoven has made throughout the concerto (another kind of syntactic puzzle; alas, there isn't space to detail them all), and when the trill changes again (m. 291), the soloist provides the root of the new V⁷ and again takes the protagonist's role in the dénouement of this little drama. Finally, A-flat major is the perfect home for the new variation of the rondo tune, since the tune's design ensures that E♭s are the most prominent notes.

It is the soloist that plays the tune in this exotic key, and it is the soloist that engineers the breathtaking return to D in the space of eleven measures. What a stroke to add that little appoggiatura at the beginning of the bar (m. 297), so that D to E♭ is brought to the fore. The E♭ passes not, as expected from the preceding bars, to a C♯ as a Neapolitan but upward to E♮, and at the same time it does not vanish from hearing, because the little appoggiatura is transposed with it, keeping it vital as a D♯ now. The harmonic progression, again, makes both meanings valid and yet indispensable. The difference from before, the difference that justifies this terrific expansion and makes it one of the great passages of concerto writing, is that it erupts in a blaze of virtuosic brilliance in which the fiddling seems to vary almost by the measure, so that the whole passage, the most intense concentration of the crucial syntactic relationships of the work, from the D♯/E♭ identity to the magnificent three eighth notes that break the runs and bring out once more the F♮ to F♯ conflict, is brought off as some fantastic improvisation embodying the very spirit of what a violin concerto is supposed to be. Beethoven brings the generic and the syntactic together and makes them embrace.

Thus, the piece is absolutely idiomatic, a true concerto for violin, and that is very much part of its genius. Beethoven depends not only on his community's willingness to grant him the benefit of the doubt at every turn regarding eccentric syntax but also on his community's perception of virtuosity in violin playing. The perception of masterful technique in playing this passage is as important to its final effect as the perception of prodigious compositional technique in solving the problems of syntax, and in that way the genre creates an analogy with the essentially technical aspect of syntax itself.[27] That is why Beethoven's own rescoring of this piece as a piano concerto fails (Ex. 4.8). Beethoven's conversion of the saucy little appoggiatura figure into more pianistic octaves is a real loss,

Example 4.8. Beethoven, Violin Concerto, rescored by the composer as a piano concerto, III, mm. 288–308.

but even if that can be forgiven, there is simply nothing impressive about the technique of the passage when played on the piano, and the attempt to make it so actually straitjackets the voice leading at the end. The ravishing, climactic eighth-note melody (D–E–F♮–F♯) is gone.

The Violin Concerto proves that genre can provide a pragmatic context for music's syntactic discourse of notes and rhythms, one that engages this discourse in a circular perception like other reflexive contexts in music and language. Genre links the Violin Concerto with the real world, with the community of listeners that inhabit it. It is essential for the effects that the composer is trying to create.

It has shown us something else, too. Those harmonic progressions in the third-movement passages are quite beyond the norms of the harmonic syntax that Beethoven inherited, and yet he has contrived somehow to make them more than simply comprehensible, but powerful, beautiful, and almost—one hesitates to say it anymore—inevitable. Somehow, Beethoven has created a harmonic syntax, but one that is good for this composition only. It turns out that music of the Classical style does this quite regularly, in a way remarkably reminiscent of poetry.

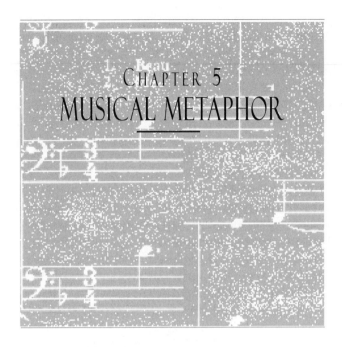

Chapter 5
MUSICAL METAPHOR

A MOODY child and wildly wise
Pursued the game with joyful eyes,
Which chose, like meteors, their way,
And rived the dark with private ray:
They overleapt the horizon's edge,
Searched with Apollo's privilege;
Through man, and woman, and sea, and star,
Saw the dance of nature forward far;
Through worlds, and races, and terms, and times,
Saw musical order, and pairing rhymes.

EMERSON, "THE POET"[1]

In this cameo of the poet's nature, Emerson alludes in the last lines to an essentially musical quality of poetry. This allusion finds almost universal sympathy among poets, and its appreciation can be quite deep. Wordsworth attributes poetry's pleasurable effects to much more than the sensual:

Now the music of harmonious metrical language, the sense of difficulty overcome, and the blind association of pleasure which has been previously received from works of rhyme or metre of the same or similar construction, all these imperceptibly make up a complex feeling of delight, which is of the most important use in tempering the painful feeling which always will be found intermingled with powerful descriptions of the deeper passions.[2]

His description of the "sense of difficulty overcome"—the impression of technique, in other words—united with the memory of previous pleasures could be taken, together with the essentials of "harmonious metrical language," as an apt précis of the psychology of musicality. Ezra Pound, less circumspect, simply defines poetry in musical terms flat out:

> Poetry is a composition of words set to music. Most other definitions of it are indefensible, or worse, metaphysical. The amount or quality of the music may, and does, vary; but poetry withers and "dries out" when it leaves music, or at least an imagined music, too far behind it.[3]

Musicians have rarely spoken with such effusion and profundity about this affinity between music and poetry, but they have nevertheless unquestionably affirmed it by their actions, which often speak louder, as the adage says. In the ages-old marriage between music and words that creates the world's songs, for example, the preference of composers for poetry is overwhelming. Even in opera, where a composer's interest shifts from the lyric to the dramatic, the libretti are almost always in verse. Only the unmetered *Gloria* and *Credo* and the canticles of the Christian tradition of sacred Western music prevent the use of poetry in musical composition from being a kind of universal law.[4] Sacred music apart, everything sung is sung to poetry.

The obvious reasons for this mutual affinity are written into Wordsworth's "harmonious metre" and Emerson's "pairing rhymes." In a song the poetic articulations of meter and rhyme of a traditional lyric match and reinforce the musical articulations of measure and phrase. Thus, songwriters, whatever value they might place in the meaning of a lyric, prize at least as much its properties of pure sound: the patterns of accent that can suggest a meter, the rhymes that define a melodic phrase, even the phonetics that inspire melodic shape. In poetry without a musical setting, these devices articulate the flow of time in a way that, for many writers, can only be "musical."[5] In 1923 the great linguist Roman Jakobson called this rhythmic element of poetry its essential *Gestaltqualität*, and Shelley wrote that "the language of poets has ever affected a sort of uniform and harmonious recurrence of sound, without which it were not poetry."[6] It is this abstract property of measuring time that has convinced many not only of the truth of this affinity between music and poetry but that poetry is the only real analog for music in the realm of human language. Donald Davie believes that "poetic syntax is like music when its function is to please us by the fidelity with which it follows a 'form of thought' through the poet's mind *but without defining that thought*."[7] And how familiar to musicians is Susanne Langer's observation that "though the *material* of poetry is verbal, its import is not the literal assertion made in the words, but *the way the assertion is made*, and this involves the sound, the tempo . . . and the unifying, all-embracing artifice of rhythm."[8]

Emerson's poet-child "saw musical order." The affinity is ultimately rooted in syntax. Rhymes, consistent line lengths, and meters come about because poetry indulges in syntactic manipulation on a far greater scale than speech, an obvious thing but germane to the essentially musical preference for sound and syntax to plain meaning. In short, syntactic simplicity is traded for a musical pattern.

> Hence loathed Melancholy
>   Of *Cerberus* and blackest midnight born,
> In *Stygian Cave* forlorn
>   'Mongst horrid shapes, and shrieks, and sights unholy,
> Find out some uncouth cell,
>   Where brooding darkness spreads his jealous wings,
> And the night-Raven sings;
>   There under *Ebon* shades, and low-brow'd Rocks,
> —As ragged as thy Locks,
>   In dark *Cimmerian* desert ever dwell.
>
> MILTON, "L'ALLEGRO"[9]

This stanza of Milton is shot through with dislocations, syntactic inversions that defer "unholy" to the end of its line to rhyme with "Melancholy" and keep the reader tensed and waiting from "There under" for three lines until "ever dwell" completes the strophe. No aspect of poetry could be commoner; indeed, it is this kind of syntactic play that, when occurring in normal speech or prose, is taken to be "poetic." Of course, the preferences for such devices change over time and mark changes of poetic style. William Baker remarks that "Twentieth century poets have markedly preferred, along with a stronger emphasis on the ordinary sentences of everyday discourse, the use of fragments—usually noun phrases or clauses—not clearly related to any one sentence."[10] But the modern preference for normal syntax does not make the poetry any less musical;

on the contrary, the systematic use of fragments in Pound and other moderns, as Baker indicates, is a weakening of grammar that must be compensated by fundamental gestaltlike perceptions of similar sounds and parallel constructions in proximate locations, musical constructions par excellence. Gerard Manley Hopkins once defined verse as "speech wholly or partially repeating the same figure of sound."[11]

But the syntactic fascination of poetry never implies a complete disregard of semantics, any more than it does in music. Syntax cannot be changed without affecting semantics, and in many works the alliance is essential. In the Milton stanza above, for example, the explicit syntactic aspects of meter and rhyme articulate the storytelling. The address to Melancholy issues from a command "hence" and a long epithet defined by the first quatrain, but ending with an unbalanced line, thus incomplete. A new command comes in line 5, but in the succeeding four lines no rhyme matches and completes it; instead, new epithets, new rhymes, and an incomplete sentence. When at long last line 10 resolves the incomplete sentence and the unmatched rhyme, holding the third essential command to the end to do both jobs at once, it articulates the entire decina as a syntactic and semantic whole. Thereafter, the poem moves into regular tetrameter couplets that address cheerfulness and change the mood. Davie remarks that "if all poems are born as rhythms, then some, it seems, may be born as rhythms of ideas, that is, as patterns of syntax rather than patterns of sound. And this would make of syntax the very nerve of poetry."[12] As it is the nerve of music.

METAPHOR AND MUSIC

If syntax is the nerve of poetry, then metaphor may be its lifeblood. Speaking of poets, Shelley has it that "their language is vitally metaphorical."[13] But in modern times they have been made to share metaphor making with the rest of us. For metaphor has found a home in other disciplines beyond the literary and its role has broadened: "metaphor plays a unique and irreplaceable part in human discourse, from poetry to ordinary conversation to scientific models. . . . It reflects a need to extend the categories embodied in generic terms the better to assimilate new domains or to cast fresh light on familiar ones by illuminating yet other similarities and differences."[14] When we reimagine the concepts that make up thought, we practice metaphor.

Precise characterizations vary, of course, among such a range of analysts, but two aspects of metaphor seem common enough to all as to make them appear essential to a general notion of metaphor.[15] The first is that some concept, variously described as "semantic field,"[16] "relations,"[17] and even "contrast sets,"[18] is transferred or grafted onto another distinct concept. The second essential is that the graft suggests some similarity between the concepts that is "discovered" or "constructed" by the perceiver at the same time that it suggests something semantically strange about the graft, a "patent falsehood or even absurdity in taking the conjunction literally. Man is not, literally, a wolf."[19] There is a third aspect not usually mentioned because it is so obvious, but quite essential for a musical analog: metaphors are temporary, their semantic imprint lasting only as long as the moment in which they are spoken, the stanza in which they are written, the oration in which they are invoked.

In the semantic framework of chapter 3, a metaphor occurs when the semantic range of one word extends temporarily the semantic range of a second to include meaning that it would not normally contain. The word "man" may mean many things, but "wolf" is not one of them. The utterance "Man is a wolf" is metaphorical because the semantic range of "man" is abnormally and temporarily extended.

True poetic metaphors that juxtapose distinct semantic ranges in this traditional way are extremely rare in music. One of the great effects of the intermittent storm music in the third act of *Rigoletto* is that, in stretching out the storm's arrival for so long, Verdi can make its rising intensity parallel the increasing tension of shorter and louder phrases in the singing immediately preceding Gilda's murder. The arrival of the storm is coincident with her brutal killing, and thus the storm music, quite traditional in its makeup of fast rhythms, dissonances, and minor mode, becomes a metaphor for the violence on stage. The same music expresses the storm literally and the murder metaphorically. But this is only possible because both meanings reside in the semantic range of the musical passage. Verdi has a prefabricated lexical item for "storm" already at hand—it must be fast, dissonant, and in the minor—and at the same time a context window in the opera scene that sufficiently narrows the same sounds to take on another meaning in its semantic range without losing the first. Most circumstances never permit such a simultaneous definition; there is enough trouble in narrowing music's expressive focus to one specific, never mind two.

No, a concept of musical metaphor works best where the linguistic character of music is strongest: syntax.

In fact, "syntactic metaphors" are common enough in poetry. "It has for long been acknowledged," writes poet Donald Davie,

> that the poet enjoys a special license in the matter of making nouns do the work of verbs, adjectives of nouns, and so on. There are abundant examples in Shakespeare. But now it can be claimed that this sort of thing is at the very heart of poetry, since it represents a re-creation by the poet of the natural patterns of experience. Allen Tate begins a poem:
>
> > The idiot greens the meadow with his eyes.
>
> and his poem ends,
>
> > the towering weak and pale
> > Covers his eyes with memory like a sheet.
>
> The adjective "green" serves as a verb; other adjectives, "towering", "weak", "pale", serve, some or all of them, as nouns. And of course the device is not uncommon.[20]

Is not this "re-creation by the poet," and necessarily by the reader, the kind of redefining, fruitful conjunction that characterizes metaphor? The contrastive concepts are now syntactic, now the absurdity resides in the very pattern of the sentence, but the work of imagination is there all the same.

A musical metaphor, then, is a passage whose "absurdity" or incongruity is syntactic, a passage that performs strangely in its context, controlling tension and creating articulations in ways unaccustomed and yet comprehensible. Because their special effects are entirely syntactic, we cannot hope to hear in such passages things that call to mind true poetic metaphors. My adopting "syntactic metaphor" as a name for them is itself a metaphorical use of the word. The analogy is perhaps strained but nonetheless justified, since the strangeness of the syntactic transfer and the grammatical absurdity are real. Such incongruities give these passages unique effects, effects that amount to much more than simply stamping a particular work with a characteristic profile. They have real work to do. What kind of work?

In vocal music, especially opera, a musical metaphor may mark a particularly profound expression of a character. For instance, in Example 5.1, there is no way to rationalize syntactically Orfeo's interruption of the Messenger's dreadful pronouncement. The G-minor triad coming upon the E major could hardly be more brutal, because it could hardly be more

Example 5.1. Monteverdi, L'Orfeo, Act II (Messenger: "I come to you, Orfeo, unhappy messenger, about a most unhappy and morbid event. Your lovely Euridice . . ." Orfeo: "Alas, what am I hearing?" Messenger: " . . . your beloved wife is dead.")

distant, harmonically speaking. The same is true for the move back, from a C-minor chord to the same E major that allows the Messenger to finish as if Orfeo had never sung aloud, as if we had somehow been privy to his inner, hidden feeling. Orfeo's brief interjection is a harmonic breakdown, "scarcely rational modulations" to use Robert Donington's phrase,[21] that expresses his emotional breakdown, so pathetic coming as it does here, after so many more rational attempts by him and his friends to come to grips with what she has to say. That rationality has been maintained with a reasonable syntax throughout. Breakdown demands something special.

Once established somehow, the invented syntax gains an integrity that is metaphorical: anomalous and temporary, but of significant power because it is so singular. Monteverdi takes advantage of it to bring to the fore of consciousness the most terrible parts of the Messenger's story—the bite of the snake:

Example 5.2. Monteverdi, L'Orfeo, Act II ("It struck her foot with a poisonous fang. And behold, immediately . . .")

and Euridice's final cry, "Orfeo," before she dies:

Example 5.3. Monteverdi, L'Orfeo, Act II ("and calling to you, Orfeo. After a deep sigh . . .")

Wasting no time for its reiteration ensures for Monteverdi and his listeners the stability of the metaphor, for its most beautiful recurrence must wait until the fourth act, Euridice's piteous cry at the last sight she will ever have of her husband:

Example 5.4. Monteverdi, L'Orfeo, Act IV ("Ah! Vision too sweet . . .")

Here Monteverdi does not spare the chromatic semitone even in the vocal line.[22]

Musical metaphors as special expressions occur on the immediate level of musical experience. At the other extreme they can operate on the highest levels of musical structure, as devices of extension. Such extensions come about when a composer wants to write a continuous movement of extreme length, longer than the normal resources of musical language would allow. The metaphor creates a perceptual frame for an additional level of structure in the hierarchy, thus extending the capacities of listeners to organize the incoming musical information. Consider two examples from the music of J. S. Bach.

Example 5.5. J. S. Bach, Fugue in B minor, Well-Tempered Clavier, I, mm. 1–7

In Example 5.5, the answer to Bach's twelve-tone subject brings all manner of syntactic anomalies when it begins in the fourth measure. How is it that the second B in the tenor, approached by leap, can accommodate not only a dissonant A but an even more extremely dissonant C♮, a pitch not even in the key? Why the direct fifth, usually avoided in two voices, at the beginning of measure 5? What about the high G in measure 6, one unmistakable dissonance that then leaps to another?

The answer to these incongruities is a metaphor in the form of an extra level of harmonic rhythm, almost a phantom level, that arises in the subject itself. The awareness of this level, like the construction of the metaphor, is necessarily gradual. In the first measure there are no strange notes and nothing seems amiss. The next half-measure introduces two pitches, D♯ and C♮, not belonging to the central key of B minor. They are at odds with the harmonic procedure of a fugue, because, while they don't belong to the tonic key, they would not normally prepare the answer in dominant of F-sharp minor either. But together they describe a diminished seventh, which, in the context of this minor-mode composition, can be easily imagined as a secondary dominant of iv, represented by the B to which the C "resolves." The next half-measure continues, then, in the manner of a tiny modulating sequence that does, in fact, move toward F-sharp minor. Already, Bach's melody has implicated a higher level of harmonic rhythm: not just the eighth-note rhythm implicit in the first measure but now quarter-note changes too.

But if the C♮ and the following D♯ "resolve" their diminished harmonies, they also force us to rehear their earlier mimics. Every single one of those eighth-note pairs, articulated by Bach's original slurs, is a half-step motion, appoggiaturas in effect. This perception conjures a yet slower harmonic pattern (Ex. 5.6). This phantom is not tangible until we hear the descending triad in measure 3, echoing and explaining in F♯ its mate in B minor at the opening, and the mysteriously long trill on the G♯. These gestures make it clear that behind the easily imaginable progressions based on eighths and quarters there is an even slower half-note harmonic rhythm. The perception of this slow motion can then make sense of all the grammatical "errors" of the following measures, since the Baroque conception of counterpoint justifies voice leading not by interval alone but by harmonic progression. In this multilayered feast of harmonic motion, the A and C♮ of measure 4 are understood to resolve the previous G♯-B-D diminished triad on the eighth-note level, themselves being subsumed into a whole half-bar of B harmony (iv and IV) that answers the second half of the first measure. The direct fifth is not "truly" direct because the chord tone is G♯, not A. And the high G in the following measure is swept into the reigning dominant harmony as a minor ninth.[23]

Example 5.6. J. S. Bach, Fugue in B minor, Well-Tempered Clavier, I, mm. 1–7, indicating half-note harmonic rhythm.

And the reason for this complex idea? Bach has in mind a very long piece, long, that is, in the context of his musical language and in the tradition of fugues for keyboard. His principal means of articulation are harmonic: syntactic progressions organized into keys. The slower he can make those progressions seem, the longer he can make each key last. In fact, his first key of B minor lasts about seventeen measures in largo tempo, better than one fifth of the composition. When he finally does modulate, he does so with the usual Baroque means, a sequence (Ex. 5.7). The phantom is gone from here, and the contrasting clarity of the quarter-note harmonic rhythm, its comparative ease of pronouncement despite Bach's exquisitely sequenced suspensions, is very much a part of the beauty of this moment.

Example 5.7. J. S. Bach, Fugue in B minor, Well-Tempered Clavier, I, mm. 17–20.

The Fourth Brandenburg Concerto offers another such structural metaphor, this time operating on the very highest levels of perceptual organization. The first movement of this concerto is huge by Baroque standards, bigger than any simple succession of keys, ritornello, or dance form would allow, so Bach invents a singular passage to articulate its highest-level organization, a kind of super-ritornello (Ex. 5.8).

Preceding this remarkable passage are sixty-seven measures that nearly make up a kind of concerto movement in miniature, and indeed, one minute in High Baroque style is a considerable space of time. Already, we have heard flashes of interplay between the three soloists and tutti; already, the music has modulated to the dominant key and returned. But this extension of the main statement is extraordinary, an extension, really, of the Baroque language itself. For the first time there are hints of subsidiary keys (E minor, mm. 69–72; C major, mm. 74–77) that generate significant harmonic tension without leaving the principal key of G major. There is also a textural tension, melodic lines straining to break

Example 5.8. J. S. Bach, Fourth Brandenburg Concerto, I, mm. 68–83.

free of the others: the two flutes constantly move against the rest of the ensemble, first by stressing the third beat in the figure in measures 69–74 while everyone else emphasizes the first, then by continuing a six-unit sequence while the strings change to a new pattern, and finally by moving opposite the ensemble in the great hemiola (mm. 79–83). These articulations of texture, staggered in the various parts, collect themselves into a giant sweep of motion that contrasts decisively with the previous music, and yet it is the harmonic stability provided by that previous music, especially its motion away and return to the tonic, that prevents everything from flying off in all directions. The pull between the texture and the harmonic gravity is wondrously strained. So characteristic are the tensions here, so unique the profile against the background of what has gone before, that Bach can use this passage as a metaphor throughout to articulate the main framing of the movement.

Metaphors as special expressions of vocal works and as structural extensions in instrumental works are the two principal ways musical metaphors are used in composition. Beyond these are the multifarious special effects that defy generalization.

The exploitation of the concerto genre in Beethoven's Violin Concerto is an example of such a special effect.[24] The quarter-note motive on the D♯ (Ex. 4.1, page 74) is syntactically anomalous because it is ambiguous and kept that way throughout the work. Only a thorough training in this particular ambiguity justifies its final comprehension, in the hands of the soloist, as the linchpin of a metaphorical progression.

The Violin Concerto offers some curious instances having qualities like that of a metaphor but without syntax. One is the mimesis of the drum beats by the violin. Here is a transfer, not uncommon, of a figure idiomatic to one instrument to another for which it is not idiomatic. The incongruity is the contradiction of the instrumental color and our expectations about what such a figure should sound like. In short, the violin is not a drum, just as Handel's bass singing "The trumpet shall sound" with a splendid solo arpeggio spanning an octave is not a trumpet. The semantic effects of such moments are not to be denied—in the Violin Concerto the match of violins and drums is essential—but they are something other than metaphor. In natural language they are more analogous with certain linguistic behaviors such as irony or sarcasm or simple mimicry, where the incongruity of use is in the situation and not in the utterance itself.

The quarter-note motive itself, however, is an example of what Charles Rosen calls classical counterpoint, the deliberate highlighting of a patently accompanimental figure for thematic significance.[25] Examples in the works of Haydn, Mozart, and Beethoven are legion and figure essentially in their Classical style, as Rosen has demonstrated so well. It is an essential aspect of the Violin Concerto's first movement: those drumbeats in the brass lurking behind the soloist's figuration in the development have a power far beyond any other idea in the movement. Again there is an incongruity between our expectations for the use of the quarter notes and its actual significance, really an incongruity in the figure-ground relationship of musical texture that finds little parallel in natural language, certainly not in syntax. It is perhaps akin to narratives in which some detail, constantly present and yet insignificant, turns out to be the key to some twist in the plot. But that is not metaphor, because the incongruity of figure-ground is not constantly sensed as it is in music.

How is it that these musical metaphors work? How do we comprehend them despite their syntactic oddity? Why do they not seem like simple mistakes?

In the eminently reasonable thesis of relevance of Dan Sperber and Deirdre Wilson, there are but two things to remember concerning the comprehension of metaphor. One is that meaning is always conditioned by the context of the utterance, and the other is that members of a language community usually communicate with one another in good faith. When faced with an incongruity in language, plain or poetic, the hearer will find the best context to justify the utterance. This process is so automatic that when Milton writes "Where brooding darkness spreads his jealous wings," using the special kind of metaphor called personification, one barely realizes the semantic incongruity of darkness being something that broods, is jealous, and has wings before the sense of the line is understood whole. Syntactic metaphors may give slightly greater pause, but their comprehension works in the same way. Consider these lines of Hopkins:

> They fought with God's cold—
> And they could not and fell to the deck
> (Crushed them) or water (and drowned them) or rolled
> With the sea-romp over the wreck.

> GERARD MANLEY HOPKINS
> "THE WRECK OF THE DEUTSCHLAND"[26]

The sentence is absolutely ungrammatical yet contains enough sense to make it comprehensible. The reader sees that the parentheticals change the syntax of previous words from object to subject, as if the relative pronoun "which" must be filled in. In this way "deck" and "water" have Necker cube-like switching properties, first one, then the other, and both at the same time. Hopkins concentrates so much action in these few lines, the syntactic confusion mimicking the mayhem of the image.

Hopkins has to his advantage the immensely powerful ally of semantics, the comparatively precise semantic ranges of all the words he uses. They point the way to how the sentence must read. In instrumental music such pointers are rare, so Beethoven must teach his listening community the operation of his syntactic metaphors gradually. They must be justified.

Justification is an endlessly variable process, but in general it requires the composer to present the musical metaphor initially in a context that underscores its special character and yet allows the listener to make some grammatical sense of it. Beethoven marks out his drumbeat D♯s by having the violins play them like the drums they are not, but unharmonized, so that the following dominant harmony can accommodate them even if the voice leading is anomalous. Bach sets up his syncopated passage in the Fourth Brandenburg so that neither its singularity nor its defining cadential effect is lost. When words are involved the task is much easier: Monteverdi can depend on our understanding of the dramatic situation to justify his irrational progression. He relies on the sense of language in the same way as Hopkins.

Once justified, the metaphor can be used ever more freely, and every proper use reinforces its artificial syntax for the life of the composition. Thus, the Messenger continues to teach us the meaning of Monteverdi's harmony even though its use is less justified than in Orfeo's exclamation. Thus, Bach can use his cadential passage, after its first hearing, without the benefit of home-key stability. Beethoven's metaphor is the most extreme, syntactically, and listeners absorb its significant ambiguity through many presentations and many contexts. Only at the last is its full power exploited.

In general, then, a musical metaphor, like the metaphor in natural language, is a means of stretching a language.[27] In poetry, rhetoric, and speech the metaphor stretches the semantic range of utterances to include meanings quite outside their bounds; in music it stretches the syntactic coherence of a composition.

Because the musical metaphor is syntactic, it affects the tension of the music whenever it is used, and I wonder whether the tension produced is as particular as the metaphor itself. The tension arising from Orfeo's exclamation is of harmonic origin, of course, but is it right to say that it is simply harmonic tension, in the sense of progressing to a dominant? The harmonic distance of Beethoven's miraculous A-flat passage at the end of his Violin Concerto is the reason for much of its effect, but surely not all of it. If our sense of that passage's coherence depends upon this justification, our previous experience of it, then the weight of all that experience comes to bear on the moment as powerfully as the purely grammatical sense of harmonic distance. The tension of a musical metaphor must be unique; indeed, that is perhaps its chief attraction.

It must have been particularly attractive to the masters of the Classical style, for it is no accident that the most salient examples of musical metaphor come from the music of Haydn, Mozart, and especially Beethoven. The musical language of the late eighteenth century combined the two conditions that make metaphorical exploitation most likely: explicit syntactic rules of composition and the necessity of syntactic invention. This necessity probably has several origins, ranging from the contemporaneous view of instrumental composition as a kind of rhetoric[28] to the habitual requirements of comic opera, but a most likely source is the simple eagerness to explore the possibilities of high-level tensions and resolutions made possible for the first time by the art of articulate modulation. How could tensions be stretched longer, big climaxes made bigger? How can they be made extraordinary?

Such questions make one think of Beethoven first of all, and rightly so, for he composed musical metaphors throughout his career, and they are responsible for musical effects particularly emblematic of his work. First, sheer length and scope of composition: the monumental nature of Beethoven's music owes so much to his power of extension, making simple musical events last a long time, and this power depends on these musical metaphors. Beethoven is famous, to choose an obvious example, for his use of keys on different levels of structure. In the midst of the D-minor theme in Example 5.9 are two cadential progressions in F major (mm. 57–58, 61–62) that establish a sense of that key without leaving, in a larger sense, the key of D minor. This kind of harmonic structure is heard in his earliest works onward, and they are metaphors. The incongruity is that the concept of key connotes a stability strong enough to organize the various turns of a melody, and yet this kind of key participates itself in a progression to a different point of stability. Now this particular example is not at all extreme, being a case of the relative major and so almost a "dead" metaphor in his language, but yet Beethoven takes the trouble to begin teaching us the syntax of this metaphor beforehand.

Example 5.9. Beethoven, Violin Concerto, I, mm. 55–64.

The foray into D minor (see Ex. 5.10)[29] is striking enough to bring to our attention some critical new pitch relations, especially F♮ and F♯, but is readily acceptable in terms of traditional syntax. Why, it is even properly introduced with a dominant.

The purpose of this technique is reminiscent of the Bach B-minor fugue. There is another level of articulation in the hierarchy, and so the fundamental opposition of two keys (D major and A major) in Beethoven's exposition can be stretched without losing its essential polarity. The structural capacities of the musical language are extended, tensions increased. And not just increased, but given special characters. The technique described here is not particularly difficult to bring off from a technical standpoint; what is nearly impossible, what Beethoven does so impossibly well, is to coordinate all the new pitch relations that

Example 5.10. Beethoven, Violin Concerto, I, mm. 26–32.

this technique brings to our ears. D minor and D major contrast F♮ and F♯, and we are not allowed to forget it. The accumulated experiences of many juxtapositions bear upon moments such as the one in Example 5.11. It is an enharmonic pun,[30] to be sure, but so much more than that, too, owing to the moment's metaphorical history.

Example 5.11. Beethoven, Violin Concerto, I, mm. 295–299.

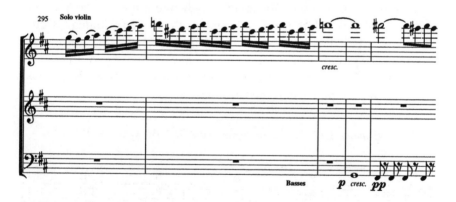

This kind of control and creation of high-level tension is at the heart of one of the most prominent features of Beethoven's music: his stupendous endings. The end of the Violin Concerto, for all its perfect brilliance for the soloist, has not the explosive Beethovenian drive to the very last measures, and in fact the end of the first movement, for all its poetic extension of the famous lyrical theme, is rather routine. But his large compositions after this one almost always find a way to delay the climactic moment of the movement, and his late career might be characterized as a series of experiments to create such concluding climaxes on ever bigger scales.

The traditional affinity between harmonic syntax and the aesthetic of Classical proportions opposed him. The musical language Beethoven learned could create high-level tension with articulate modulations from a home tonic to its dominant and resolve that tension with an even more articulate return, in effect the normal syntax writ large. As Rosen has described, the Classical aesthetic of returning to the home key midway or, at most, three-quarters of the way through the composition generally placed the climax there.[31] Beethoven could not, or would not, do without that elegant symmetry of proportion in his music, but his powers of metaphor could perhaps subvert Classical syntax without losing all coherence.

His Seventh Symphony, composed three years after the Violin Concerto, is a showcase of the kind of end climax for which Beethoven is famous. There is a tremendous one that closes the first movement and, incredibly, an even greater one that closes the symphony.

In its harmonic pattern the finale is remarkable for its complete abstinence from the key of E major, the dominant of the home key of A major. The exposition of the movement moves, not to the dominant, but to the mediant minor, C-sharp minor, an extremely rare if not unique harmonic goal in Beethoven. Here is our subversion. Beethoven's strategy is quite clear now: avoid all structural use of the dominant key, not sparing even the point of recapitulation, thus saving its power for the end. In fact, the sound of the dominant is never established as a key, even at the end, but instead grows to immense power in the ostinato:

Example 5.12. Beethoven, Symphony No. 7, IV, mm. 388–397.

Classical proportions are preserved, the form is as articulate as ever, and the last page explodes as never before.[32]

Beethoven's vaunted strategy of the substitute dominant, this syntactic subversion, is a metaphor in action. He begins teaching this syntax in the exposition of the first movement when, before the music settles into the dominant key (E major) as usual, it makes a feint toward the key of C-sharp minor (Ex. 5.13). This is not all. The first movement rehearses

Example 5.13. Beethoven, Symphony No. 7, I, mm. 109–114.

the strategy of the finale in provisional form, first by short circuiting the resolution of the tension at the recapitulation, only hinting at the dominant without spelling it unequivocally. In fact, the tonic A-major chord arrives ahead of its time, blurring the articulation in the manner of his late style:

Example 5.14. Beethoven, Symphony No. 7, I, mm. 272–278

Then he builds an elastic tension around another ostinato, this one centered not on the dominant E but on the mediant C-sharp (Ex. 5.15). As

Example 5.15. Beethoven, Symphony No. 7, I, mm. 403–408.

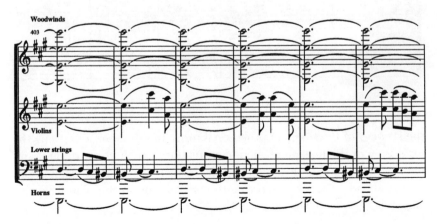

the bass line twists and turns around the C♯, the upper orchestra merely plays with a few triadic motives on tonic harmony. A steady crescendo and ever faster note rhythm do their part, but the fact is that this prolonged tonic chord comes to beg for release, for the torrent of motion into traditional progressions that end this movement so brilliantly. Beethoven has already convinced us that C-sharp is a viable dominant substitute, and he looks forward to the extraordinary finale.

Without a treatise on the Seventh Symphony it is impossible to describe the difficulty of this feat, this gigantic harmonic sleight-of-hand. It is almost as if Wordsworth were to write a poem without any finite verbs and make it seem natural. The quotations from the first movement show the most obvious gestures, but they hardly begin to tell the story. The metaphorical relation of C♯ to A is but part of a nest of such metaphors that coordinate different levels of structure large and small. To give but one example, as A is constructed as a stable concept with respect to C♯, so is C♯ with respect to C♮ and D.[33] Thus, the ostinato in the coda of the first movement plays on three relations at once, with C♯ as the stable goal of the immediate figure while always itself bursting to resolve to A:

HIERARCHICAL RELATIONS OF STABILITY IN BEETHOVEN'S SYMPHONY NO. 7.
(ARROWS INDICATE RESOLUTIONS OF TENSION ON TWO LEVELS.)

Wordsworth, of course, cannot write so artificial a poem and make it seem completely natural, and to tell the truth, Beethoven cannot do the same in his symphony. Metaphors are incongruities, and incongruities in syntax, almost by definition, have a roughness about them, because syntax controls the ease of handling information. The poetry of Hopkins quoted above is not gentle with readers; they must struggle to come to terms with it, and probably that is part of the intended effect. In experimenting with his syntactic metaphors Beethoven gives up a certain grace for certain powerful effects, a similar kind of tremendously beautiful struggle.[34]

Beethoven's ancestors in composition rarely wished or needed to stretch the powers of their musical languages in this way. There are exceptions of course. Texts demanding extraordinary expression, like Monteverdi's opera, and texts of extraordinary length, like Josquin's

Psalm 51, demanded extraordinary means and their composers had the imagination to find them and make the most of them. Particular inspirations such as the opening chorus of the St. Matthew Passion or the closing "Amen" of *Messiah* are singular monuments indeed. But in musical languages where high-level tension was not really possible there was simply not much point in tampering with a beautifully ordered syntax in a metaphorical way.

After Beethoven, the Romantics' irresistible individualism made tampering de rigueur, but the precise musical syntax required for the salient presentation of metaphor slowly began to weaken. Original harmonic and melodic ideas were always justifiable by chromatic voice leading in the embrace of ever slower harmonic rhythm. By the last part of the nineteenth century incongruities in syntax become too hard to identify, because most everything, with respect to the perceiving community, is incongruous. This does not imply in the least that "intra-opus norms," the particular motives, ideas, standards, and procedures of a composition, were any less important. On the contrary they are more important than ever in perceiving the course of a composition, but there are far fewer singled out for special learning or special effects. Or one could say that all the ideas are special, all are individual. Does metaphor make any sense, have any impact, in a language where nothing is plain? This is what happens at the turn of the twentieth century, at least in the learned styles. Metaphor becomes impossible, because syntax in the communal sense has disappeared. Syntax is no longer community property. Syntax has become artificial.

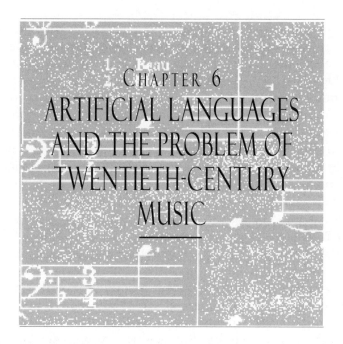

CHAPTER 6

ARTIFICIAL LANGUAGES AND THE PROBLEM OF TWENTIETH-CENTURY MUSIC

The twentieth century is the age of artificial languages. History records no other time when so many men and women, each working alone, invented complete linguistic systems, seeking to build a worldwide linguistic community or to control with ever greater precision and imagination the awesome power of the digital computer. Esperanto, machine language, and BASIC are signal artifacts of our time.[1]

So are serialism, minimalism, chance music, *musique concrète*, and countless other nameless kinds of musical composition. The artificial systems of twentieth-century composition are by far the most prominent feature on the face of its troubled history, and nothing else has so greatly affected the character of that history.

The twentieth century is the first in the history of music to wall off the music of popular culture from the most seriously cultivated styles. While Josquin could make folksongs the foundation of his most sublime masses, while Bach glorified the simple churchgoer's Lutheran hymns, while Haydn invented popular material at will for his symphonies, and Verdi songs that suited both café and La Scala, virtually all the important art composers since 1900 except the nationalists have avoided any taint of popular music in their compositions. The suspicious regard has been mutual; devotion to Schoenberg and Springsteen rarely coincide in one person.

Thus alienated from popular venues, serious composition in our century has retreated to the academy, where it takes its place alongside other disciplines as one more exercise of the intellect. Composition supersedes the mere fashioning of sounds and becomes the fashioning of ideas.[2] But "idea" here is not simply a strategy for a piece, a central theme or determinant device. No, the twentieth-century compositional idea is idea on grand scale, the scale of musical language. An architect in an analogous situation could no longer be content with designing new, even radically innovative buildings, but must invent entirely new principles of engineering. After Schoenberg, a composer cannot hope to win distinction merely by creating within an accepted tradition; a great composer must invent a new language.[3]

That is why the twentieth century has incubated so many kinds of music theory that give birth to the various compositional systems.[4] Older music theory, for the most part, struggled breathlessly to keep up with the marvels that it sought to explain, beautiful music that arose from musical communities with apparent spontaneity, and certainly without help, beyond the most rudimentary grammatical instruction, from the speculative wing of the art. But now theory precedes composition, describes how music might be fashioned. The invention of musical languages is a patently rationalist enterprise "based on an assumption that valid structural logic is accessible to any reasoning person."[5] It is no accident that composer Milton Babbitt chose "the midnineteenth-century revolution in mathematics and the twentieth-century revolution in physics" as the models for his own situation.[6] Compositional ideas must now be logically grounded and rationally defended, the province, of course, of theory. "In the construction of individual compositions, composers were confronted with an unprecedented amount of 'precompositional' or theoretical advance work."[7] The music comes only after the homework has been done.

MODERN INDIVIDUALISM

The modernist fascination with this kind of explicit creation of idea—making artificial languages for music—grew quite directly from the nineteenth-century preoccupation with a composer's personal originality, a stylistic individualism. The dictum that every composer must create an individual style to establish credentials as Artist is so widely taken for granted in the modern world that it is worth emphasizing how recently the Western community has demanded this kind of originality. In earlier days, composers didn't worry about that sort of thing; if anything, their attitude was the opposite. If one was talented enough to make music like Josquin's, so much the better. The trouble was, no one was that talented: the technique of Josquin's personal syntax posed too high a hurdle.[8]

The roots of the individualist impulse go back to the turn of the nineteenth century, to one of the true revolutions in the history of Western musical communities: the composer's move from the patron's palace to the concert hall and salon. This appeared to be a great liberation. Now the composer was free to create at will; now the Romantic concept of musical inspiration became practical. But this freedom of movement and concomitant broadening of the musical community to include the middle classes who could buy tickets and scores only replaced the composer's servitude to a patron by another kind of bondage, to the harsh economics of public concerts. In the old days the good positions at court or chapel were limited, as Mozart knew all too well, but later the chance to earn a living was limited by space on the concert stage. And that space was increasingly crowded by a competition from a group that had never before bothered new young composers seeking to establish themselves: the dead. Impresarios and managers began to notice that the symphonies of Beethoven and operas of Mozart did not pale with age. Mendelssohn brought back Bach's choral masterworks in the 1820s after nearly a century in the attic, and thereafter there was no stopping the growth of this magnificent collection of music called the standard repertory. The musical "classic" was born.

But to newcomers repertory was a threat—Brahms muttered about "the footsteps of Beethoven" as he delayed the composition of his first symphony until the ripe old age of forty—so they created aesthetic distance for themselves through stylistic innovation. Better to be found different than to be found wanting. A new, more exalted social position vaulted the composer from mere craftsman to Artist, and this consciousness of music as Art naturally stimulated a consciousness of music history, a new sense of responsibility to the past and to the creation of Original Thoughts worthy of the Tradition. "No Baroque composer weighed on Haydn as Beethoven did upon Schumann," as Charles Rosen aptly concludes.[9] Innovation became an ideal, the quest for uniqueness an obsession.

The crisis came in two decades at the turn of the century. The greatest thinkers among the young generation of composers came to believe that the traditional musical language had reached its limit of innovation.

Nothing else sufficiently original, sufficiently individual, could come from it any longer. So Debussy in Paris, Bartók in Hungary, Stravinsky in Russia, Schoenberg in Vienna, and Ives in New England began to undertake sustained experiments in composition that gave birth to new musical languages. This is the defining mark of modernism in music. In the twentieth century the West sustains for the first time a polyglot musical culture.

The experiments now called impressionism, expressionism, and the various nationalisms were intuitive ones, slow and radical innovations justified by the composers' own ears, by their intuitive musical sensibilities. But Arnold Schoenberg became famous for founding a system of composition during the 1910s whose terms seemed completely rational and explicit, and this intellectual audacity set the pattern for a great deal of new composition for the next half-dozen decades of the century. The compositional idea, idea on the scale of language, became the key to originality, which continues to be the sine qua non of modernist composition. It was a logical step. Rather than follow Debussy's course, developing works slowly, one by one, and justifying them carefully only by "sound sense," apparently, why not think up a new compositional theory that could directly generate a whole class of new works? As the measure of originality became ever coarser, the need for it ever greater, rationality became the shortcut to linguistic invention.

INVENTED LANGUAGES

Invention and experiment are the very stuff of artificial languages. All languages are artificial, of course, insofar as they are products of the human mind and conscious, creative things are done with them every day,[10] but the systems referred to as "natural" languages—English and Japanese, for example—are the products of evolution by successive linguistic communities. Shakespeare and other extraordinary individuals may occasionally claim some influence on their development, but the most systematic aspects of syntax and phonology owe their shapes only to slow development from some mysterious origin in the very distant past of which virtually nothing is known. Having no birth, English and Japanese seem as natural to us as the mountains and sea.

Artificial languages of the twentieth century, by contrast, owe their origins to single individuals, or small groups, who consciously design the entire phonological, syntactic, and semantic components at a stroke.[11] In this sense Zamenhof's Esperanto of 1887, Kemeny and Kurtz's BASIC of 1964, and Schoenberg's serialism of 1923 are true artificial languages. Some artificial systems such as symbolic logic precede the modern era. A striking example of this in music, a paradigm, really, of much twentieth-century practice, occurred in fourteenth-century France when modern rhythmic notation developed almost overnight by a kind of rational extrapolation of two concise ideas: that duration can be expressed in notation by its shape, quite independent of a note's neighbors, and that these durations can be related by ratios at many levels. Conscious, repeated applications of these principles created the language of the Ars nova.

What was the necessity that mothered all these inventions? There are many, really, as many as the languages themselves.

Lazar Ludwik Zamenhof's Esperanto grew out of his experience of ethnic conflict in his hometown: "In Bialystok, the population consisted of four diverse elements: Russians, Poles, Germans and Jews; each spoke a different language and was hostile to the other elements."[12] His handbook of Esperanto's complete grammar, published when he was just nineteen, is Zamenhof's solution to a divided humanity, a solution traceable to his native Lithuania, his brilliant talent for languages, and his Jewish heritage. "No one can feel the need for a language free of a sense of nationality as strongly as the Jew who is obliged to pray to God in a language long dead, receives his upbringing and education in the language of a people that rejects him, and has fellow-sufferers throughout the world with whom he cannot communicate. . . . My Jewishness has been the main reason why . . . I have given my all for a single great idea, a single dream—the dream of the unity of humankind."[13]

Computer languages owe their invention to sheer pragmatism. Alan Turing's breakthrough idea in 1937 of a rigorous logical process—the Turing machine—that required only two symbolic elements, coupled with Claude Shannon's discovery the same year that the basic Boolean operators "and," "or," and "not" could be expressed by certain simple arrangements of on-off switches, made the fundamental theory of the digital computer. But it was a computer necessarily based on binary code, whose "words," made up of long strings of 0s and 1s, lack sufficient discreteness to be used easily by humans. In other words, it is hard to tell 001000101001 from 001001010001 at a glance.[14] The higher-level computer languages known as FORTRAN, COBOL, and the rest are essentially translating devices that transform instructions conceived in natural human languages into machine code that can control the operations of the binary switches. Thus, the machine "understands" the artificial language. The individual languages all fulfill this primary practical need but in addition respond to particular needs imagined by their inventors: Jean Sammet's Common Business Oriented Language for processing commercial data;[15] John G. Kemeny and Thomas Kurtz's BASIC for college students; John McCarthy's LISP for artificial intelligence; Niklaus Wirth's Pascal for all-purpose structured programming. "All of the programming languages . . . that have survived and left their mark . . . share at least one common trait: a well-defined *raison d'être*."[16]

The composers and theorists of fourteenth-century France simply became fascinated with the implications of a simple, revolutionary idea. The expression of a note's duration could be completely independent from its neighboring notes for the first time.[17] More than that, any duration's subdivision into shorter notes could be controlled and specified at will. Duplets and triplets were possible at any metric level, and different subdivisions and meters could be combined at the same time. Essentially, the composer-theorists of the Ars nova invented the entire rationale for modern rhythmic notation at one stroke. They had a brand new toy, and they wanted to play.

Leading composers of art music in the twentieth century made their own toys out of their own heads. But the necessity seems different somehow. In the earlier period the fascination with the new rhythmic techniques seems to come from the joy of serendipitous discovery. In modern times the playing has become serious, driven by a compulsion to sing in one's own language.

In short, artificial languages arise when someone perceives a problem—computational, social, aesthetic—and invents a language to solve it. In theory, artificial languages may share many essential similarities with natural languages in the manner of parent to offspring, as do Esperanto and the Ars nova, or hardly any, as in some computer languages and *musique concrète*. But regardless of the reason for invention, there is one inevitable challenge to every new artificial language: it is alien. At the beginning of its life, the linguistic community of any artificial language is but one member, the inventor. How well this first barrier is overcome is one critical measure of its success.

Overcoming it was certainly Zamenhof's principal concern when he designed Esperanto. Most of the lexicon comes from what he judged to be the most accessible roots in the Romance and Germanic languages. The grammar arises from sixteen principles that are a model of syntactic efficiency and consistency. All singular nouns end in *-o*, plural in *-j*, and the accusative case is always made by adding *-n*. All adjectives consist of a root word with -*a* added. The syntax of verbs is completely regular. Words are pronounced with accent on the penultimate syllable and spelled exactly as pronounced according to phonetic rules.[18]

Niklaus Wirth designed Pascal so that computer programming could be taught as a process of defining a large problem in terms of successively smaller problems of computation. Pascal forces the programmer to use such "structured programming techniques," and a Pascal program shows the breakdown of the big problem and the method of solving each part at a glance. But in 1971 such advantages were not enough to guarantee success, because existing computers could not "understand" the new language without new compilers—translating programs—that could transform its instructions into machine language. Fortunately, one of Wirth's disciples, Kenneth Bowles, invented a kind of first-stage, transportable compiler whose output could be easily adapted to the new wave of microcomputers coming on in the 1970s and 1980s.

The early stages of Esperanto and Pascal teach an obvious lesson. Learning a new language is a lot of work, as everyone who has tried it well knows, and yet any artificial language demands this radical upheaval, a new linguistic community, if it is to succeed. Above all, learning it must be highly beneficial, and that benefit—whether it be an altruistic one of uniting humanity or the purely practical one of solving computational problems—is always weighed against the cost by prospective converts. Zamenhof and Wirth labored to make their creations appealing to their intended markets, their future linguistic communities who had to invest the price of learning their languages. Zamenhof's choice of a European-oriented lexicon and Latinate grammar shows his origins, to be sure, but it was also the wisest strategic choice. If Esperanto did not catch on in Europe at the turn of the century, it would not catch on anywhere else. Wirth had to persuade a community of programmers already satisfied with what they had. The greatest obstacle to artificial languages is inertia.

To shock listeners out of their lethargic trance, born of a fascination with old music, and compel them to vault this obstacle, music in the twentieth century has traded on two things. One is novelty: music promised sound colors never heard, melodies never imagined, rhythms and harmonies of such complexity that the repertory could not match. The second is the sheer beauty of its compositional systems, its ideas. The reasons to learn its musical languages are the same as those for learning abstract mathematics or symbolic logic. Was there ever a time when composers volunteered to explain so much of their music?

MUSIC AS IDEA

Modern criticism and theorizing about the traditional repertory—the same repertory that helped bring about the modernist composer's peculiar position—has remarkably underplayed the aspect of music as "idea." Instead, the dominating view is of music as a listening process. To be sure, Schenker posits his *Ursatz* as the ultimate compositional ideal to which all aspire, but the most interesting aspects of any Schenkerian analysis concern themselves with the progression of melodic lines toward a goal.[19] Leonard Meyer's implication-realization model is an explicit treatment of listening processes, and much less formal criticism plays on listening expectations, pattern fulfillment, and so forth. This is all quite reasonable. Process plays to the common intuition of music as an art that lives in the ongoing stream of time and appeals to the metaphor of motion that seems essential to musical thought.

Then again, there is a lot of musical thinking that implicates rather concrete "things" such as motives, melodies, binary forms—in short, any kind of articulation. Beyond that obvious rejoinder, music as idea addresses the composer's imagination and, more important, our appreciation of it, appreciation that magnifies the listening experience. When Handel signals the oncoming end of his magnificent "Amen" fugue in *Messiah* by bringing in the voices on top of one another at the interval of a single beat, we can admire the very idea of it almost as a static object, not so much what it does as what it is, a sculpture in sound (Ex. 6.1).[20]

Is this the sort of sensibility to which modern composers appeal?

Medieval historian Richard Hoppin, describing the late fourteenth-century compositional experiments in France known today as the Ars subtilior, writes that "not until the twentieth century did music again reach the most subtle refinements and rhythmic complexities of the mannerist style."[21] His colleague Jeremy Yudkin agrees that "one of the most characteristic features of the late fourteenth-century style is its rhythmic complexity, a complexity not found again in Western music until the twentieth century."[22] This music, however, parallels that of our own time not only in its inherent complexity but in its artificiality, its roots in the conscious inventions and rational extrapolations of the new rhythmic notation. A contemporary observer, one Arnulf de Saint-Ghislain, writing about 1400, describes compositional seminars dominated by scholarly sages who could not sing but who "keep the glorious treasures of the art and discipline of music in the sanctuaries of their breast" and

Example 6.1. Handel, Messiah, *"Amen," mm. 139–143.*

who "instruct [others] according to rule."[23] Theory dictates practice; how familiar it all sounds.

Some of these glorious treasures can be glimpsed in an excerpt from a member of the Avignon school, Anthonello de Caserta (Ex. 6.2). In the score the touted features of sustained cross-meters and various subdivisions of the beat are immediately apparent. In the hearing "the overall effect is of an improvisatory rhapsodizing."[24] Missing is a sense of constraint that traditionally attends polyphonic composition, either in the relations among the voices or within the voices themselves.

The handling of dissonance, to begin with, is always a principal syntactic aspect of a polyphonic language.[25] This music has dissonant notes

Example 6.2. Caserta, Beaute parfaite, *mm. 1–17. Harmonic dissonances, including m2, M2, P4, T, m7, and M7, are circled.*

sprinkled rather liberally throughout. What is their character here? Regarding melodic motion, they do appear limited to step motion, but on closer inspection, not entirely. Dissonances may be approached by leap (m. 13) and resolved by leap (m. 14). Regarding metric stress, they can occur on strong beats without special preparation (mm. 6, 8), although this music projects such a weak sense of meter one might argue that a metric constraint is ineffective in any case. It is true, though, that dissonances occur only in notes of short duration.

One place where dissonance is certainly banned is at phrase endings. The articulation of phrases is brought about by open-fifth concords of relatively long duration, as in measures 5, 11, and 16. As analysts of the Ars nova have known for a long time, however, there is little in the way of pitch syntax in the approach to the cadences. There is no way to judge from the notes composing the phrase whether the phrase is to end on a G final (mm. 5, 16) or an A final (m. 11).[26] And when there are no dissonances, the individual melodic lines can leap about as they please; fifths and even sevenths (mm. 7–8, 15) abound in the middle voice of *Beaute parfaite*. Parallel octaves among voices seem not to be taboo (mm. 4, 6, 16–17). Finally, there is no apparent syntax of metric changes and subdivisions of beat, save that the voices arrive together at a phrase ending. This is surprising, since those things form the core of the experiment.

This rhythmic freedom is less extravagant in music of the Ars nova proper, but the syntax of the polyphony, or lack of it, actually, is much the same (Ex. 6.3). The same liberality of dissonance treatment, although with somewhat more conservative voice leading, can be heard in this famous work of Machaut of the generation preceding Caserta. The fifth measure is particularly rich in dissonance, with its parallel sevenths approached by leap from the F that is already itself contradicting the G in the tenor.

The creators of the Ars nova reveled in the potential of their new rhythmic notation but at the same time carried on the polyphonic traditions of the Ars antiqua, assuming all along that music should be polyphonic, that melodies should be combined. Their theoretical notion that duration and proportion could be notated in a way independent of pitch—their revolutionary discovery—failed to recognize that in the practice of composition, the pitches of one melody would continue to sound against those of another. The melodies might be metrically independent and with various subdivisions, but nothing would prevent them from sounding together in some way. As their rhythmic fancies took

Example 6.3. Machaut, Messe de Notre Dame, *Agnus Dei I.*

flight, they failed to control for this harmonic aspect, or failed to control for it adequately. In the harmonic dimension the Ars nova has a syntactic gap.

The plain truth is that it would be extremely difficult for anyone to notice a mid-phrase performance error in this particular Caserta, as is so easy in other music, even if that listener were well familiar with the tradition. The polyphonic syntax is not sufficiently defined; there are too many degrees of freedom. Jeremy Yudkin, in his analysis of *Beaute parfaite*, argues that the "hazy outline and transparency of texture is carefully controlled, however, for the underlying cadence structure is completely regular and provides points of stability and response for the shifting and flexible flow of the music."[27] This is to argue in the twentieth-century mode: high-level structure is all, details do not matter. But as we have seen in other styles, if syntax is important to music, then details matter very much, at least as much as high-level structure.[28] The patterns of Ars nova composition, after all, are eminently clear. *Beaute parfaite* is a French ballade, one of the traditional *formes fixes*, whose standard AAB pattern is articulated interiorly by occasional "points of repose" at phrase endings and, incidentally, at the end by a recapitulation of the music that ends the A section. But within the phrases? Precious little can be said.

Where there is no sense of error there can be little sense of the technique that accompanies and masters a strong syntax. The "idea" of the music cannot compare with the kind admired in Handel and cannot elicit the same response. As the rational extensions of the Ars nova language grow bolder and freer, they, paradoxically, become less impressive.

The syntactic gap of the Ars nova was quickly redressed by a conservative reaction to "medieval permissiveness" in most every aspect.[29] Unprepared dissonances disappeared. Voices were coordinated in consonant progression, which required in turn the restriction of cross-metric effects so highly prized in the fourteenth century. By the fifteenth century the grand experiment had fallen into disrepute, ironically so, since the new music of the early Renaissance could not have existed without the essential Ars Nova invention of independent rhythmic notation.

But the rejection of the Ars nova after its relatively brief time on the center stages in France signals more than a change in musical taste of the cultivated classes. The Ars nova, though an artificial language driven by rhythmic innovation, actually forced the whole question of polyphony as the primary signature of Western music. The question it bared was this: if there is to be no coordination, no syntax, among the voices in a polyphonic texture, then why have the texture at all? What is there to be appreciated? After all, once the implications of the Ars nova discovery dawned on composers and theorists, there was no a priori reason why polyphony had to continue in vogue, why the essential line of development could not have followed a rhythmic path instead. Indeed, the French Ars nova blazed just such a trail—Machaut himself experimented with monophonic chansons—but ended up taking with it the baggage of polyphony. The consensus was clear: polyphony was too valuable to give up. The French court composers never lost their taste for the independence of vocal lines and broad schemes of rhythmic organization— witness the persistence of isorhythmic motets well into the fifteenth century and the distinct contrapuntal art of chansons in the sixteenth.

But on the close levels of detail, syntax would rule in the harmonic realm, with rhythm in its service, when the Ars nova finished its course. As the historians have remarked, not until our own century have experiments in rhythmic design again received such attention.

The worst problems of the Ars nova experiment would appear to have been solved by the most influential artificial musical language of the twentieth century, serial composition, whose very creation was the inspiration for the radicalized thinking about composition that led to all the other later attempts at language building. The Ars nova began with new ideas about rhythmic organization but never developed a syntax to control the new harmonic structures it produced. Serialism began with new ideas about pitch organization and articulated a precise syntax from the outset.[30] Moreover, this syntax could be extrapolated to all the salient aspects of music, including duration, dynamics, and even tone color, as the work of Milton Babbitt has shown us. Thus, there would be no dangling elements, like the polyphonic aspect of the Ars nova, that loom large in the ears of the listener without any apparent organization. The explicit theory of serialism should make it easy to tell if a note is wrong. And it is rich in the complexity of its ideas: the compendium of row manipulations, complementarity, interval vectors, and other theoretical constructs can be a fascinating study, even for a single piece.

Well, then, what happened? Why is serialism, three quarters of a century old, still an alien language for most modern listeners?

A speech consisting of English words pronounced in the exact reverse of their normal word order could claim a syntax just as precise as the normal one, but that is no guarantee that a play written in "retrograde English" could be comprehended by native English speakers, or by anyone for that matter. Logic—in the form of consistent rules and their rational extensions—is but one aspect of natural-language syntax, and probably not the dominant one. The innate capacities of human linguistic cognition, acoustics, and life's experience of cause and effect have at least as much claim on syntax as has logic.

Like the Ars nova, serialism began with certain premises and then extended them logically to create a system. Chief among these premises are, first, that a strict sequential arrangement of the twelve available pitch classes is an integral musical organization sufficient to supplant the perceptual anchor of a tonal center, and, second, that inversions, retrogrades, and other subset relations of this sequence are also sufficient. The sequence need only remain intact. This logic produces an articulate syntax; one can always say which pitch class is required and why.[31] If the concept of serial order is transferred to durations and other musical aspects (a very logical thing to do), then one can say why the note F♯ should be an eighth note played loudly by the violin.

But whether this logic can be heard, can be experienced directly, is quite another matter. To say that explicit serial theory makes it easy to identify a wrong note and to justify a right choice is to talk about the score, not listening, to invoke a judgment that is purely intellectual, rational, and logical. It is not the instant, intuitive, almost reflexive judgment one exercises when hearing a mistake in Handel or in speech. Some recent thinking about human cognition of music, particularly the thinking of composer-theorist Fred Lerdahl, suggests why this is so. Seralism, because it stakes all on the pitch-class sequence (the tone row, or series), "is a permutational rather than elaborational system. Pitch relations in virtually all 'natural' compositional grammars are elaborational," by which Lerdahl means that musical information can be chunked into groups using the same or similar cognitive strategies over and over.[32] Hierarchical relations—the construction of pieces out of sections, sections out of themes, themes out of phrases, phrases out of notes, to pick one illustration—are harder to articulate in serialism. Second, Schoenberg's "emancipation of the dissonance"—the logic of justifying a note only by its position in the series, not against a criterion of consonance—"in effect defines musical consonance and dissonance out of existence. . . . But this strategy, while perfectly logical, does not neutralize sensory [acoustic] consonance and dissonance."[33] In short, one cannot wish away Pythagoras and his simple whole-number ratios. They are acoustically more stable, and in natural "listening grammars," to borrow Lerdahl's term, they act as natural points of articulation. The Ars nova insisted on very little in its polyphonic syntax, but it did insist on that point in its open-fifth phrase endings.

Finally there is the matter of context. As for the broad cultural contexts that aid in linguistic comprehension, one can argue whether serialism was the logical endpoint to nineteenth-century chromaticism or whether it broke radically with all Western tradition (and most others, too) by creating music without a tonal center.[34] Schoenberg himself seems to have been of two minds on this: "this music was distinctly a product of evolution, and more revolutionary than any other development in the history of music."[35] But there is no question that serialism has shunned the advantages of immediate contextual effects.[36] Indeed, the most striking characteristic of all artificial languages, from Esperanto to LISP, is their syntactic consistency, an absolute logical system that tries to eliminate all local or unpredicted effects of intercourse among the elements inside the utterance, those mysteriously ambiguous meanings and functions that arise in natural languages. That is why composer Benjamin Boretz points with pride to the "context-free" quality of the serial language:

> And the absence of "aboutness" in the languages of the musical and visual arts, at least, frees them from the constraints of conventional norms of syntactical and lexical formation and association. As a result, they are free to create their own norms contextually from much simpler perceptual-assumptive bases. Hence, for example, works of music are constructable from a general notion of "music" without the *essential* intervention of stages identified as, say, "tonal" or "twelve-tone," which would be analogous to the construction of a particular English utterance wholly from a system that defines "language" in general, without the essential intervention of an English dictionary or grammar.[37]

In other words, for music to be truly free, it must begin from scratch. Like machine language for computers, only the primitives are really necessary.

None of this means that serial music must be impenetrable, nothing more than a rationalistic conceit of Schoenberg. Indeed, one cannot read him for very long without being moved by his sincerity and conviction. Surely the brilliance of some of his followers is persuasive of something real there, and there is even some empirical evidence that some fundamentals of the language come with experience.[38] But the experience of the century leaves little doubt that learning serialism in the way we expect to learn other musical languages is far from easy. Schoenberg himself admitted Gustav Mahler's reaction to his First Quartet of 1905: "I have conducted the most difficult scores of Wagner; I have written complicated music in scores of up to thirty staves or more; yet here is a score of not more than four staves, and I am unable to read them."[39] And this a pre-serial work! If the likes of Mahler cannot enter, then the musical community of Webern, Berg, Babbitt, and the other luminaries must be a tiny elite indeed.

Perhaps the whole problem of perceptibility is irrelevant, as voices as diverse and learned as those of Carl Dahlhaus, Jean-Jacques Nattiez, and Nicholas Cook have advised.[40] "After all, there is no evidence to suggest that Machaut or Isaac or Bach was worried if his listeners failed to perceive the contrapuntal devices in his music."[41] No, indeed, since the devices of canon, ostinato, and the like were just the icing on the cake made with a much more fundamental recipe of melody and harmony whose syntactic comprehension was taken for granted. If the comprehension of the root musical language had been in question, they certainly would have worried, for they quickly would have found themselves unemployed. For his part Schoenberg proclaimed that "composition with twelve tones has no other aim than comprehensibility."[42] Certainly Babbitt thought it important: "Inability to perceive and remember precisely the values of any of these components results in a dislocation of the event in the work's musical space, an alteration of its relation to all other events in the work, and—thus—a falsification of the composition's total structure."[43] But perceptibility is only relevant as long as one assumes that some form of communication with a musical community is part of the act of composition. Perhaps the designers of twentieth-century artificial languages make no such assumption. "I'm the only listener with whom I'm concerned when I compose," declared George Perle in 1990.[44] "Such a scenario, plausible enough in relation to the music of Schoenberg and his successors, stresses the completeness of the breaks and the self-enclosure of the systems. . . . No longer ostensibly a form of shared or communal expression, composition could be viewed as a form of self-indulgence."[45]

Or perhaps they simply don't care how big their audience is. Milton Babbitt, writing his notorious "Who Cares If You Listen?" in 1958, prefers the tiny musical community of cognoscenti. Serious composition, like scientific research, belongs exclusively to the expert, who, like the pure researcher that he is, need not worry about its practical applications in the wider world.[46]

Outsiders are left, then, with music as idea, pure idea. The composition is an object, a design, a thought, to be contemplated, not an activity to be engaged. Read Schoenberg's own images: "Just as our mind always recognizes, for instance, a knife, a bottle or a watch, regardless of its position, and can reproduce it in the imagination in every possible position, even so a musical creator's mind can operate subconsciously with a row of tones, regardless of their direction, regardless of the way in which a mirror might show the mutual relations, which remain in a given quality."[47] This is *Beaute parfaite* expressed as musical computation. Indeed, historians of the Ars nova emphasize with justice that the design of individual compositions plays with much more than the newfound rhythmic notation but also with obscure coordinations of the multiple texts, allusions to the patron, even the visual presentation of the music in manuscript. But these things rarely participate in the musical experience; rather, they are the frozen architecture. And they are far from Handel's "Amen" fugue. The sculpture of Handel's stretto is an intellectual appreciation, no doubt, but, strangely enough, here it is hard not to instantly bind that cool beauty to the fact that it was a human being who thought of such a stretto with this very subject, which heretofore was thought incapable of such a device, and how it accomplished its task of crowning the fugue with such grandeur. The perception of "a great idea!" fuses recognition of the passage as a profound thought originating in Handel's mind with the experience of its effects as it is played out. Listeners live through the idea, feel Handel thinking, and sense the technical triumph of its solution as immediately and intuitively as we sense a poem's rhyme. The moment reminds such listeners of their membership in Handel's community and makes them glad of it. Artificial languages that exclude real-time cognition as a consideration exclude as well this kind of communal participation. The computer languages are fine examples: their syntaxes are consistent to a fault, they are relatively context free by design, and their linguistic communities are populated only by machines.

The problem is not that composition should avoid confronting listeners with new things. On the contrary, it must. But can it do so in a way that invites listeners along for the experience? Consider Debussy.

Debussy was one of the greatest innovators of his age, but he is not the author of an artificial language in the sense of Schoenberg or Carter or Stockhausen. There is no logical system grown by deduction from premises. Debussy was a slow composer and not at all prolific. His method of innovation was trial and error and his justification was his musical sensibility.

In the passage from his first Prelude for piano (Ex. 6.4), it is easy to discern a specific syntax for the harmonization of the melody: every note

Example 6.4. Debussy, Prelude No. 1, "Danseuses de Delphes," mm. 15–16.

Example 6.5. Debussy, Prelude No. 1, "Danseuses de Delphes," mm. 21–24.

of the theme becomes the fifth factor of a major triad. Similarly, in the passage in Example 6.5, every melody note is the third factor of a major triad. The clarity of the syntax ensures a kind of intelligibility, the basis of technique, simple as it is. The resulting progressions are freshly non-functional, yet it is not hard to hear an error in performance, even on first hearing. The listener can be brought along.

Indeed, the music invites the listener to help create the local dialect for this work. There is no reflexive intuition as there is for Handel, but rather food for the imagination. The interpretation of the harmonic progression in Example 6.6 affords several interpretations and leaves many questions. Is the F pedal the local tonic? Are the parallel chords a kind of multiple melody? Is that an old-fashioned contrary counterpoint they make with the high melody? Such a nod to the past is hardly rare for Debussy. In the opening gesture of the prelude, Debussy does what Beethoven does so often: he creates a syntactic metaphor (Ex. 6.7).[48] The augmented F triad is an artificial dominant. Because its root is the same as the traditional dominant in this B-flat context, and because Debussy

Example 6.6. Debussy, Prelude No. 1, "Danseuses de Delphes," mm. 11–12.

Example 6.7. Debussy, Prelude No. 1, "Danseuses de Delphes," mm. 1–2.

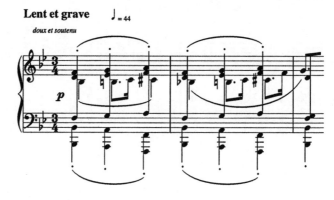

places it on the upbeat leading back to a B-flat "tonic," the augmented triad, traditionally a weak and dissonant passing chord, begins to acquire the traditional function of preparing the tonic. The prelude reinforces this legerdemain so consistently that there is no other way to conclude the piece (Ex. 6.8). Try playing a traditional F-major chord in place of the augmented ones here; it is the very image of triviality. And yet, while syntactic metaphor is one of Beethoven's hallmarks, the technique here is not Beethoven's. Debussy does not bother with the definition of the metaphor in a traditional context. There is no gradual teaching of the idea; rather, it is presented as a fait accompli, leaving us to make sense of it as best we can.

That is how Debussy feeds our imagination and brings us along. There is no consistent and logical system that informs the piece, never mind one for his oeuvre, but by taking advantage of fundamental perceptions he creates a highly original syntax that is nonetheless negotiable.

Example 6.8. Debussy, Prelude No. 1, "Danseuses de Delphes," mm. 25–27.

Acoustic dissonance marks relative tension, consonance resolution. Longer durations and pauses create phrasing. A faint tonic of B flat begins and ends the work.

The syntax that arises is extremely fragile. There is no weight of tradition behind it, and Debussy cannot depend on his listeners having been prepared by years of learning. That is why the tensions and resolutions in Debussy are comparatively mild affairs. Even that F augmented triad, whose role is defined unmistakably, has nothing like the force of a true dominant. That was sacrificed for freshness of sound. Because he depends so much on what might be called innate, as opposed to cultural, syntax, Debussy's tensions are less articulate and nuanced. Once the sound is struck, however, this impressionistic kind of tension—some would say mood—can be sustained for remarkably long periods. Perhaps that is why filmmakers have found this language so useful.

Film music reminds us that the twentieth-century musical languages that have planted the strongest roots in the culture came equipped with a strong semantic component. Debussy's pieces have fanciful titles for listeners to think about, as have Ives's. Stravinsky's career took off via the ballet; whatever we think about them today, *The Firebird*, *Petrushka*, and *The Rite of Spring* originally referred to real actions and plots. It makes sense, for a new musical syntax takes a long time to learn: better give listeners an additional mode of understanding while that learning goes on.

But semantics has apparently not sugared serial music in the same way. Schoenberg wrote *Moses and Aaron* and many other vocal works, but the semantic component of their texts seems not to have diminished the "opacity" of the music for the culture at large. Serialism remains respected at arm's length. Are the inventors' logical methods then to blame? An uncomfortable position, that, for it indicts rationality itself and implies that any serious thinking about composition brings the kiss of death to the ensuing music. Rather, try the premises from which the systems grew, not the logic that cultivated them. "Coherence in classic compositions is based—broadly speaking—on the unifying qualities of such structural factors as rhythms, motifs, phrases, and the constant reference of all melodic and harmonic features to the centre of gravitation—the tonic. Renouncement of the unifying power of the tonic still leaves all the other factors in operation."[49] Such was Arnold Schoenberg's premise, and from it the logic of serialism is incontestable. But if "all the other factors" are insufficient? Flawless logic can bring about flawed results then and tries the patience of even a sympathetic community. Serialism presents a kind of obverse case to the late Ars nova. There the ideas of rhythmic and metric invention are easy enough to sense, but, without sufficient syntax of their own and none in relation to the polyphonic medium, there is little technique to appreciate in their working out. Serialism leaves nothing to be desired in its technical virtuosity and syntactic precision, but few can *experience* the ideas directly with any immediacy.

All these experiments in this century of artificial languages, in their attempts to solve practical problems in the world, have founded linguistic communities that are articulate, even passionate, but small and elite. Esperanto struggles to unite its speakers' power, but its dispersal around the globe renders it nearly impotent. Computer programmers, fluent in their many tongues, use them to speak only to machines, never to one another. And the composers who invent languages to ensure that their music bears resemblance to no other in history create musical communities that exist in relative isolation from the culture at large. The exceptions are those languages that are not so "artificial," that accept for their premises only the premises of hearing, which, incidentally, cannot be wholly rational because they are but dimly understood. Debussy has shown us how this school of hard knocks can teach. But Debussy's manner of invention is an old-fashioned kind. Invention in some degree has always been a part of Western musical tradition, but it is traditionally carried out, for the most part, in contact with the musical communities that it concerns. There is an essential cooperation to this invention, the give-and-take of linguistic evolution.

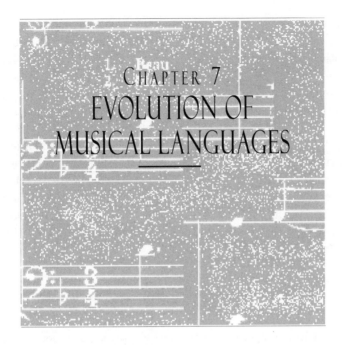

CHAPTER 7
EVOLUTION OF MUSICAL LANGUAGES

How and why do languages change over time? Modern linguists, after a considerable absence, have only recently returned to ponder evolution.[1] In the nineteenth century the history of languages was the centerpiece of "philology," and such scholars painstakingly examined inscrutable fragments of writing and other clues to deduce ancient pronunciations, etymologies, grammars, and even great chunks of ancestor languages such as Indo-European, of which nothing survives. But when Ferdinand de Saussure, with his slice-of-life synchronic approach to language, established modern theoretical linguistics in the second decade of the twentieth century and Noam Chomsky began to specify its machinery in the late 1950s, the problem of language change became passé. Some linguists such as Leonard Bloomfield believed that serious study of it was impossible, since change was too slow to be observed in the field.[2]

For musicians, on the other hand, the succession of musical languages, one seeming to change into another like Latin changing into French, has always been a fascination ever since consciousness of music history arose in the nineteenth century. In our own century of charitable attitudes toward all music, earlier notions about evolutionary "progress" toward musical perfection have given way to less prescriptive accounts: music evolves to suit the culture, or because great composers venture down "new roads" or to take advantage of new instruments, or, perhaps the most frequent explanation, because the languages tire out, all their possibilities exhausted by geniuses.

Anyone looking for a precise explanation of any particular turn in music history—say Mannerism in the sixteenth century, or Romanticism in the nineteenth—is bound to be disappointed by such easy, all-purpose accounts. Many historians, perhaps skittish of any theory that smacks of prescription or direction, would deny that explanation is possible anyway. Music changes, that's all. We only need know when and how. But that defeatism does nothing to satisfy music lovers who believe that there are verifiable and rational causes at work here, who want to understand evolution. Recent inquiries into evolution of spoken language have begun to touch on the question "why" as well "how" and "when." Can they help?

A SAMPLER OF LINGUISTIC CHANGES

Languages can change in any or all of their principal aspects: in phonology, semantics, and syntax.

On Martha's Vineyard, an island off the coast of Cape Cod in Massachusetts, the sociolinguist William Labov recorded some changes in the pronunciation of vowel diphthongs. In the word "house," for example, the native islanders once used a diphthong closer to the front of the mouth than the normal American one: [hɛus] instead of [haus]. The first half of this century saw the pronunciation begin to move backward, matching the mainland sound. Recently, however, the sound has begun to return to the original frontal diphthong among certain islander groups, particularly elderly fishermen in the village of Chilmark and a large number of other men aged thirty to forty-five.[3]

This is a purely phonetic evolution, a change of sound that has no effect on syntax or meaning, leaves the phonemic inventory untouched, and does not affect the speaker's ability to be understood. It affects only the "color" of the speech, and that is its precise analog in music. A phonetic change for a musical language could be the introduction of a new instrument or, more subtle, the slow advance of a particular instrumental or vocal technique, such as vibrato. These things change the color of the sound but leave the set of usable pitches within the octave and all higher-level syntax unaffected.

When changes in pronunciation alter the perceived meaning of utterances, usually over long time spans, the evolution in sound is phonemic. Everyone who studies French as a second language quickly becomes familiar with its characteristic nasal vowels: *an*, "year"; *coin*, "corner"; *fin*, "end"; *brun*, "brown." Once the final *n* consonant was pronounced clearly without a preceding nasal. During the period from the ninth to the fourteenth centuries, the final *n* slowly disappeared, and the preceding vowel turned into a nasal sound.[4] The difference is important: the vowel in *an* must be distinguished from the one in *ananas* ("pineapple") and so counts as a phonemic change.[5] This evolution helped to add the nasals to the modern French phonemic inventory, contributing to its unusually high sixteen different vowel sounds.

An analogous phonemic expansion occurred in Western music from the fourteenth to sixteenth centuries. The medieval pitch inventory was seven or eight within the octave, depending on how one considers the "soft B" or B$^\flat$ that replaced B$^\natural$ in certain circumstances. The following centuries gradually added the other "black key" chromatic notes in auxiliary contexts. By the seventeenth century they had attained full status in the inventory, functionally indistinguishable from the older notes.

More often, a phonemic inventory will not expand but simply change, substituting new sounds for older ones that disappear completely from pronunciation. The Chinese language lost its stop consonants at the ends of words (e.g., [p] [t]), which turned into glottal stops and then into tones. That is why pitch is a critical distinctive aspect of modern Chinese vowels. The German gutterals once were prominent in English but gave way to stops: [k] and [g]. Most famous of all is the Great Vowel Shift of the fifteenth century, which moved all the long vowels systematically forward and upward in the vocal tract, leaving the gulf between modern English pronunciation and Chaucer's.

The most significant phonemic change in Western music arrived with the system of equal-tempered tuning, beginning in the sixteenth century. This system aimed to allow keyboard instruments the same radical harmonic progressions that occurred in the secular vocal genres by eliminating the acoustic clashes that inevitably resulted from tuning by pure Pythagorean intervals. A harpsichordist playing an instrument tuned so that the fifths around F, the tonic for the madrigal in Example 7.1, were pure, would find it impossible to play the passage.[6] Because the acoustic fifths based on the 3:2 harmonic ratio are not symmetrical with respect to enharmonics—in short, G$^\sharp$ will not have the same pitch as A$^\flat$—the G$^\sharp$ that is tuned to sound good in measure 36 will assuredly sound wretched in measure 46, when it must be A$^\flat$.

Example 7.1. Cipriano da Rore, Dalle belle contrade, *mm. 35–48. ("What will become of me all dark and grieving? Ah! Cruel love, how dubious and brief are your sweetnesses . . .")*

Singers can make the adjustment, but instruments whose pitches are fixed in advance cannot. Equal temperament divided the acoustic octave into twelve equal parts; pure fifths were lost, but passages like the Rore became accessible to such instruments, since G♯ and A♭ now signified the same note on the keyboard. The change is phonemic, since it altered the syntactic significance and potential of every tone, although the cognitive distinction between enharmonics remained real, like homonyms, enforced by context. When the serialists declared this distinction null and void in the twentieth century, music's phonology changed again.

No change in language is more familiar to everyday speakers than the sprouting of new words. Inventions, discoveries, new fields of inquiry—in short, any unfamiliar contexts—bring along new words to describe them. Words also disappear as their relevant contexts disappear: "talkie," once common, is now used only by historians of cinema; how long before we lose "ditto," "phonograph," and expressions such as "half-past seven"? The capacity of a language to add to its lexicon and of its speakers to keep up with its growth is remarkable. While most obvious in compounding languages like German, whose speakers can create new words almost at will from a constellation of roots, prefixes, and suffixes and simply by jamming established words together, English is not so far behind in this regard. How often does someone make a temporary new adjective by adding -ish, -like, or -y to the end of a noun? Music is generally much less fecund in its semantic creativity. Certain languages—the Baroque, for instance—have acquired detailed lexicons of sighing motifs, weeping motifs, and so on, and the nationalist idioms establish symbols such as the augmented second for gypsy music and modal progressions for Russian, but compared to spoken language musical vocabulary is a rock of stability.

More common than additional words are words whose meaning has changed over time. Any page of Shakespeare will show how many of our familiar words had different, sometimes contrary, meanings in the sixteenth century. The circumstance for this kind of change is similar to that for a new word: instead of distinctively new contexts requiring patently new expressions, a word is continually used in an evolving context and its meaning—always a product of its initial semantic range and that context[7]—evolves with it until its semantic range is different. Thus, "gentleman" and "maid" do not have nearly the same range in modern American as they had in the English of two centuries ago.

The most striking analog to this kind of lexical change in music is the rise of the major/minor distinction, once more in the sixteenth century. There were once eight to twelve kinds of scales (modes) in Western music owning different patterns of half-tone and whole-tone sequences. Half of these had the major third above the tonic and half had the minor one, and they were semantically indistinguishable, at least in the sense that there is no correlation between their use and the meaning of song texts, for example.[8] Then the songwriters and madrigalists of the sixteenth century began to use the modes with the major third to set texts with happy, humorous, or otherwise light emotions and to use modes with the minor third for the darker ones. The distinction was slow in developing consistency and never became an iron-clad rule, if only because a composer can marshal so many other contextual factors besides the mode in the service of semantic expression. Thus, as late as the eighteenth century Handel's magnificent elegy in *Saul* is centered on the major mode and Bach's Easter cantata *Christ Lag in Todesbanden* can accommodate a minor mode hymn tune composed before the major/minor distinction was born.

That evolution is striking because it is so rare. Why is it that musical semantics is so stable compared to the mercurial fancies of speech? The stability probably derives from two important differences in the semantics of the two systems. First, natural-language semantics is infinitely more specific in both reference and connotation than is musical semantics. The system that can so precisely distinguish among "paper," "sheet," "leaf," "page," and "folio" will suffer change as soon as their proper contexts do. A small change, a little time, and "folio" becomes antique. Musical semantics is saved from similar wear and tear by its generality. Musical meaning, presentational in character, without truth value, and so difficult to specify to common agreement in any particular case, has a semantic range so broad and deep that changes of context in its setting or in the community that hears it have the effect of fog drifting about an obscure view. If we can't agree on what we see, we can hardly pinpoint alterations.

Second, the objects of musical semantics may be more inherently stable than most of the objects of speech semantics. After all, speech must concern itself with all the material world, and that changes all the time. But music, traditionally, is supposed to express the ineffable, the intangible, the emotional. Whether or not one gives "love," "pain," or "divine" objective status, such ideas probably do not evolve very much, even over centuries. If such things are a main concern of musical semantics, then stability would be built right in.

If the analogs for semantic evolution between music and language seem a little poor, surely those for syntax, that most dynamic and languagelike aspect of music, should be rich. But here is a surprise: there appear to be none at all.

Syntax is perhaps the most conservative feature of language, but, given enough time, the syntax of most any language will evolve. English once had an extensive set of inflections for nouns that indicated case: nominative (sentence subjects), accusative (sentence objects), singular, plural, and so on. Now only a few vestiges remain in the plural and possessive endings. Word order in Old English was a much more flexible affair than it is in modern English. Historians consider this to be an obvious trading relationship. As inflectional endings dropped out of pronunciation, syntactic ambiguities arose in sentences, ambiguities eventually corrected by fixing the word order to a subject-verb-object form.[9]

The verb system, too, has evolved, from a large number of irregular or "strong" verbs to just a few. The vestiges here are seen in irregular past tense forms: "spoke" instead of "speaked," "sang" instead of "singed," and so forth. Other changes in verb usage may be occurring right before our ears. One possibility is the use of progressive tenses in English. This form of the verb indicates an action in progress:

> Raimondi *is singing* that opera.

The form emphasizes the immediacy of the action and the present state of the subject, as compared with:

> Raimondi *sings* that opera.
>
> Raimondi *does sing* that opera.

which normally imply a habitual or repeated action in the first case and emphasis of fact in the second. These sentences say little about the present state of Raimondi. Now, as Jean Aitchison reports:

> there used to be a set of verbs expressing mental states which were never normally used with the progressive, even when they indicated an action in progress, as in:
>
> Ursula loves God (not *Ursula is loving God).
>
> Angela knows my brother (not *Angela is knowing my brother).
>
> I understand French (not *I am understanding French).

Nowadays, however, one hears an increasing number of sentences in which mental-state verbs are found with the progressive:

Billy is kissing Petronella, and *is loving* it.

Charles *is understanding* French a lot better since he's been to France.

The matron does not know all she should *be knowing* about this affair.

We're certainly hoping they'll *be wanting* to do it again.[10]

Might we extend this tendency to the curious use of the present progressive, common among the youth of the 1990s, to describe past action?

So they fixed my car two days ago and I'*m saying,* "How much will this cost?"

Or to its more distressing abbreviation?

So they fixed my car two days ago and I'*m like,* "How much will this cost?"

There are no credible analogs to this sort of evolution in music, because there are no specific analogs to the components of natural-language grammar: nouns and noun phrases, verbs and verb phrases, and their modifiers.

It is true that one might find analogs to general patterns of syntactic evolution. For example, teachers of harmony often like to introduce the dominant-seventh chord by demonstrating its "etymology" deriving from a common voice-leading pattern (see diagram below). The acceptance of the dissonant chord as one of the most stable elements of eighteenth-century harmonic syntax came about when strong harmonic functions took over much of the job of regulating the coordination of simultaneous

"ETYMOLOGY" OF THE DOMINANT SEVENTH.

melodies. Melodic leaps and dissonant combinations that in Josquin's music would have threatened its comprehensibility became organized and justified by harmonic forces in Bach's.[11] There is a trading relation reminiscent of that between the disappearing noun inflections and more rigid word order of early modern English.

Similarly, some writers have pointed to certain recursive features in music that act like the embedding of sentence structures in generative grammar. We have seen how Bach can construct a multilevel harmonic syntax with just two voices (see Example 5.6, page 105).[12] In order for the strange dissonances, odd leaps, and long G♯ in measure 3 to make sense, we must understand the higher levels of progression even as we perceive the more immediate ones. And if we are to understand something as simple as:

He knows he doesn't understand what is going on.

we must parse it on several levels as in the diagram below. But embedding appears to be a universal feature of language,[13] and while many aspects of musical structure lend themselves to multilevel descriptions, it is required in no one particular aspect and in simpler musics perhaps not at all. And can we be sure that the harmonic functions replicate essentially on higher levels, as grammatical ones do in language? What exactly in the Bach is to correspond with the noun and verb phrases? Without the analogies of specific syntactic components, recursion sug-

GENERATIVE DIAGRAM SHOWING SYNTACTIC EMBEDDING

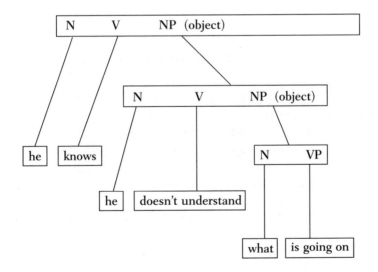

gestions little more than a basic cognitive strategy of hierarchical perception, a kind of divide-and-conquer approach to organized hearing.

Analogies of syntactic evolution can be no more specific, because the fundamental purposes of syntax in music and language are different.[14] Language syntax, in its regulation of word patterns, conveys information about relationships in the world outside the speaker. Musical syntax, in its regulation of sound patterns, controls musical tension and resolution in its many kinds. Histories of syntactic change in music, having nothing to match up with nouns and verbs, must describe the sources, uses, and effects of musical tension.

The description at any given point is complex, indicating, among other things, the sources of tension, including the locus at a given level of structure; which tension predominates and what is the effect of that? how finely is each source controlled? what is its place in the organization of the music? A history of syntactic change chronicles the shifts and trade-offs among these and the resulting effects. Bach has more freedom in his voice leading than Josquin, but he must order his triads with greater care. The gain is precise control of an articulate harmonic tension, but he loses a quality of contrapuntal tension that might be metaphorically described as ebb and flow.

So the comparison of change in music and language so far merely confirms already suspected similarities and differences. That is by no means a null result; confirmation is always welcome. But a survey of suspected causes of linguistic evolution does reveal something new: how these changes interrelate and arise from one another within a communal laboratory.

SOME CAUSES OF LINGUISTIC CHANGE

Conquest and colonialism have presented historians of language the best opportunities to observe the most drastic occasion for change: the collision of two linguistic communities. Language, perhaps more than anything else, gives people a sense of social identity and nationhood, as we see all too well in Québec, Sri Lanka, Belgium, and many other places. When invasion or political annexion forces communities together, a linguistic competition ensues as two peoples try to converse. Often a kind of working linguistic compromise called a pidgin arises, an apparently haphazard mixing of isolated words and expressions from two languages with little in the way of sophisticated grammar that the parent languages possess. If the pidgin persists, a fully grammatical daughter language called a creole develops, sometimes within a single generation.[15] Thus, a language with completely new features may be born. Otherwise, social or political dominance of one community may cause the decline and disappearance of the other language, but not without the winning language having borrowed many words from the losing one.[16] The case of English is interesting in this regard. After the Normans conquered Britain in 1066, French dominated in the upper classes and in fact remained the language of Parliament until the fourteenth century. Normally, such social prestige would be the trump card in the language competition, but because French speakers never overwhelmed the country either geographically or numerically, Old English was able to hold on and eventually triumph. But several centuries of cohabitation had passed, and the English that survived had been enriched by thousands of Latinate words while retaining Anglo-Saxon equivalents. This accounts for innumerable pairs such as "brotherly" and "fraternal," the great richness of English vocabulary today.

Of course, communities borrow language from one another all the time without any animosity at all. Despite the objections of cultural organizations such as the French Academy, the increase of the lexicon by wholesale adoption of foreign words is part of the natural growth of virtually any language. All that is required is a useful expression in one community that has no analog in another. Then the latter simply "borrows" the original expression. The rule of "minimal adjustment" applies: everything is made to conform as much as possible to the norms of the borrowing language.[17] So when American speakers say "crêpes" or "chauffeur" or "bon bon," they blithely scandalize French ears just to conform with American phonology.

Less drastic changes of social origin can come from within the language community itself. William Labov thinks that the reversal of the diphthong trend on Martha's Vineyard is caused by the subconscious desire of the old fishermen and their admirers to set themselves apart from the hordes of "summer people" that invade the island each vacation season. The older pronunciation has become a symbol of tradition and a simpler island way of life, above all an efficient means of identity.[18]

Very often, the cause of a change can only be guessed. What, for example, accounts for the broadening usage of the English progressive present tense and its various colloquial sports? Linguists have little to say. Remembering that every change of syntax causes a change in meaning, however slight, one might suppose that the appeal of the progressive, particularly to younger people, is that it emphasizes the fact of the matter less and the experience of the matter more.

> So I went to school yesterday . . .

> So I'm going to school yesterday . . .

Though grammatically paradoxical, to say the least, the speaker might unconsciously choose the second expression because it brings the listener into the narrative in a more urgent, immediate way. It does not report the experience to the listener so much as re-create it for him. But who really knows?

Some particularly interesting causes of evolution come not from social forces but from within the language itself. The loss of case endings in English pronunciation is a case in point: fixed word order in phrases and a whole class of auxiliary verbs arose to prevent the ambiguities that inevitably resulted when one could no longer hear whether a noun was the object or subject of a sentence by its inflected ending. "For the same reason, prepositions and auxiliaries like *of* and *do* and *will* and *have* were bled of their original meanings and given important grammatical duties. Thus, many of the signatures of modern English syntax were the result of a chain of effects beginning with a simple shift in pronunciation."[19] Something similar happened in French, because of an apparently universal tendency to underpronounce final consonants of a word when no vowel follows. The silent consonants that are the bane of foreign students trying to learn French are fossils of an antique pronunciation. When these consonants dropped off, crucial syntactic features such as plurals could no longer be heard: thus, *enfant* and *enfants* became identical. To compensate, distinctive articles marked the plurals: *les enfants*. "Nowadays, therefore, plurality in French is no longer marked at the end of a word, but at the *beginning*."[20] In short, when an evolutionary trend within a language threatens its ability to communicate, the language corrects itself by making adjustments elsewhere.

The same kind of adjustment can take place within a musical language. The syntactic gap that opened up when the rhythmic experiments of the Ars nova made the polyphonic strands of their music more independent of one another than they had ever been became an urgent pressure requiring compensation as the fourteenth century progressed.[21] At first glance it might appear that the reaction of "la contenance Angloise" that set in was simply a regression to the status quo ante, at least in harmonic terms, but clearly the rhythmic innovations remained in their essence, only curtailed in their most disintegrating practices. The end result was a new language, an adjustment of harmonic and rhythmic syntax that compensated for a rapid destabilizing change in rhythmic syntax a century before.

Seldom are the causes of change so urgent and so precise. More often they are in the nature of opportunities, small changes that accumulate in succession to a large one by creating new possibilities at every turn, possibilities that could never have been foreseen from the perspective of the first link in the chain.

> For example, it has recently been noted that, the world over, there is a natural tendency to pronounce vowels on a slightly higher pitch after voiceless consonants such as [p], [t], [k], than after voiced consonants such as [b], [d], [g]. This tendency became exaggerated in Chinese many centuries ago, and the exaggeration was followed by a loss of the distinction between voiced and voiceless consonants. The result is that Chinese is now a tone language—one which distinguishes between words by means of variations in pitch.[22]

The phonology of European music began to change when pitches auxiliary to the main notes of a mode appeared, as in Example 7.2. The tones C♯ and G♯, both foreign to the A mode of Josquin's motet, decorate the standard cadence formula of this language, the 7–6 suspension cadence

Example 7.2. Josquin, Miserere mei, Deus; tertia pars, *mm. 26–29.*

with syncopation. The "unofficial" or auxiliary status of these notes in the mind of the fifteenth-century community is implicit in the lack of a specific notation.[23] Editors add the required auxiliaries to modern scores, following theoretical treatises of the period, although then, as now, the inferred practice was often misunderstood and variable. Such confusion is the signal of evolution in the making.

In any case, as with the English progressive, one can guess the reason for auxiliary notes. The sound of the traditional suspension cadence formula varies with the mode being sung; the F modes contain the half-tone under the final (E to F, *subsemitonium modi*) as part of its normal pitch set. Other modes have a whole tone under the final (e.g., the D modes, C to D). Perhaps the articulations provided by these cadences became important enough to require a uniform syntax to aid in their perception.

Whatever the reason, this phonological change had two immediate consequences: it created a standard harmony, what we will later call the major triad, to precede the final in suspension cadences, and it clarified cadences made on notes other than the final of the mode. In Example 7.2 Josquin makes a cadence on A, the mode of this motet, in measure 29 only after having made an identical one on D in measure 27. So, the phonological evolution affects the syntactic, as it did with English word order, and it is not hard to look down the road to see other changes ahead. The major triad employing degrees 2, 5, and 7 of the mode eventually becomes the authentic cadence, one of the principal functions in the harmonic syntax that develops in the next century, a syntax so stable that the rhythmic inflection of the syncopation can be let go.[24] As this new functional harmony gains power to articulate tonal centers, the practice of cadencing on alternative degrees of the mode becomes the practice of establishing alternative tonal centers: modulation. The last link is syntactic embedding, whereby tonal centers organize small spans of time within other tonal centers that reign on the higher levels of structure, the essential harmonic construction of the eighteenth century.

Now it is too strong to say that the universal tendency to heighten vowel pitch after voiceless consonants caused Chinese to turn into a tone language. In that case, all the world's tongues should be tending toward tone languages. The tendency provides the opportunity, the entrée for change only. Whether it actually affects the evolution of a language must depend on other factors. Likewise, the half-tone suspension cadence did not cause the authentic cadence and harmonic embedding in any teleological sense. It was an essential link in the chain that eventually formed, but a link that, given other cultural conditions, might have developed in a number of directions, or perhaps not at all.

Musical languages also respond to pressures from their own communities, pressures that are more social than linguistic in nature. They can be very specific. When the Council of Trent declared shortly after 1560 that sacred composition must abstain from secular practices, it ensured the survival of two separate languages—one sacred, one secular—at the end of the century. The language for sacred music virtually stopped evolving, like Latin, and has remained distinct ever since.

As with spoken languages, other community influences are much harder to pin down. The swing of opera fashion away from traditional opera seria toward Gluck's reform opera and to opera buffa above all is widely credited with supplying new melodic and rhythmic effects whose adoption broke down the Baroque language, specifically its foundation of motor rhythm. Perhaps we should similarly credit the broadening interest of Continentals in Shakespeare and other "serious" literary figures in the early nineteenth century with the attention given to German Lieder and the tragic opera lirica in Italy. But why then did Beethoven, who so appreciated Shakespeare and Goethe and Schiller, contribute so little to these movements?

From here it is but a small step to the idea that culture at large can change a musical language, an idea that is taken for granted by many and that has been articulated at length by no less a voice than Leonard B. Meyer's. In his 1989 book *Style and Music* he attempts to establish a direct link between the ideology of a culture–"beliefs about mind and body, nature and society, freedom and necessity, genesis and goals"—and what actually happens in its compositions: "But most often and most importantly the effects of the parameters of action (politics, economics, social arrangements) reach music through the mediation of ideology. That is, the constraints of the parameters of action are translated into the concepts, beliefs, and attitudes that constitute the ideology of the culture (or subculture), and these are in turn translated into the constraints that govern musical choices."[25] Such a reasonable and attractive idea, but how hard to apply with convincing rigor. The problem, of course, is with the translation device that will connect any cultural aspect or change with some answering aspect in a musical language. To speak of a specific change in the musical environment—the Council of Trent or the taste for comic opera—is one thing, but to cite, as Meyer does, something like "egalitarianism" of the nineteenth century as the thing that rotted closed Classical forms and strict harmonic syntax is quite another. Ideological notions are notoriously vague and can therefore accommodate almost any kind of effect one would like to adduce. If Verdi is troublesome to Meyer because he refused to abandon traditional aristocratic forms and syntax, at least he wrote tunes that could be sung by commoners in the café.

It is silly, of course, to insist on the other extreme, that musical development is somehow insulated from its harboring culture, but great care must be taken with cultural cause and musical effect, because even when formulated specifically enough to be convincing, too much time may have passed to make the connection meaningful. Consider the French Revolution and the Enlightenment, the key cultural and political events of the eighteenth century, perhaps of the modern era. What are their effects on musical language? Perhaps they led to a reappraisal of class and other social relations. Perhaps this reappraisal resulted in more people having access to aristocratic accoutrements such as professional music making. Perhaps this access stimulated the growth of public concerts somehow. Perhaps the great numbers of concerts cultivated the new concert repertory.[26] And perhaps Brahms felt the weight of this repertory as a cultural responsibility unlike that felt by any Baroque composer. Even if this chain is reasonable, it seems a bit of a stretch to say that the French Revolution can be heard in Brahms or that it affected his composition in any immediate way. Then again, perhaps public concerts of the nineteenth century were simply the logical result of a steady trend that began with the opening of the first public opera houses in Venice in 1637, quite a while before Rousseau and Danton.

Specifically musical influences, much easier to link up in a causal chain, are at the heart of contact between communities. Since western Europe constitutes in practice one great big musical community with a number of regional accents, opportunities for foreign contact are comparatively rare, but the borrowing that does occur can be a salient aspect of many kinds of composition. The cymbals and drones of late eighteenth-century "Turkish" music and the exposed augmented seconds of "Hungarian" dance melodies do stand right out, marginal though they may be. When a language continues on in some limited role, like church music after the seventeenth century, it is like a separate community and can contribute commonplaces such as the "Amen" cadence or chantlike effects that have equally specific connotations when the situation requires. Occasionally, whole authentic melodies can be borrowed, as Beethoven did from Russia for his opus 59 quartets dedicated to Count Razumovsky. Then there is the curious case of the wholesale importation of the Italian madrigal to England in the 1590s, where it was given a new language and flowered briefly and gloriously before dying out with the rest of the tradition.

In such cases, as when English borrows "crêpes" and "chauffeur," there is no respect for the niceties of authenticity or original context. The attractive, stereotypical aspects are lifted and adapted to the traditional sounds and semantic requirements of the borrowing language. The "Turkish" effects are given a new robe of Western harmonic syntax; simple Russian folk songs are treated to counterpoint that peasants never dreamed of.

By far the most sustained, complex, and dramatic result of interlingual competition in music of the Western experience is American jazz. As in the case of the Norman invasion of England, a strict division in American society allowed two utterly distinct musical languages, the African and European, to survive side by side. The ground was fertile for the growth of the creole that we now call jazz, a new musical language in its own right, neither African nor European, with a full-fledged system of phonology, syntax, and semantics. Some elements of the language such as triads or the predominant role of improvisation can be traced directly to the linguistic parents, but, as with any creole, there are new elements that neither parent language contains: the sense of "swing," the distinct phonology of blue notes, the syntactic stability of dissonant seventh chords, just to name the most prominent.

Because music generally accords sound and syntax so much greater priority than the explicit meaning that is the province of natural language, the genres of composition that contain and determine the sound and syntax play a part in language change that has no apparent analogs in speech. Research on this question in linguistics seems not to exist, but it is unlikely that the forms of conversation and oration have corresponded with the change in English itself over the centuries.[27] The evolution of musical genres, however, is clearly a principal reagent in language change.

Consider the case of the Italian madrigal. In the 1520s a confluence of revived interest in Italian lyric poetry, particularly Petrarca, a growing awareness in the lighter song genres of functional harmony's articulative power, and a sharp interest in the semantic problems of textual expression fashioned with remarkable suddenness and unanimity the first madrigals. The new genre quickly came to dominate the sphere of secular music in Italy and commanded the attention of its foremost composers, all of whom, until rather late in the century, were foreigners from beyond the Alps, *oltremontani*. Having begun its life from the most basic premises of secular music, the madrigal then became the proving ground for experiments in chromatic writing, word painting, rhythmic discontinuity, harmonic dissonance, and intimate relations between text and music that made its sound utterly distinct from the tranquil sonorities heard in church. Its prestige became so great that Heinrich Schütz, a young German come to study with the master Giovanni Gabrieli in Venice, felt compelled to crown his completed apprenticeship with Opus 1 of 1612, a book of Italian madrigals. Then, within two decades or so, the madrigal was no more. Once again, the musical language had changed, this time more radically, and again under the aegis of a new genre, this time opera.[28] By 1630 the leading young composers wrote operas, not madrigals, and the last efforts of Claudio Monteverdi, the last and perhaps greatest practitioner of the madrigal art, bear closer resemblance to opera's small relative, the cantata, than to anything called "madrigal" in the previous century.

Genre and language: clearly in the case of the madrigal they fed off one another in a way complex and yet definite. Rarely is the relationship even as clear as that. Instead, it is vexed by tangled chicken-and-egg questions. Is it true, for example, that comic opera was encouraged by new sensitivities for periodic phrasing and rhythmic transition that obviously suited the musical dramatization of comic action? or rather, that interest in comedy fostered a new kind of musical language based on phrasing and transition rather than Baroque motor rhythm? It is attractive to think that the experiments in high-level harmonic tension made possible the striking new genres of string quartet and symphony, the first major kinds of instrumental composition that could do without an outstanding "external" contrast such as a singer or virtuoso soloist. The new technique supplied an "internal" contrast made of the fabric of the musical material itself. That these genres find success just when the Classical language achieves an identity seems just too neat for coincidence; it demands an explanation, but could it be simply that string quartet and symphony, attractive ensembles in themselves, pointed the way and made the solution a necessity?

What comes to mind here, particularly in periods of historical transition, is the feedback model, the circular relations that are so necessary to the interaction of perceptual information and context.[29] Rather than look for a single, decisive cause and an inevitable effect, consider instead a series of small interactions between genre and language, each one changing the other in a small way, groping toward a synthesis. The idea of a uniform string ensemble covering the traditional four voices, a quartet in short, encourages compositional experiments that will make it work. Partial successes encourage in turn the continuance of the genre, developing the language along the lines of probable success, with trial and error, and so on. Some experiments run into dead ends, of course: guitar quartets have practical problems that were never overcome. How similar this is to the circular perception that allows us to assimilate raw data with contextualizing information in milliseconds, now writ large and slowed down, a kind of community perception.

That musical languages and genres have some degree of mutual dependence implies something important: musical languages are not equally good for every kind of compositional task. Linguists these days are not fond of that kind of comparative evaluation; every language is sophisticated beyond description, and none is especially primitive or complex. Perhaps so on the level of fundamental linguistic functions, but a more detailed comparison makes it clear that natural languages do differ in certain capacities. Rhyming in Italian, for instance, is simply easier than in English, and there is a simple explanation for it. The accent so critical to the sense of rhyme falls on the inflection of Italian verbs but on the stem of English ones. So even though "singing," "finding," and "multiplying" all end with the -*ing* inflection, they do not rhyme, because the accent is on the stems where the sounds differ. But in Italian they do rhyme: *cantando, trovando, moltiplicando*. The stem vowels differ just as much, but when the accent occurs on the inflection -*ando*, as well as all other inflections, Dante's achievement seems just humanly possible. Similarly, everyone who speaks a second language knows expressions that are impossible to translate accurately into the first; one chooses between the literal meaning and the right context. For example, it is not possible to translate this simple exchange into Italian:

> Student: So we'll have lunch on Friday.
> Student: Yes, I'm looking forward to it. Bye.
>
> Studente: Allora, facciamo la colazione venerdì.
> Studente: Sì, ????????????????????. Ciao.

Literally, one could say "sono in anticipo" or, more idiomatically, "non vedo l'ora," but the first is far too technical and the second connotes too much excitement. Italians just do not have the casual "I'm looking forward to it."

The failure of jazz and rock music in church liturgies, despite their prominent position in modern culture, is due to a similar semantic lacuna.

A sense of the sacred is missing from the semantic repertories of those languages, as it may be missing from all musical languages developed since the Baroque. That would explain why masters from Haydn to Brahms felt compelled to borrow so heavily on imitative devices and other signifiers of earlier, more "sacred" languages. Semantic differences among musical languages are most apparent in definite contextual settings such as religious services or, in particular, the theater. It is hard to understand why Mozart, who knew the nature of music drama better than anyone, could not bring off an opera seria that can stand with his comic and tragicomic masterpieces, without speculating that there is some kind of cross-purpose, a misfit, between opera seria and the musical language of the late eighteenth century. The dearth of comedy in the following century invites thinking along the same lines.

One might point out that so-called semantic effects of the various languages are but conventional associations with nothing rational behind them, but that is precisely how the elementary semantics of any language begins, with arbitrary and hence conventional associations.[30] To say that jazz connotes little sense of the sacred is no more or less rational than to say that the star of David or the expression "Trinity" connotes a lot. It is probably true that a great amount of semantic formation gets done during the period of a language's inception. The cultural context and immediate reasons for the rise of jazz or eighteenth-century Classicism determine to a great extent the original associations, and therefore the original semantics of the language. Thereafter, the inheritors of a linguistic tradition take what they get.

Semantic effects, of course, arise mainly through the syntactic techniques that make the music possible. More technically, the precise quality of the tension created by the syntax affects the semantic dimension in very particular ways,[31] and effects that depend on those techniques, again, may be well within the province of one language but not in another. Fugue and passacaglia in nineteenth- and twentieth-century music have a curious reminiscence about them and little sense of the amazement and wonder that comes of a technical tour de force, because the harmonic syntax against which they must struggle is comparatively loose and free in those languages. Similarly, the endless melody of the Romantics is inconceivable in music of earlier centuries because harmonic rhythm was far too fast to allow chromatic technique any of its delaying effects, even if those composers owned it. If certain syntactic techniques are beyond the reach of a language, then their associated semantic effects are likewise.

In extreme circumstances it may be possible to get any language to express almost anything, just as an American, at a loss for anything else, might insist on replying "I'm looking forward to it" in Italian somehow. But it will not be easy, smooth, and fluent, any more than it will be for jazz to fit into a Mass, and ease of expression means a great deal to musical art. It is hard to imagine why anyone would want to make the struggle of composition obvious.

So what, in general, causes musical languages to change? With the exception of this influence of musical genre, the lessons are largely the same as have been learned by linguists about natural language.

Causation is rarely a matter of simple cause and predictable effect. Causation is much more in the nature of a stimulus to which language may respond if conditions are right. The conditions can be purely linguistic—like the dropped inflections of English or the syntactic gap of the Ars nova—and that is when evolution seems most systematic, but more often conditions arise from the culture that uses the language, and they shape the probabilities of change in ways difficult to predict, since precise cultural states never replicate themselves. Here we have once again a pervasive context, now on a big scale. Linguistic features certainly exercise no priority, with phonological changes leading to syntactic, which lead to semantic changes. Pervasive evolution can originate in any aspect and spread out to the others, and interaction between internal and external factors is normal. Thus, the phonological adjustment of equal temperament made possible a tremendous change in the relation of keys; thus, jazz-improvisation syntax provoked a reconception of standard phonology, what counts as a note; both had semantic effects. Even these cases are simplifications; such large changes in a musical language are likely the results of a series of small changes, a chain of causes. The situation is reminiscent of the old question about what caused the auto accident: the fog, the sharp curve that the driver missed, the cat that distracted him, or the two drinks he had before leaving? Complex linguistic features such as harmonic embedding or blue notes clearly have many forebears, each one necessary in sequence, yet without any single one leading inevitably to the result at hand.

But if it is not systematic and predictable, evolution is not random either. It must respect, at least, the physical and cognitive apparatus of speakers and listeners: the shape of the vocal tract, limitations of tone categorization, and preference for hierarchical organizations among other things.[32]

Furthermore, a change does not happen for nothing; it responds to a need.[33] A trend causing ambiguity and misunderstanding may need to be fixed; a musical form may need to be extended in length; some piece may need to be louder so that it can be heard outdoors. The catalog of what music may need to do is virtually infinite. If the need is acute or widespread, a number of solutions may be tried, with the most effective one spawning imitators. Here the evolutionary process seems closest to Darwinism, with the environmental pressure taking the form of the need that has arisen, and natural selection taking the form of imitators copying the best adaptation, ensuring its survival.

Whatever it is, the need for a change in the musical language comes from the musical community using it. A look at its nature shows a surprising dynamic.

EVOLUTION AND THE MUSICAL COMMUNITY

A musical community is nothing more than a group of listeners who share musical perceptions in all their phonological, syntactic, semantic, and pragmatic aspects.[34] The perceptions of a jazz community in 1925 New Orleans obviously differ from those of Bach's parish in 1725 Leipzig. The discriminations can be as fine as anyone wishes: the community of "swing" perceivers versus the community of "sighing-motif" perceivers. Membership in a community requires learning its musical language in some sense. In the twentieth century, made polyglot by recording the past and by its own linguistic invention, listeners typically belong to more than one community, and serious listeners can negotiate many languages.

A need for a change in musical language can then be described this way: when someone desires the language to do something it is not doing, the stimulus for change is born.

Such a picture does nothing to simplify the myriad cause-and-effect relations that can obtain in the history of a language, but it does clarify one crucial aspect of the dynamic. A musical community does not even pretend to be a democratic organization. Voices are not equal. Some carry a lot of weight and others close to none. Membership in a musical community is not really analogous to citizenship of a nation, which is an all-or-nothing affair. Musical communities admit of degree.

Linguistic communities have their occasional members of great influence. The plays of Shakespeare and the King James Bible were major players at the end of the period of tumultuous change that began in the fifteenth century and have been credited with no small part of the vocabulary and character of early modern English. On the conservative side, the great lexicographer Samuel Johnson reined in changes in usage and haphazard spelling by recommending conformity with the learned classes. "Johnson's dictionary rightly had enormous influence, and its publication has been called 'the most important linguistic event of the eighteenth century.'"[35] A close second would be the 1762 publication of Bishop Robert Lowth's *A Short Introduction to English Grammar*, which prescribed a number of rather arbitrary rules, such as not ending a sentence with a preposition, that still shape our aesthetic sense of English today. In small matters, one need not have linguistic expertise to have special influence, only prominence. It is thought that President Jimmy Carter did nothing for the distinction between "flaunt" and "flout" when he told the United Nations: "'The Government of Iran must realize that it cannot flaunt, with impunity, the expressed will and law of the world community.'"[36]

But the shape of a musical community is vastly more pyramidal than any linguistic one, if only because the stratifications of skill, while similar in kind, are vastly more pronounced. Everyone speaks, and while poets and orators may speak better and more beautifully, sheer weight of numbers is against them. In a Western musical community, everyone listens, some with intelligence, the expert few produce, and the stratifications among them are again all too clear. In addition there is a tremendous difference in the significance of individual speech utterances and musical compositions. Every composition, no matter how minor or modest, is in some sense an aesthetic event, and community members pay attention to its artistic aspects and wonder at them if they are beautiful, whereas the vast majority of speech is workaday communication. Form matters little as long as one is understood. It is no wonder at all, then, that the great composers, impresarios, performers, and other highly trained and gifted musical artists speak with thundering Olympian voices from the top of the pyramid, no wonder that a single passage, such as Wagner's prelude to *Tristan und Isolde*, can change the course of a musical language while Lincoln's Gettysburg Address, equally moving for different reasons, leaves little trace in American English.

This great diversity of status for members of a musical community allows a paradoxical state of affairs that could never obtain in natural language, namely that rather abstract features of a musical language may be extremely important to the minority at the top of the pyramid and quite irrelevant to a considerable majority of listeners. In 1987 the prominent music theorist Nicholas Cook published the results of an experiment which indicated that first- and second-year music students at the University of Hong Kong, judging musical criteria of "coherence," "completion," "pleasure," and "expressiveness," did not prefer passages or compositions that ended in the same key in which they began to similar ones that did not.[37] The result would disown the venerable principle of tonal unity, an aesthetic postulate that claims that compositions should end in the same key in which they began, regardless of whether there are key changes during the course of the music, in order to give listeners a fundamental sense of coherence based on the perception of the governing, unifying tonal center.

Is the tonal unity principle then a fiction, a figment of music theorists' imaginations? What then of the overwhelming majority of compositions in every genre, from chant to the Beatles, that put the principle into practice?[38] The only answer to the evidence of musical composition itself is the obvious one: tonal unity is an essential fact of compositional art for those who practice it, but it is a rather abstract one, perceptible in a meaningful way to a minority of composers, performers, conductors, and other sensitive listeners for whom it is an all but indispensable part of Western art music, the only music of the world that makes changing its tonal center a significant part of its syntax. Cook's experiment showed that this perception was not all or none; rather, the aesthetic sense of tonal unity declined with the length of the passage. For those with the deepest aesthetic sense, only tonal unity throughout a composition will suffice. For them, it more than suffices: it provides an essential structural constraint against which they can play off some of music's most telling effects.

The deepest aesthetic sensibilities reside at the top of the pyramid, the few whose decisions about what pieces to perform, which to publish, and, above all, what kind of music to compose rule the day for the entire community. In the practical terms of evolution this means that the dissatisfactions of Richard Wagner, though he be but one individual, can direct linguistic changes that bring all Europe under his spell, if his intuitions about his inherited language's faults and their righting are only persuasive.

That is where the community at large plays its role, as the final arbiter of changes initiated by individuals. "So long as we try to communicate a new idea, it is necessary to be modest in our linguistic

demands—otherwise we will be misunderstood. So the need to communicate acts as a conservative force" on the impulsive conceits of creators.[39] In short, composers and listeners, sharing in the musical
language of their community, share alike in a tacit agreement to ensure
comprehension, as do the members of any natural-language community. Invention is constrained by the limits of cognition and perception,
first of all, and then the amount of play in the syntax of the language,
particularly as regards those low-level syntactic forms such as scales,
keys, metric patterns, and so on, that experienced listeners comprehend all of a piece. So even a titan like Wagner has to make sure that
his listeners can follow his discourse, persuade them of the aesthetic
benefits of his new road. But again, the dynamic is not that of an executive proposing to a congress. The community, even when ratifying a
change, is still pyramidal, and Wagner succeeded because he convinced the most perceptive.

It is not happenstance that he chose the medium of music drama to
do this. Many of the most extreme syntactic changes in the history of
music—experiments with dissonance and chromaticism in madrigal writing, the swing from opera seria to buffa in the eighteenth century—took
place in genres that provided the most explicit semantic context of a text,
which could at one stroke justify syntactic innovations and explain what
they were for.

Failure to satisfy the community at large has strewn the history of
music with the corpses of innovations rejected for one reason or another: the quarter-tone pieces of the twentieth century, which assumed that
people could categorize twenty-four pitches to the octave; the glass har-
monica, an instrument whose initial fascination was eclipsed by its clum-
siness and inability to perform to the potential of the language already at
hand; the chromatic madrigals of Gesualdo, forgotten when opera turned
the semantic goals of music to an entirely different purpose. Yet this kind
of failure does not always entail aesthetic failure, as Gesualdo proves, nor
does immediate community ratification always yield lasting aesthetic value. The last quartets of Beethoven exercised virtually no influence on the
later communities of the nineteenth century, which ignored them for
decades. Individual compositions in the last analysis count, not for what
they contribute to the development of a language, but how they handle
their own native language, and it remained for a later perspective to
rediscover the intrinsic value of these strange quartets, at a time when
the current language was too far removed from them to respond. They
are one of the great dead ends of music history.

It is a cliché to say of a great composition that it appeals on many levels, but the stratified nature of the musical community makes the cliché a real, almost indispensable virtue. The health of a musical community depends upon great numbers of people who simply listen with sensitivity and intelligence, waiting for the tuneful melodies in a Schubert symphony or the atmospheric effects of a Debussy tone poem, as well as upon the conductor, some of the players, and a few gifted listeners who may attend to the more abstract effects of syntax as well. This stratiform aesthetic should imply no condescension. Everyone loves a great melody, and it is a great achievement of musical art to compose one. Still less does it imply any simplistic demarcation between an intellectually oriented high level of structure and an emotionally oriented lower level: ethereal music for the ultra-perceptive cognoscenti and digestible scraps for the unwashed, all made palatable somehow in a single composition. The fact that no one has come close to writing a convincing theory or aesthetic for a beautiful melody shows all too plainly how little we understand about where the most subtle effects of music lie.

Even though musical communities naturally curb all but the most persuasive changes in their language, evolution is still as inevitable as it is in natural language. That is because the communities themselves, groups of actual people, change continually, providing ever new contexts that require new expressions, new tasks, or simply new ways of saying "I love you" in musical terms. Such needs cause change, most often in small and proximate ways, taking advantage of a potential already present in the language that ensures a high degree of intelligibility. There is rarely any necessity about the eventual outcome, but there is surely a rationality to the outcome. Rarely can we predict what will happen; often we can explain what has happened.

Linguists have no comprehensive theory or model for the evolution of language. Neither will historians of music. The wild card that makes such theories unlikely is the same one that undermines any deterministic theory of syntax or semantics: context, always powerful, always unique. But we can at least dismiss the worst of the vague generalizations about why musical languages change, particularly the weakling explanation that they become "exhausted," all their potential used up by the genius composers, leaving their successors no alternative but to start afresh with something else. Nothing known about the nature of language, natural or musical, suggests that any one can run out of unique utterances. They are infinite systems. Linguistics can offer instead a number of little models for proximate changes, modes of explanation that will classify changes at the very least and often provide a specific link between music and culture. Good enough for a start.

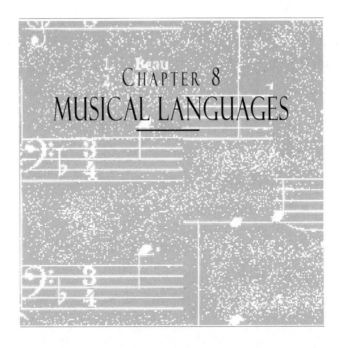

CHAPTER 8
MUSICAL LANGUAGES

By now we have seen something of the many ways that music deeply resembles the spoken word: how musical elements are gathered and understood like speech elements; how that understanding is specific to a community of speakers and listeners; how the meaning of music may now broaden and now narrow, ever responsive to its context; how composers can use that context to teach their listeners to hear syntax that endures but for one piece, an ephemeral syntax that is music's answer to metaphor; how composers have imitated linguistic idealists in the production of artificial systems in our century; how music and language have similarly evolved.

And yet I do not conclude that music is a language. I conclude, rather, that if spoken language engages a singular mental activity, even, as some would have it, a particular "module" of cognition, then music engages a parallel module, a parallel kind of mental activity that shares cognitive mechanisms, strategies, and just plain habits, conscious and unconscious, that language depends on.[1] Moreover, it is a mental activity with a universal social dimension: every culture talks and every culture sings. That is why all kinds of music lovers, from circumspect aesthetician to amateur rock guitarist, have always talked and written about music in linguistic terms, even after thoughtful debates have called it into question and misguided efforts to apologize for it have failed. The intuition of a deep, almost inevitable resemblance is natural.[2] Why else is the metaphor "musical language" such a commonplace in writing from everyday reviews in the popular press to the most erudite criticism in academic books? The depth of the resemblance makes for convincing analogical argument, a treasury of images, models, and hypotheses for thinking about music. That is why the notion of musical language itself is worth this much contemplation. But if a musical language is not a natural language, what exactly is it?

A good many readers are no doubt irritated that this matter was not taken care of with an explicit definition right in the opening chapter. That "musical language" has appeared in every discussion as a real thing without a proper introduction goes against all formal protocol, which prefers, of course, that definitions and postulates be stated outright so that deductions can follow therefrom.

After all, a definition at the outset might have fended off any number of criticisms of the analogy of music and language by effectively ruling them out of bounds. Defining "musical language" as void of semantic content, for example, would immediately render quite irrelevant all the complaints about the missing specificity or propositional content in musical passages, the lack of agreement among listeners, and the inability of music to translate. Writing flexible syntax into a definition might have parried Nicholas Cook's argument that the "grammar" of music, if such it can be called, is far too fluid and flexible to bear fruitful comparison with language, and somehow including even simple musical systems could have ducked Harold Powers's charge that no known language has the simplicity of, say, folksong. Indeed, the right definition could have saved a lot of trouble.

The omission was deliberate. The great philosopher of language Ludwig Wittgenstein has shown that the formal definition of a great many, if not all, common everyday concepts such as "game," his most famous example, is fiendishly difficult or impossible.[3] In other words, setting explicit boundaries—which is what "defining" means—around the concept "game" so that all the items that people call games are inside the fence and none of them outside is something that no one has been able to do. To see what he means, try defining opera so that the term includes *The Magic Flute* and the Italian warhorses but excludes *West Side Story*. Other examples abound. Concepts evidently do not always follow explicit rules.[4] And that makes a lot of sense, since the most common and compelling concepts arise not from anyone's careful definition of them but from the community that needs them. That is exactly why they are compelling but also why they are fuzzy in outline. Long use in many contexts overlays a concept with any number of connotations and subconcepts, some of which can indeed be mutually exclusive. Psychologists have proposed that people measure objects against cognitive "prototypes" in deciding how to categorize something: *Aida* can act as a prototypical example of opera, so how similar is *The Magic Flute* or *West Side Story* to *Aida*? Philosophers offer another solution, to which I have often resorted myself: the "cluster concept," a kind of mental checklist of characteristics. A reasonable number of aspects need to be present to call something an opera—trained singing, dramatization through music, staging, and so on—but not all: that Mozart uses spoken dialogue will not singlehandedly disqualify *The Magic Flute*.

Trying to define musical language, particularly as a means to avoid serious criticisms of the concept, would have created many more problems than it solved and smacked of intellectual cowardice besides. Any credible analogy of music and language and any useful concept of musical language will have to find a way to come to terms with these criticisms. Studying the nature of something before knowing exactly what makes it that something is hardly rare; natural scientists do it all the time. Often, such study will turn around and change the working concept of that something. In this way we have explored musical language. Now what can we say about it?

THE IMPLICATIONS OF MUSICAL LANGUAGE

Let's start with what is most often taken to be the foundation of a language: its phonology. Every musical language must have a finite inventory of discrete pitch classes. That the notes are conceptually discrete limits severely the number of different notes available within the octave, because when the octave becomes too crowded listeners lose the ability to tell which note is which.[5] Remember, too, that the production of these notes is never a matter of pinpoint precision, even in the highest professional circles, therefore requiring the listener to have some cognitive "margin of error." Musical languages, like spoken ones, have this margin in an instinctive categorical perception that instantly makes "this or that" decisions by the dozens every second.[6] So, despite all the possible gradations between the phonemes /æ/ or /ɑ/, our linguistic audition rudely corrals all those low vowels into one group or the other. Similarly, the D played by the bassoon differs remarkably in its acoustic makeup from the

D of the timpani that immediately precedes it in the opening of Beethoven's Violin Concerto, and yet everyone unconsciously understands the two to count as the same note. The term "pitch class" (as opposed to "tone") is clumsy, but it does the job of connoting a conception of tone rather than a purely acoustic event. To keep these concepts from disastrously blurring into one another, the spoken languages of the world limit their vowels and the musical languages their notes within the octave.

Acoustics, however, is by no means irrelevant. The presumption of the octave range as the field of operation here only reflects the practice throughout the world of using octaves as principal signs of articulation and stability. In general, Pythagorean acoustic consonance based on small whole-number frequency ratios has a role in the fundamental design of the inventory and syntax of musical languages, although, as is well known, it may exercise little influence over their most interesting details.

The production of notes in a musical language often has a semantic dimension, as it does in speech, ranging from rather neutral, as perhaps when a single mid-range note is sung or played on the piano, to rather specific, as for instance an organ note, to colored but undefinable, as the timpani opening for Beethoven's concerto. Moreover, the means of production can be essential in the sheer identity of a musical language, which is why it is possible to identify a nineteenth-century symphony as soon as the radio is turned on. There is simply nothing else that makes that sound.

In a larger sense, because it is so elemental, the inventory of a musical language is a measure of how close a relative that language may be to others. The inventories of the art musics of the seventeenth, eighteenth, and nineteenth centuries are identical in pitch class—they share the common-practice set of twelve notes to the octave. But sixteenth-century sacred music uses only seven notes with auxiliaries, and the twentieth-century's artificial languages establish radically different inventories, either by redefining the phonemic status of the twelve notes, so that E♭ no longer differs from D♯, or by simply carving up the octave in new and far different ways. And so listeners perceive a link between Allessandro Scarlatti and Chopin that does not obtain between Scarlatti and Palestrina or Chopin and Schoenberg, closer historical neighbors.

The discreteness of the notes in an inventory is essential if they are to be organized into the structural patterns that we know as music, as they must be: every musical language must have a syntax. Some of the features of any particular syntax may derive from universal gestalt tendencies of perception—the use of silence to mark phrases, for example, or shorter notes to group motives—but others must be learned through the cultural medium that finally delimits musical communities. In other words, basic grouping strategies may make the outline of a composition available to a newcomer, but the appreciation of the really interesting and most edifying aspects of syntax such as cadence types, pitch patterns such as scales and arpeggios, phrase grammars, and metric patterns—not to mention the integration of all these—can come only from experience. These complex patterns, once learned, are a chief means of organizing musical information into hierarchical orders, one of the two principal functions of musical syntax. That is why a foreign musical language seems to be most times a formless, unpredictable blur of sound. There is plenty of form there, but the listener has not yet learned the patterns that would allow its extraction.

The other function of syntax is the single most outstanding aesthetic aspect of musical art: the control of tension and resolution, which shapes not only the essential musical dynamic, the metaphor of motion, but also the very character of every musical language. Thus, the Baroque language differs from all others not just in what its practitioners do in terms of musical construction but in the effects those constructions have on listeners, which are so much more directly sensible. If, as I suggest in chapter 2, the various sources of musical tension contribute not only an amount but a particular *kind* of tension, then musical languages become still more distinct, since their various syntactic organizations will create unique tension compounds. The motor rhythm and functional harmony of Baroque music, to name just two of its principal components, together concoct a particular flavor of musical tension, steady and yet simmering with controlled energy. Particular syntactic gestures inform every individual composition made in that language, and the patterns of its tensions and resolutions, complex and inimitable as turbulence, form that composition's indelible, utterly unique profile. A theory of these tensions and their compounded effects would be the most significant project to come from the analogy of music and language.

All these sources of tension must be coordinated so that the syntax can do its job of controlling information flow. But this burden is actually a great blessing, since the coordination it requires is the very impetus of compositional technique. The aesthetic dimension of tension and resolution is twofold, at least: the sense of dynamic ebb and flow, and the more static sense of an obstacle surmounted, a problem solved, a loose end tied up with consummate grace.

The *effects* of syntax are probably the only indispensable semantic aspect of every musical language. In other words, the meaning of every musical passage is, at the very least, the effects it makes on its musical community, principally the effects of tension and resolution. This conflation of syntax and semantics might seem to be bizarrely unlinguistic, until we remember that the form of every utterance in speech influences its meaning to some degree. No syntax can change without some semantic reflection. Musical languages put this property of form as meaning in first place in its semantic system, and this arrangement thus replies to the analogy's critics who say that music has no communal meaning as has language. Its communal meaning is in its syntactic effects: everyone senses Beethoven's climaxes at the same moment.

Some musical languages may have more meaning than that: lexicons of affect, word paintings, leitmotifs, and the like. Many musical languages of the West boast a capacity to match an accompanying text that focuses the semantic range of a passage at the same time that the passage magnifies the surface meaning of the text in a complex interplay that is by now familiar. But other musical languages, the sacred ones of the Middle Ages and Renaissance, never developed such capacity or perhaps unconsciously avoided developing it in order to retain their mystical qualities. Chants and motets can be as beautiful as any music we have, but why a given psalm inspired a given setting seems beyond explaining. Such diversity arises from the presentational semantics associated with word meanings: it can give meaning to a musical passage, but with a degree of precision that is much less definite than speech, and in some music—chant, Palestrina motets, and Bach fugues come to mind—tends to obscurity. Beyond the effects of syntax, in the last analysis musical semantics is only a potential of a musical language, something that can distinguish one from another.

Skeptics have ruled out this potential with the charge that no musical passage can be translated into speech without destroying its essence, a thing routinely done between spoken languages. The truth of this remark again underscores the preeminence of syntax over semantics in most musical art, which in turn suggests a parallel case in natural language: poetry. When translators take up Homer or Dante, they face a Hobson's choice. What shall be left out, the meaning of what the poet has said, or the beauty of the way he has said it, the meter, the rhyme, the alliterations, all of those things that poetry critics often call "music"? For as surely as natural languages are amenable in an all-purpose way to translation, no two of them will match up in sound *and* meaning, since the arbitrariness of the sound symbol and its meaning is the very foundation of semantics. So which will it be? Perhaps a compromise between the two. Perhaps that is why there are dozens of attempts to translate Homer and Dante into English. "It were as wise to cast a violet into a crucible that you might discover the formal principles of its color and odor," wrote Shelley, "as seek to transmute from one language into another the creations of a poet," and Robert Frost once said with rather less delicacy that "poetry is what gets lost in the translation," but would either say that his art is not linguistic?[7]

Richard Wagner has shown us that the semantics of music can be downright propositional—if the context is just right. Context is the great player behind the operation of any musical language, and every musical language must take advantage of it, if only in its role in immediate perception, in the top-down processing of the rapid fire of musical information. The recognition of individual notes and essential syntactic patterns completely breaks down without it. Only in the twentieth century have certain artificial languages taken up "context-free" symbols as an ideal; all others depend upon context to make understanding easier and, above all, to profoundly enrich the syntax of any language. When Nicholas Cook criticizes the notion of musical grammar by observing that "Music . . . is much more fluid than language. Before you start a conversation, you know what the grammar is going to be; in music, you can never be sure of the grammar until you have heard the piece,"[8] he oversimplifies the situation in natural languages. It is true that everyone in a linguistic community knows the grammar tacitly, but what most would take to be the rules of that grammar are routinely abbreviated, extrapolated, choked off, and otherwise violated as a matter of routine. A transcript of a real conversation, such as the Watergate tapes, is barely legible in written English,[9] yet the president and his men had not a bit of trouble understanding one another. And any conversation can be incomprehensible if one doesn't have the background to its subject. It is context that repairs the damage to all these deficiencies. But context guarantees not just the comprehension but the creativity of language, even allowing people to make up words on the spot, complete with syntactic function and form, like the plumber who decided "We'll ess that pipe right over to that vent there." And what is "ess"? Well, to shape the flexible tubing into the shape of a letter S so that it would reach the vent properly, of course. Such a verb had perhaps never been uttered before and possibly never will be again, but the meaning was perfectly clear at the moment. Context allows that kind of fluidity. It happens in music and it happens in language, and both are much the richer for it.

Such linguistic contexts are generally unique. Context is thus the inevitable wild card, the X factor in any theory of music that takes perception into account. This is perhaps the most important theoretical consequence of the music and language analogy. But a certain kind of context does repeat itself, the kind called genre. Unlike casual speech, music is almost always produced as a kind, a particular form, which connects with the musical community in terms of what is expected from it. The material of Beethoven's piano sonatas lose their power when played by orchestras; Palestrina cannot be transcribed for the wind band. Instead, there can be a tight relation between abstract musical ideas—themes, progression, rhythmic motives—and the means of their presentation. This is hardly news to music lovers, but it might be news to analysts.

Genres persist in part because they are expected by the listeners who share their presumptions. Every musical language entails a musical community whose members share that language, whose members share the perceptions that found it. But the perceptions are ordered, in a sense, from the most practical to the most abstract, and all members need not share all of them with equal competence. In most musical languages of the West, for instance, all listeners need to be able to locate the tonic, but far fewer must notice its changes and remember them. The community is pyramidal. So are the communities of natural languages, although their pyramids are wide and flat, those of musical communities taller.

In the West this is particularly so. In fact, the peculiar extremes in the West—our distinct class of professional performers, another of composers, a repertory that is static, not a basis of improvisation—have made music seem less like language here than elsewhere in the world. Harold Powers makes a good case that Indian classical music is much more like speech, particularly in its capacity for extemporaneous expression and improvisation.[10] But improvisation is less alien to the West than it appears at first glance. Until recently, all composers and expert musicians could improvise; jazz musicians still can, and of course, children always have. It is true that our culture discourages that particular facility and rewards rote performances, but that is a momentary characteristic of music's place in the modern West, not of its nature. Powers's point about the variety of musical complexity—that there are simple musics but no simple languages—may likewise implicate community environment rather than the nature of music. Obviously, natural language is more essential to practical human existence than music, and that accounts for the greater stratifications in musical communities: not everyone needs to do it in the same way that everyone needs to talk. The complexities of Indian ragas and Renaissance motets are founded upon stable societies, traditions handed on through notation or precise tutelage and professional classes of musicians. The so-called simple musics may belong to those communities that cannot afford those things.

In any case, the musical community provides the standard of reference, the best approximation to objectivity, for discourse about music. Beethoven's odd progressions may be heard this way, that way, and another way, but that fact never implies that one analysis is as good as another. The opening of Mozart's C-major Quintet has a semantic range of a breadth typical for instrumental music, but that does not automatically mean it is fair game for gender assignment, social analysis, or other fancies of the critic. Interpretation is constrained; criticism is responsible. The arbiter is the musical community to which such discourse is directed, and the virtually infallible arbiter is the musical community over time.[11]

Sound over meaning. Mutual interference of notes, syntax, semantics, and community. Context shaping all. The essential components of a musical language—sounds, syntax, semantics, genre, and community—are wrapped up in these essential and pervasive characteristics, and that is the package.

LEARNING MUSICAL LANGUAGES

The idea of musical languages entails that they are learned by their community members, at least to the extent that allows some appreciation of music, if not its creation or performance. Moreover, in the modern Western world it is obvious that most music lovers have this minimal competence in several, if not many, musical languages and turn from one kind of music to another with the ease of United Nations interpreters. Twentieth-century culture is in that respect the oddest in the history of Western music. At no other time have musicians resurrected lost languages of the past with such energy and respect, as if we had just come into possession of some Rosetta stone for music, and yet at the same time, with equal energy, invented additional ultramodern languages from scratch. Modern music lovers are true polyglots.

How is it that listeners acquire these various languages and keep them cognitively separate, as bilingual people keep their Italian vocabulary from peppering their sentences in English? Why does it not all run together in some vast musical experience? There is no research that I know of on any of this. But the musical language model suggests some questions, the first of which is: what does it mean to "know" a musical language? Consider the passage of Palestrina in Example 8.1. Someone who has grown up on Brahms and Broadway and heard little music composed before 1700 may well be puzzled by this passage, wondering why the piece finishes with a dominant harmony left hanging in the ear. Most listeners, even Palestrina lovers, will be unable to remember that the final harmony is the same one that opened the motet six minutes ago, but nonetheless, assuming that Palestrina did not wish his hearers to be puzzled on Christmas Eve, the chord grammar must be conclusive somehow. Knowing Palestrina's sacred musical language, then, at least at the elementary level, means understanding chord progressions in a different way, divorced from the powerful functions they have in later music. This is but one aspect of the matter, of course—there is the syntax of texture manipulation, so much more variable and critical to the final effect, and

Example 8.1. Palestrina, O magnum mysterium, *conclusion.*

the general association with religious function—but the harmonic syntax makes particular difficulties for the modern listener.

For how does a listener reform that kind of habitual expectation? Obviously, no one unlearns it; otherwise, we would only trade ignorance of Palestrina for ignorance of Brahms. I should guess, rather, that the listener naive to the sixteenth-century sacred tradition begins from scratch and eventually constructs a separate cognitive "module" or space for that language.

The steps in that process are unknown. Research in the linguistics specialty of second-language acquisition suggests some possibilities. Most enticing is the discovery that adult students of a foreign language profit by a "silent period" in which no response, no active use of the new language is expected. They listen and evidently absorb more linguistic knowledge than others who are forced to speak.[12] This, of course, is exactly what we would expect of people coming to terms with a new kind of music, and indeed, most never graduate from the silent period, unless they undertake intense study to become practicing musicians. Yet, such silent people can become very competent listeners. Another more commonsense conclusion is that learners of new languages learn better by contextual experience, seeing how the phrase is used, speaking the language in actual social situations.[13] It seems common sense because it capitalizes on the essential purpose of language, to refer to the world. Neophyte listeners likely take similar advantage of context: visual cues by performers, the setting of the performance, and "natural" markers such as silences and rhythmic decelerations. The motet's final silence that caused puzzlement at first is soon turned into an arbiter of closure, and in that way one learns that such a progression may indeed end a composition. Meaning is shaped by context, as it is in all language experience.

That is perhaps why the "affects" of the Baroque and other explicit semantics are often unavailable to the modern listener. It is not at all that we don't know what they stood for; it is that we can but weakly re-create the context of their learning, which counts for so much. A similar situation obtains in foreign-language learning. When a native Italian speaker tells us that Orfeo's "Ohime" upon the death of Euridice is a very strong expression of grief in Italian, we accept the fact but cannot feel its depth, because we have no "Ohime" experiences that have taught us its connotations. That is why it is dangerous to take translations of slang and profanity at face value and then use such words in real situations: one has no idea of their real impact. So when we learn that Josquin uses the "Requiem" chant in his famous lament on the death of Ockeghem, we accept the fact but can rarely feel what Renaissance listeners may have once felt. They had the experience of hearing that chant countless times at real funerals, and we have not.

Moreover, no one can be sure that reception studies and other accounts of the thinking of any composer's original audience and culture, for all their historical interest, have much effect on the way we moderns hear the music now. To think that it does entails that simply reading about a cultural listening context is enough to reform our own contexts along similar lines, so that we can "hear the music as they did." If cultural orientation arises from immediate experience, as language does, then such benefits are highly unlikely, to say the least.

Hearing Palestrina's final harmony as an inconclusive, unresolved dominant is an example of negative interlingual transfer, a kind of interference caused by one's native language on correct performance in a second language. One often hears students in early stages of Italian study say *mio libro* rather than the correct *il mio libro*, because the latter would literally translate as "the my book." The erroneous form is closer to English. Transfer is a controversial matter among the researchers of second-language acquisition, but estimates of errors caused by interference of the native language run from 8 to 20 percent or so. In the end good learners get over it and learn to distinguish the ways in which one's native language can help make the right constructions from the ways in which it leads to the wrong ones. Eventually, the habit of *il mio libro* is second nature, while the other grates on the ears; eventually, we accept Palestrina's final harmony as a resolution.

Do listeners grow up with a "native" musical language? The question arises only because for Chomskyan linguists the native language is special. Because it is learned by all children, virtually without exception, in definable stages and without explicit instruction, the first language is promoted as the prime evidence of innate language circuitry in the brain, a cognitive apparatus that only awaits some switches to be thrown, like the settings on a computer, by minimal exposure to language in the first few years of life.[14] But this apparatus does not wait forever. Many linguists and psycholinguists believe in a "critical period" of native-language learning during which children learn languages fluently almost as easily as they breathe and after which adolescents and adults learn them only with arduous effort, and then imperfectly at that. Jamshed Barucha has carried out a line of experimental research indicating that musicians, even modernistic composers who swear to their facility with dissonant combinations, process major triads fastest and, furthermore, that this processing reflects the traditional harmonic relations along the circle of fifths.[15] This is interesting, but not too discouraging. After all, thousands of adults learn to speak beautiful Italian, and they can learn to love Palestrina motets.

Wherever this line of thinking might lead, the very fact that listeners can learn to negotiate and then find beauty in different languages should reform certain historical and critical habits. One of the more unfortunate commonplaces heard from time to time is that a kind of dissonance saturation is the agent behind the steady march of music history toward ever increasing dissonance. Certainly, the most familiar trends in harmonic syntax over the last four centuries and the "emancipation" of the dissonance in the twentieth encourage such a view, but, even without the fifteenth century as an exception on purely historical grounds, the process of human hearing becoming ever more coarsened to dissonance, like a soup taster who always wants more salt, cannot stand up to the language model. If it were true, no one today could ever enjoy the Palestrina, or perhaps even much Bach. The supple sixteenth-century control of dissonance would strike the modern ear as a long hum of barely articulated boredom. Perhaps that's the way it does sound to some first-time listeners, and learning a new language does take effort. But eventually that cognitive space arises, and a new sense, a whole new scale of consonance and dissonance, takes effect, rendering the wonders of Palestrina's polyphony palpable at last.

Another change of habit that polyglots point to is the way we think about style.

MUSICAL LANGUAGES AND MUSICAL STYLE

"Haven't we really been talking about style all along?" is the question that will have occurred to many readers by this point, if not before. Indeed, in common parlance the expressions "musical language" and "musical style" are near synonyms and used interchangeably without much worry. I believe that this is a mistake, a confounding of distinct notions that has prevented, among other things, good criticism and appreciation of earlier music, even including the high Baroque, for which many acquire their taste later in life.

The confounding of the two is, in a way, logical, for both ideas entail the notion of commonality. Language implies a system that entire groups, cultures, and nations use in common, the community dimension that is so critical to its proper function and regulation. Style, too, connotes things that practitioners do in the same way, whether it is composing, writing poetry, or batting a baseball. But already there is a difference that hints at trouble: the common elements in a language are required for any kind of participation, active or passive, speaking or hearing, composing or listening, while the common elements in a style are active only, made by practitioners with no account of observers. If Walt Whitman wishes to write poetry that will reach his readers, he must use a natural language that they understand. To that extent he meets them halfway, an implicit agreement is struck. But he alone determines his poetic style.

When writers on music have treated style as a serious, even theoretical matter, they have generally made the aspect of commonality central to their conception rather than judiciously limiting its role. The first and only thoroughgoing theory of style is Leonard B. Meyer's *Style and Music: Theory, History, and Ideology,* published in 1989. Like all his work, it is a great piece of thinking and follows from much of his earlier theory, but its commitment to style as common traits is explicit from the opening pages: "I begin, perhaps somewhat unceremoniously, with a definition," Meyer writes, and the analytic definition that follows sets the course for the theoretical part of the book. As a definition it is logically incontrovertible but nevertheless leads to conclusions about style and music that contradict the listening experience in very material ways. Such is the danger of formally defining a concept that is already part of the language. *"Style is a replication of patterning, whether in human behavior or in the artifacts produced by human behavior, that results from a series of choices made within some set of constraints"* (emphasis in original).[16] There are three operative terms in the definition: replication of patterning, choices, and constraints. All have a certain common sense about them, yet all are problematic. A detailed analysis of Meyer's theories of constraints and choice can be found elsewhere;[17] here it is the heart of Meyer's concept, the replication of patterns, that captures the aspect of commonality.

He states that "Style analysis begins with classification" of these replicated features. Then, to his great credit, Meyer quickly moves on to say that a deep understanding of style means much more than compiling lists of features that serve as identifiers or marks on a timeline: "Style analysis is more ambitious. It seeks to formulate and test hypotheses explaining why the traits found to be characteristic of some repertory—its replicated melodic patterns, rhythmic groupings, harmonic progressions, textures, timbres, and so on—fit together, complementing one another."[18] In short, we study replications to find out what the rules of composing might be.[19] That knowledge in turn explains composers' choices in compositions. So these inferred rules make it possible to describe how traits discovered by classification fit together. Meyer summons the analogy of a biological organism whose characteristic traits work together in mutual interdependence. He then provides an excellent illustration of what he means in a "sketch-analysis" of the style of Richard Wagner, which begins with a list of ten characteristic Wagnerian traits and then describes a system that unites them all, that shows why they work so well together.[20]

So what could possibly be wrong with this total reliance on replication? Isn't a sense of the typical one and indivisible with a sense of style?

Equating replication and style implies such indivisibility, and it implies furthermore that unique features of a composition have nothing to do with style. In short, anything not replicated is eliminated: "Style analysis . . . is not concerned with what is nonrecurrent."[21] Taken in the extreme, it implies a style analysis that is impossible because of our constant companion, context. The surroundings of any given pattern make any instance unique. Everything is eliminated because there are never any perfectly precise replications. But let's cut Meyer a little slack and allow some abstraction: divorce some phrase pattern, some procedure of imitation, some formal structure from its immediate context—observing that fugal imitations generally occur at the fifth, for example. The result is still an analytical position that is uncomfortable at best and at worst unworkable and false to the intuitions of the experienced listener.

If style is essentially replication, then many of the most memorable moments in music must be "unstylistic," and the list of these would be considerable indeed: the fantastic discursus into A flat for the solo violin at the end of Beethoven's concerto; the chains of descending, overlapping scales that completely replace the standard and obligatory suspension cadences at the very end of Josquin's *Miserere mei, Deus;* the extraordinary length, even surpassing that of *Eroica*'s opening, of the first movement of Mozart's String Quintet in C, K. 515. This tiny selection comes from a few principal examples of this book; it's not hard to think of a lot more.

Now, the obvious counter is to argue that only certain aspects of these patterns have no replication, while other aspects have extensive replication. The harmonic setting of the violin passage is wild, but the tune is the same as before; the cantus firmus returns to the tonic at the end of Josquin's motet; the opening of K. 515 may be long, but its form is replicated throughout Mozart. Isolating musical aspects in this way, however, means throwing out Meyer's conception of stylistic features working together as they do in an organism, falling back on the impotent model of style as a laundry list of sundry items whose interconnections are of little consequence. But any composer knows that extraordinary length in a composition is not simply a fact fit for the record books but an essential characteristic that materially influences the design of all the interior components, and that Mozart realized this can be heard in his very first *five-measure* phrase of the quintet. Similarly, to pretend that Beethoven's strange harmonies are theoretically dispensable is to miss the significance of the timpani's motto.[22] If style is indeed replication, then unique characteristics such as these that permeate entire compositions in procedure, structure, and sound are not only unstylistic themselves but render the pieces containing them unstylistic too. Josquin's great motet becomes just a great oddity and a poor example of his style.

Is the experience of style so banal that it can do without these moments? Do not our memories of Beethoven's style have that violin passage deep inside?

Putting the idea of replication into practice seems guaranteed to conjure stylistic ideals that are indeed as banal as can be imagined. Defining the style of the first half of the eighteenth century in western Europe, for example, would require polling the works of all active composers in that time and place. Because style can only contain replicated features, the result would be a list of the "greatest common features," which assuredly would not be very many, nor very great. Now the organism model is quite dead, because while it is clear that the life-supporting components work beautifully together in the great majority of sharks, horses, and musicians, it is equally clear that such concordant coordination is all too rare in musical compositions, except in the most pedestrian sense of linking one phrase to another or one key to another, the things that any good harmony student can do. If replications are the arbiter of stylistic features, the resulting analysis is assured of bringing out not only what is in common but what is, simply, common.

This normative view, the indivisibility of the typical and the stylistic, led Meyer some time ago to make a distinction between style analysis and music criticism: while the former discovers what is in common among compositions in some repertory, "Critical analysis seeks to understand and explain what is idiosyncratic about a particular composition."[23] Such a characterization might correspond with a goodly portion of critical activity, but the idea that criticism itself is a search for the weird would be deservedly scorned by most any critic or critical listener. Critical listening is at root a form of perception, a deep appreciation of what a composition attempts to do and has to offer in all its facets, which include "the meaning it conveys, the pleasure it initiates, and the value it assumes, for us today," as Joseph Kerman once wrote.[24] Surely, unusual music attracts attention, but just as surely what is most familiar and expected can also be very beautiful. The cadential progression that ends the French overture in Bach's Goldberg Variations is brilliant, perfectly appropriate for its position, and as typical as could be. Similarly, every listener would expect, in Renaissance Italy and now, the drawn-out suspension cadence that articulates the first section of Palestrina's sublime *Sicut cervus*, and yet, as we shall see, that takes nothing away from its extraordinary effect.

It is not that criticism should avoid distinguishing between the typical and the unusual, but rather it should not place some arbitrary value on either one before beginning. Meyer allots to criticism everything that cannot be accounted for by style analysis, that is, anything unreplicated. In his theory of style analysis, on the other hand, Meyer elevates the typical to the status of a norm, which he needs to regulate the counting of replications:

> what I have in mind is something like what physicians mean when they speak of a normal heart. What is meant is not an average heart, for most hearts are faulty or at least peculiar in some respect. Rather, the term *normal* means that the components of the heart function properly with respect to one another and to the circulatory system of which they form a part. And physicians know how the heart should function because they have a theory about the relationships among the constraints that govern its behavior.[25]

So, replicated features are verified, in a sense, by their capacity to be incorporated into a system. But this kind of normalcy differs from the typical, the sort of sampling that Meyer had earlier implied. For the normalcy of a heart is ultimately tested by an exterior criterion, that is, whether it continues to beat and keep someone alive, and not by its match with any theory. There is no criterion exterior to the lists of replications that could do the same thing, that is, measure and assure the successful workings of a stylistic model.

Or is there? The closest analogy in music to the cold facts of the life or death of an organic system would be the cultural survival of a composition. In other words, the "ideal types" for which Meyer searches are found in the best compositions we have, which are at once the supreme exemplars of interrelated features that work together and the practical limit of such workings, since anything beyond them is unimaginable. If the understanding of such style systems is to have any depth and validity, then the strategy of conducting some disinterested Gallup poll of a historical repertory must be scrapped because it is impossible to be disinterested and because it would result in either no interrelated system at all or one of stunning mediocrity. When style has no connotation of value or artistic integrity, then oft-used phrases such as "proto-Classical style," "Mozart's immature style," or "transitional period" lose all meaning because all patterns have equal claim to value as long as they are replicated. The antidote to this hopeless relativism is to let criticism inform style analysis, the kind of criticism that is made not by individuals touting their personal canons, which after all is the activity in which critics have the least practice and least success, but by the culture at large, which through the centuries and generations selects its classics.

The rejection of an empirical approach for one that is, one could say, elitist or prescriptive actually embodies the act of critical listening and indeed the way communities carry out musical life. Meyer's insistence that stylistic norms must be known before extraordinary choices can be revealed hints at the old saw that masterworks are heard as such against a historical background of unimaginative and timid mediocrity, a notion that cannot be taken seriously if only because its image of musical life is so unreal. No one comes to appreciate Bach only after listening to dozens of his contemporaries; rather, the culture promotes his music quite directly. If by chance we come across a performance of Graupner or Graun or some other forgotten competitor, our appreciation of Bach is increased, perhaps, not because we have learned more about the norms of eighteenth-century style but because we are grateful for not having wasted time on them previously. No music historian teaches a style period by offering a syllabus of random selections or even a rather broad range of selections. No artistic director programs concerts without considering quality. On the contrary, the musical community practices criticism in virtually everything it does. Why deny that community its power to identify, as a culture, its classics, when such power provides a practical and legitimate sample on which to build style analysis?

But identifying the sample, the classic repertory, is one thing, and understanding it in critical fashion is another. Here is the logical problem: if the normative account cannot deal with uniquenesses in music, how else can we understand them? In this sense Meyer's intuition is exactly right. There must be some connection between them and the listening culture. In short, how do listeners both make sense of a unique moment's place in musical continuity while maintaining the sense of its peculiar, special quality? How can we understand what should be impossible to abstract?

Connecting the unique with the norm is precisely what language does so well. Utterances are unique yet comprehensible. What if the notions of musical language and musical style are made distinct?

The first to make this distinction seriously was Charles Rosen in a rather metaphorical clause in his monumental *The Classical Style*: "A style may be described figuratively as a way of exploiting and focusing a language."[26] The key term "focusing" I take to mean not riveting one's attention but bringing various components into a felicitous relationship. The allusion is technical: one focuses a telescope by setting its lenses at distances of the proper proportion, so that they work together, support one another.[27] A musical language offers the composer resources—means of construction, sources of tension, a semantic potential, and so on—as well as a guarantee of comprehension of those resources by the knowledgeable community. But obviously they are in many ways incommensurate, incompatible, seemingly intractable, as anyone who has tried composition well knows. A composer who somehow tames these independent natures and accomplishes such feats of coordination that the linguistic aspects no longer inhibit one another but strengthen each other's effectiveness has created a style.

The idea of focusing a musical language is a rich insight whose full theoretical and practical significance awaits a complete theory of musical style, but it is worth trying to get a better sense of it through one last example (Ex. 8.2). This motet is outstanding, first of all, in its utter normalcy. Glancing over the score, or hearing any isolated bit of it, no unusual feature strikes the eye or ear. Its patent imitation is standard procedure for sacred counterpoint, and its four-voice texture is even old-fashioned for a mid-sixteenth-century composition. The passage is completely diatonic; not one altered tone is either signed by Palestrina or demanded by the conventions of musica ficta. Progressions are modal, of course, and center so much on the tonic that the ear is fairly saturated with F harmonies by the time the first important cadence in measure 23 comes around. The melodies step placidly and their rhythmic design—fast in the middle, slow at beginning and end—is strictly by the book. Their ambitus is so conservative that the whole motet takes up but two octaves and a fifth. All these are commonplaces of the musical language that Palestrina inherited. There is nothing here that would raise the eyebrow of a critic hunting for the great original thought,[28] and yet, anyone conversant with sixteenth-

Example 8.2. Palestrina, Sicut cervus, mm. 1–23. ("As the deer longs for running water . . .").

century sacred language will experience a climax at the end of this passage as epiphanic in its terms as any in the Western repertory.

The flash of illumination occurs in measure 20, when the choir suddenly brakes its contrapuntal motion on that long-held B-flat sonority, their mouths full open with rounded vowels. It signals the oncoming cadence, by now long awaited, and the gentle stretching of the motion toward that goal is exquisite in its slowness. What *maestro di cappella* could resist holding his choir on that B-flat chord an extra fraction of a beat, indulging just a little in the great resolution of these measures?

How can such a moment be critically explained if there is nothing unusual, no invention of Palestrina to point to? Only by remembering that the greatness of this cadential passage emerges from the language. It is not the elements but the focusing of the elements that makes the style.

What at first seemed to be a regular pattern of imitation is in fact just slightly irregular. The entrances come every four beats on average, but the third one in the soprano comes after only three, and the sixth one in the alto (m. 11) and the last one in the soprano (m. 15) take five. The same story is true of the pitch of the entrances: mostly on the tonic, but two, the alto in measure 3 and the tenor in measure 8, are on the dominant. The semantic effect of this irregular regularity is a kind of orderly yet mystical freedom. The listener soon realizes that an entrance will come with regularity on the tonic, and yet it is impossible to predict precisely the onset of any one of them. The effect on the listener is like that on a boat in a choppy sea. There is an "average" level of tension, like the average sea level, a real thing to be sure, but, to the one trying to avoid capsize, surely less immediate than the crests and troughs bounding in from all directions. Palestrina, more subtly, gradually lets loose a steady flood of sound but never lets the listener quite relax.

Yet underlying this constant overlap of imitation is an imperceptibly rising tide of tiny tensions. Quarter-note motion slowly increases. Motion in harmony, too, becomes more palpable after measure 15 when the bass breaks out of step motion, leaping instead to triad roots. Then there is dissonance. The first seven measures hold but two innocuous passing tones; everything else is consonant. The next seven sound sixteen disso-nant tones and the first suspensions—longer, strong-beat dissonances, appear in measures 10 and 12 and then more rapidly in measures 15, 16, and 17. Suspensions, of course, indicate cadences, and there are in fact what might be called theorists' cadences in the sense that the counter-point fulfills the contemporary prescription for cadence by suspending one voice against another in syncopation, resolving downward to conso-nant sixths (m. 10 soprano and bass) or thirds (m. 12 soprano and alto; m. 17 tenor and soprano). But Palestrina's imitation ensures that no one hears these cadences as anything stronger than interior articulations, cer-tainly no cessation of the tension. If anything, they feed the listener's desire for a real cadence with their tantalizing faint images of one.

Control of imitation, and musical texture in general, determines musi-cal effect more than anything else in the sacred language of the sixteenth century. The tension of texture has some strange features. Clearly, full texture is the only one acceptable for complete resolution, so imitative music actually begins from a point of tension. Listeners hear voices enter gradually and await the texture's fulfillment. How a composer enacts that fulfillment determines a great deal about the shape of the composition. In *Sicut cervus* Palestrina does not use Josquin's favorite device of inform-ing the listener about the full texture, usually through imitative pairs, but refusing the satisfaction of it until the climactic moment. That means a spare, two-voiced sound much of the time, decidedly out of fashion by Palestrina's generation, and besides, paired imitation creates a highly articulated and audible order to the motet, nothing like the seemingly random, mystical wash of sound that Palestrina wants here. Instead, he adopts a subtler version of the same strategy; he allows the four voices to be heard intermittently, for no longer than three beats until the approach to the real cadence occurs. This allies perfectly, of course, with his con-stant entrances. Voices drop out after giving the ear just a taste of the full texture, only to arouse it by reentering with the subject.

Imitation itself is a paradox of melodic perception. The subject, of course, is perceptually salient. We hear it time and again and at first alone, without any distractions, so that the listener easily learns to recognize this melody. Yet the listener cannot be said to know the melody, because the end is never learned. The continual iterations of the familiar beginning lure the attention, and if the texture builds to three voices or more, as it does in this motet, there is no tracking the subject's end. That is why all those cadences are cadences in theory only; Palestrina overlaps every one with a new entrance that undermines its effect. It is like watching familiar figures walk past, one after the other, into the fog, never seeing where they end up. It is almost as if the melody is infinite. And yet, for perception's sanity, it must end, and therein is the composer's great good fortune and great challenge. The good fortune is that imitative technique automatically ensures a delay of cadence and a strong desire for it at the same time. The challenge is that when so much of the sense and force of the interior articulation depends on the salience and activity of the subject, what is to be done in the moments when the leading voices must continue to sound in the approach to the cadence, hanging around while the following voices catch up?

Palestrina's magnificent solution begins in measure 18, when three textural tricks that he has not used heretofore converge. The first is a missing subject. We have waited as long as five beats for a new entrance, but here we are six beats past the last soprano subject, and each passing moment increases the tension produced by the composer's irregular, calculated, and (until now) incessant imitative pattern.[29] The second is that the alto voice, now the "oldest," having begun its subject back in measure 11, has its hanging around justified by following the soprano in parallel motion for the first time, amplifying the most active motive of the motet's subject. Finally, the bass reenters, but on an offbeat. This simple deformation of the subject, echoed by the tenor one measure later, refills the texture without heavy articulation. On the contrary the offbeat naturally propels the motion forward, and when the bass voice leaps to further acceleration with the first four quarter-note group, preparing and giving way without respite to the motet's first six quarter-note group in the soprano, Palestrina achieves the momentum that assures our astonishment when it collides exquisitely with that rock-solid B-flat triad initiating the long-awaited finish.

Why that chord? The century's emerging syntax of the subdominant comes to mind, of course, to argue for its propriety here, but there is more to it than that. Look back at the original subject and see how simply Palestrina creates the motet's governing tension pattern. A long tonic note gives way to a shorter one, the melody then tensing to the G and resolving back down. Follow the tenor part—still possible with but two voices in—and hear that pattern transposed up a third and truncated rhythmically. Now it is the B-flat, longer than its surrounding notes, that is the tensor, at the very moment when the first complete triad, a B-flat triad, is sung. The great moment in measure 20 is simply an amplification of that effect; in fact, the soprano has been singing an extended version of the very same melody, echoed by the tenor a sixth lower. The chord is less a harmonic object—though Palestrina again has the bass leap to the root—than a fantastic coincidence of melodic tensions. So many details, so great a coordination. The B-flat triad is by now a lightning rod for tension, and that is why all Palestrina's rhythmic momentum can be suddenly suspended there with such breathtaking effect. The transmutation of this momentum into tension of another kind absorbs its force without losing any of it and at the same time provides the brake that makes the dénouement of the first great cadence, long overdue, now possible. That chord, with its acquired semantic of melodic tension, is the only one that could make such a radical change in rhythmic motion so convincing, an instance of the seemingly effortless musical logic for which Palestrina is justly famous.

These details in their fineness elude the newcomer: that an entrance is delayed by a few beats; that the bass does not step but leaps to the scale; the few extra quarter notes. In Brahms such things would hardly be perceptible, never mind be noticed or considered important. The Renaissance sacred language is indeed full of subtle details, and the appreciation of its compositions depends on feeling that the entrance of a voice or the slightest quickening of a rhythm has the perceptual magnitude analogous to—not the same as—a surprising modulation or rapid accelerando in music of later times.

Sicut cervus offers, then, an extraordinary moment constructed out of the most ordinary linguistic materials. Imitation, rhythmic acceleration, use of dissonance, and the notion of textural control are the fundamental syntax of the sixteenth-century sacred language that is still taught in counterpoint classes today, but the cadential passage owes its magic to the focusing of that language.

The idea of focusing has two immediate logical problems. First, where is the line between focusing a language and a commonplace of the language itself? Rosen himself suggests the process of fossilization that must be common when he writes that a style "becomes a dialect or language in its own right."[30] In other words, after a composer hears how the ordinary elements of his language fit together to make something extraordinary, it may then be imitated by others in the community. The focusing, now a device, passes into the language, does it not? Does originality, in the historical sense, affect the perception of the device? The other logical problem is the old fallacy of circular proof, or assuming the consequent. If we rely on the community over time to select the exemplars of style, how can we then criticize the same works by showing how focusing has made them exceptional? If I choose *Sicut cervus* because it is one of Palestrina's best-known motets, as an exemplar of his style, can I then reveal anything worthwhile when elucidating its great moments?

There is no logical circle here, because there are two different inquiries going on. The musical communities of a culture over time identify exemplars of style, but the critic explains their effects on the community. Criteria for these inquiries can be kept separate. There can be one criterion to identify diamonds—the hardness scale, for example— and a completely different theory—crystal structure, perhaps—to explain why they are hard. What can ensure that critics make real explanations, not dressed-up identifications?

Criticism is served well, once again, by an appreciation of technique. Before, it justified the aesthetics of musical syntax in the complexity of the whole matter of tension and resolution. Here it may loosen some of these logical knots by acting as an external criterion of focusing, since focusing is above all a technical concern, as it is in the telescope. Much of the effect of *Sicut cervus*, for example, turns on Palestrina's irregular regularity of subject entrances, now three beats apart, now five, usually four. This idea has a technical implication: Palestrina must design an attractive subject that can be overlapped at three different time intervals and a counterpoint to house it. Easy? Try it. That observation, of course, does not even consider the other rhythmic, harmonic, and textural coordinations that Palestrina makes sound as natural as grace itself. Criticism should aspire to describing, whenever warranted, technical accomplishments that cannot be duplicated, cannot be copied, and therefore cannot be fossilized into the language, because they are beyond the ingenuities of all but their creators and perhaps a few of their most gifted followers. Then critics will have found a definitive break between language and style and some insurance against the critical vicious circle.[31]

Obviously, this passage is not Palestrina's style, at least not by itself. It is perhaps an example of the kind of focusing that characterizes his style across his work; only more criticism will tell. The old notion of style as commonality is still there, but the new notion of style as the focusing of a musical language gives it the richness and critical dimension that it deserves.

In any case, the idea of style as the focusing of a musical language, entailing an essential distinction between the two, goes a long way toward solving the conundrum of uniqueness in musical experience, and it does so along the lines of language. Passages like the cadence approach in *Sicut cervus* are understood, as all unique utterances are understood, as products of a common language and the relevant contexts large and small. Thinking of the passage as a particular focusing of Palestrina's language preserves its uniqueness *within* the sense of style and, no less important, grounds a critical understanding, while hearing it as an instance of sixteenth-century sacred language explains why the listening community can negotiate and appreciate it even though it be the first performance.

Perhaps this distinction can shed a little light on one of the stranger chapters in the history of music, the invention of opera at the beginning of the seventeenth century. A new genre appears on the scene and within a few decades so changes the Western conception of music, from an essentially lyrical and contemplative to a dramatic art, that the moment must rank as one of the few real revolutions in music since the Middle Ages. And yet, there is nothing in the phonology or syntax of Euridice's heartbreaking lament that is new or different from anything that Monteverdi and his contemporaries wrote in their madrigals. But the semantics of the lament is beyond anything that any madrigalist dreamed of; when, before this, could a melodic gesture reach so far back as a whole hour in time to specify a meaning so precise and so profound? This is what we now call music drama. What has changed is not the secular musical language of the Renaissance but its focus. Traditional phonology and syntax are set into a new pragmatics, the new genre of opera, and the change of effect is so salient and powerful that we speak of a change of style. But despite the efforts of some historians to pinpoint the new musical element that heralds this change, I don't believe there is any to be found. To be sure, the possibilities opened up by opera soon caused composers to demand new things of their secular language, things that the sixteenth-century language was not capable of. Paramount among these was the desire to be able to sustain and deepen a dramatic character's expression for long stretches of lyric melody. Technically, that required something that would give the clear monodic texture of the solo singer a range in time that previously only the overlapping kind of counterpoint could reach. The solution, which of course does signal a great linguistic change, was the system of integrated motor rhythm and harmonic rhythm that is the mainstay of the high Baroque. But that came later, in the middle of the century. For that puzzling period at the beginning it is fair to speak of an early Baroque style of Monteverdi that is really a radical refocusing of his native secular Renaissance language.

Perhaps the speculations of these last few pages indicate some of the utility for criticism and analysis, even historical understanding, of a conceptual distinction between musical language and musical style. Bringing such thoughts to a point beyond speculation I think demands a comprehensive theory of style that is substantially different from Leonard Meyer's and from the normative approach in general. It may seem strange to build such a theory on so metaphorical a pillar as "musical language," but the concept of style, while it can be—no—should be shot through with the technical, has always itself been something of a Platonic abstraction. Charles Rosen himself wrote that style is an essential fiction.[32] Metaphors can be powerful things, and the one that compares music with language is truly powerful because the analogy is deep and language itself, like music, is so close to the human identity. That depth, that richness is sorely wanted for an understanding of style.

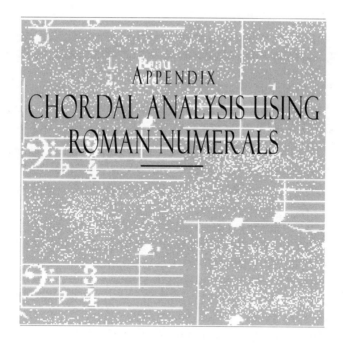

APPENDIX

CHORDAL ANALYSIS USING ROMAN NUMERALS

In this traditional method of harmonic analysis, each significant chord is assigned a Roman numeral that identifies certain qualities of the chord.

The numeral first locates the chord within a set of chords belonging to the key in effect at the moment. The set of seven chords for the key of G major is as follows:

The basis of the set is the G major scale. A three-note chord, or *triad,* is constructed on each note of the scale by superimposing two notes at the intervals of a third and a fifth above the scale note, or *root.*

In actual music, chords need not be heard in the simple forms of the figure; rather, their constituent notes are nearly always transposed and recombined in a great variety of ways. To construct a specific Roman numeral analysis, we look for the presence of the three constituent notes—regardless of the octave in which they are heard—that make up the original triad. A simple example follows:

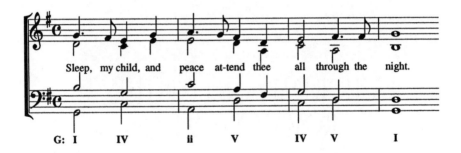

In the most common Roman numeral system, the case of the numeral indicates the quality of the triad: upper case for major, lower case for minor. The addition of a degree sign to the lower case indicates a diminished triad, and a plus sign to the upper case an augmented triad. Arabic superscripts may be added to the Roman numeral to indicate which of the three constituent pitches is sounding lowest.

In its simplest conception, harmonizing a melody means selecting triads whose constituent notes contain the melody note at any given moment. In Figure 2, for example, the first G of the melody is accommodated by the I chord containing G, B, and D as its constituent tones. Both the E and the second G in the first measure can be accommodated by IV, containing C, E, and G. Not every melodic note need match the sounding triad (e.g. the F♯ in measure 1), but the introduction of such *non-harmonic* tones is governed by a fairly strict syntax.

The choice of harmonies is greatly constrained, however, by syntactic relations betwen chords known as *functions*. Traditional theorists identify three functions: the tonic function of stability, conclusion, and rest, associated most clearly with the I chord; the dominant function of instability and motion, associated most clearly with the V chord; and an intermediary subdominant funtion, associated with the IV and ii chords. That is one reason that the end of measure 2 of "All through the night" has a tense, restless quality while the end of measure 4 sounds stable and finished. These syntactic functions control the harmonic tension and resolution of a phrase and give it coherence.

CHAPTER 1

1. The literature that discusses the history of the analogy is extensive. For a general survey along with analytical models for vocal music, see Walther Dürr, *Sprache und Musik: Geschichte, Gattungen, Analysemodelle* (Kassel: Bärenreiter, 1994), especially 18–21. See also Charles Batteux, *Les Beaux arts reduits à un même principe* (Paris: Durand, 1746), 253–55, and Jean-Jacques Rousseau, "Essai sur l'origine des langues" [1781], in *Écrits sur la musique*, vol. 5 of *Oeuvres complètes*, ed. Bernard Gagnebin and Marcel Raymond (Paris: Gallimard, 1995).

Rousseau's opinion is part of the intense debate among intellectuals at the end of the eighteenth century over the origin of human language. The musical implications of this debate are treated in Mark Evan Bonds's *Wordless Rhetoric: Musical Form and the Metaphor of the Oration* (Cambridge, Mass.: Harvard University Press, 1991) and in Charles Rosen's *The Romantic Generation* (Cambridge, Mass.: Harvard University Press, 1995), 58–78.

For a discussion of the Enlightenment thinking on the origins of music and language, see Thomas A. Downing, *Music and the Origins of Language: Theories from the French Enlightenment* (Cambridge: Cambridge University Press, 1995). For a modern defense and review of the hypothesis that "language and music evolved out of a common 'proto-faculty' which was primarily musical in nature" (147), see Bryan G. Levman, "The Genesis of Music and Language," *Ethnomusicology* 36 (Spring 1992): 147–70. For an extensive summary of the literature treating the relation between music and language in anthropological and ethnomusicological studies, see Steven Feld and Aaron A. Fox, "Music and Language," *Annual Review of Anthropology* 23 (1994): 25–53.

2. Oxford University Press reprinted Cooke's 1959 *The Language of Music*, prompting a negative review by Stephen Smoliar, *Computer Music Journal* 18 (1994): 101–5. Bernstein's Norton lectures were published as *The Unanswered Question: Six Talks at Harvard* (Cambridge, Mass.: Harvard University Press, 1976).

3. See Godwin's *The Mystery of the Seven Vowels* (Grand Rapids, Mich.: Phanes Press, 1991), 16,

and W. Jay Dowling and Dane L. Harwood, *Music Cognition* (New York: Academic Press, 1986), 63–74.

4. These spectrographs were generated by an Apple Macintosh computer running Macromedia's Soundedit 16 software. I thank Dr. Williams for introducing me to this software and for his invaluable advice on the interpretation of the graphs and on other matters of phonology.

5. Categorical perception has received a great deal of attention from psychoacousticians. For summaries of the research see Stephen Handel, *Listening* (Cambridge, Mass.: MIT Press, 1989); Rita Aiello and John A. Sloboda, eds., *Musical Perceptions* (New York: Oxford University Press, 1994), chap. 2; and Dowling and Harwood, *Music Cognition*, 91–92.

6. This distinction is indicated in Italian orthography (spelling) by the double consonant. In English the double consonant indicates no difference in its pronunciation.

7. This conflict originates simply enough in the stark contrasts of the parallel modes of D major, containing the F♯, and D minor, the F♮. Much of the thematic material in the exposition is presented this way. See chaps. 4 and 5 for a more detailed discussion of this conflict.

8. David Carroll, *Psychology of Language* (Monterey, Calif.: Brooks/Cole, 1986), 113.

9. The most prominent multilevel model based on this idea is Fred Lerdahl and Ray Jackendoff, *A Generative Theory of Tonal Music* (Cambridge, Mass.: MIT Press, 1983).

10. Roger Lass, *On Explaining Language Change* (Cambridge: Cambridge University Press, 1980), 77.

11. Ibid., 5.

12. David Cruse, *Lexical Semantics* (Cambridge: Cambridge University Press, 1986), 35.

13. *The Merchant of Venice*, Act II, Sc. viii, 39.

14. Carroll, *Psychology of Language*, 130.

15. Lass, *Language Change*, 34.

16. This distinction evidently develops early on in life. Esther Beyer, in *Musikalische und sprachliche Entwicklung in der frühen Kindheit* (Hamburg: R. Krämer, 1994), 211, indicates that children learn individual words before phrase intonation for speech, but in music the order is reversed. Children reproduce contour shapes for melodies long before they reproduce the individual notes accurately.

17. For more detail on this independence of levels, see Ray Jackendoff, *Consciousness and the Computational Mind* (Cambridge, Mass.: MIT Press, 1987), 81.

18. More technical versions of these chapters have appeared as "The Concept of Musical Syntax," *Musical Quarterly* 79 (Summer 1995): 281–308, and "The Range of Musical Semantics," *Journal of Aesthetics and Art Criticism* 54 (1996): 135–52.

19. This position is essential to Roger Scruton, *Aesthetic Understanding* (London: Methuen, 1983), 170: "It is a general rule, indeed, one fundamental to music criticism, that no account of a piece of music is of aesthetic significance unless it is also an account of what we can hear." Indeed, it would seem essential to any phenomenological position.

20. For more details see Joseph P. Swain, "What Is Meant by 'Musical Structure'?" *Criticus Musicus* 2 (1994): 20–44, and "Musical Communities and Music Perception," *Music Perception* 11 (Spring 1994): 307–20.

CHAPTER 2

1. Take any harmonic sequence, for example, that contains a suspension or some other dissonance as part of its pattern, such as that in Example 5.6. If the suspension in the third occurrence is removed and replaced by a chord tone, the change will stand out clearly as an error, and yet the third version will be more acoustically consonant than the previous two versions. The immediate context of the music is critical for detection of errors. That is why that, although the broad historical categories I outlined are generally valid, the salience of wrong notes varies greatly even within a single piece.

2. Arguments against the music and language analogy may be found, among many other places, in Susanne K. Langer, *Philosophy in a New Key: A Study in the Symbolism of Reason, Rite, and Art,* 3d ed. (Cambridge, Mass.: Harvard University Press, 1956); in Harold Powers, "Language Models and Music Analysis," *Ethnomusicology* 25 (1980): 1–60; and in Peter Kivy, *The Corded Shell: Reflections of Musical Expression* (Princeton: Princeton University Press, 1980).

   A representative sample of writing on music that makes syntax an important operative term would include: Benjamin Boretz, "The Construction of a Musical Syntax," parts 1 and 2, *Perspectives of New Music* 9, no. 1 (1970): 23–42, and 9, no. 2–10, no. 1 (1971): 232–70; Werner Breig, "Zur musikalischen Syntax in Schütz 'Geistlicher Chormusik,'" in *Alte Musik als aesthetische Gegenwart: Bach, Händel, Schütz; Bericht über den Internationalen musikwissenschaftlichen Kongress, Stuttgart 1985* (Kassel: Bärenreiter, 1987), 123–31; Edward T. Cone, "On Derivation: Syntax and Rhetoric," *Music Analysis* 6 (1987): 237–55; Peter Faltin, *Phänomenologie der musikalischen Form: Eine Experimentalpsychologische Untersuchung zur Wahrnehmung des musikalischen Materials und der musikalischen Syntax* (Wiesbaden: Franz Steiner Verlag, 1979); Sarah Fuller, "Tendencies and Resolutions: The Directed Progression in Ars Nova Music," *Journal of Music Theory* 36 (1992): 229–58; Hugo Riemann, *Musikalische Syntaxis: Grundriss einer harmonischen Satzbildungslehre* (Leipzig: Breitkopf und Härtel, 1877); and Martin Wehnert, "Zur syntaktisch-semantischen Korrelation in den Streichquartetten Leoš Janáčeks," *Deutsches Jarhbuch der Musikwissenschaft* 18 (1973–1977): 185–94.

3. For example: D. J. Allerton, "Language as Form and Pattern: Grammar and Its Categories," in *An Encyclopaedia of Language,* ed. N. E. Collinge (London and New York: Routledge, 1990), 68–111; Hadumod Bussmann, "Syntax," in *Lexikon der Sprachwissenschaft* (Stuttgart: Alfred Kröner Verlag, 1983), 527–28; and David Crystal, *The Cambridge Encyclopedia of Language* (Cambridge: Cambridge University Press, 1987), 88–99.

4. An analysis of this widespread but problematic concept can be found in Swain, "What Is Meant by 'Musical Structure'?"

5. Benjamin Boretz, "Nelson Goodman's *Languages of Art* from a Musical Point of View," in *Perspectives of Contemporary Music Theory,* ed. Benjamin Boretz and Edward T. Cone (New York: Norton, 1972), 43.

6. William A. Foley and Robert D. Van Valin, Jr., *Functional Syntax and Universal Grammar* (Cambridge: Cambridge University Press, 1984), 7, also 14. See also Nicholas Ruwet, *Syntax and Human Experience,* ed. and trans. John Goldsmith (Chicago: University of Chicago Press, 1991).

7. Eric F. Clarke, "Issues in Language and Music," in *Music and the Cognitive Sciences,* ed. Stephen McAdams and Irene Delière (London: Harwood Academic Press, 1989), 17.

8. Curtis Roads, "Grammars as Representations for Music," in *Foundations of Computer Music,* ed. Curtis Roads and John Strawn (Cambridge, Mass.: MIT Press, 1985), 431.

9. It could be that I have not entirely eliminated syntax even in this strange circumstance, for a hypothetical speaker would have to have some concept of grammatical qualities—"objectness," tense, person, etc.—in order to choose the correct word to express the desired thought. But the evidence of such concepts is no longer in the formations of the words. I thank Daniel Brown for this insight.

10. Two hundred is simply the product of (number of foul types) x (number of available players) x (number of shot options).

11. Terry Winograd, *Language as a Cognitive Process,* vol. 1, *Syntax* (Reading, Mass.: Addison-Wesley, 1983), 75.

12. Donald Davie, *Articulate Energy: An Inquiry into the Syntax of English Poetry* (London: Routledge and Kegan Paul, 1955), 125.

13. This account is greatly simplified of course. See Jackendoff, *Consciousness and the Computational Mind,* 150ff., for a much more detailed account of semantic features.

14. Roger Brown, "The Development of Language in Children," in *Communication, Language, and Meaning: Psychological Perspectives,* ed. George A. Miller (New York: Basic Books, 1973), 112.

15. Davie, *Articulate Energy*, 96.

16. Fred Lerdahl, "Cognitive Constraints on Compositional Systems," in *Generative Processes in Music: The Psychology of Performance, Improvisation, and Composition*, ed. John Sloboda (Oxford: Clarendon Press, 1988), 239; Nelson Goodman, *Languages of Art*, 2d ed. (Indianapolis: Hackett, 1976), chap. 4.

17. This is the conservative end of an estimate that remains under study in cognitive science. For further discussion see Joseph P. Swain, "The Need for Limits in Hierarchical Theories of Music," *Music Perception* 4 (Fall 1986): 121–48, and the introduction to William L. Berz, "Working Memory in Music: A Theoretical Model," *Music Perception* 12 (Spring 1995): 353–64.

18. This limit on memory for abstract information seems to have influenced metric structures down to the lowest levels, for we strongly prefer levels of meter to have only two or three divisions (beats within) all the way up to the phrase, which in certain musical languages often contains a number of measures equal to some factor of two, again like meter, which can easily be divided into smaller subphrase units of equal length. Some research on accent patterns in speech suggests similar groupings, though the regularity is far less strict than it is with traditional meter. See Ray Jackendoff, "Rhythmic Structures in Music and Language," in *Phonetics and Phonology: Rhythm and Meter*, ed. Paul Kiparsky and Gilbert Youmans (New York: Academic Press, 1989), and Alvin Liberman and Alan Prince, "On Stress and Linguistic Rhythm," *Linguistic Inquiry* 8 (1977): 249–336.

19. Chess players will no doubt point to the various phases of a match, including opening, and endgame. But these are not articulate in the same way that a clause or musical cadence is articulate, and since they do not share this discreteness they cannot be considered components of a hierarchy.

20. Edward S. Klima and Ursula Bellugi, *The Signs of Language* (Cambridge, Mass.: Harvard University Press, 1979), 194.

21. This point is elaborated in chap. 4.

22. Jeremy Campbell, *Grammatical Man: Information, Entropy, Language, and Life* (New York: Simon and Schuster, 1982), 119.

23. Eugene Narmour, "The Top-Down and Bottom-Up Systems of Musical Implication: Building on Meyer's Theory of Emotional Syntax," *Music Perception* 9 (Fall 1991): 1–26; A. Rakowski, "Context-dependent Intonation Variants of Melodic Intervals," in *Music, Language, Speech, and Brain*, ed. Johan Sundberg, Lennart Nord, and Rolf Carlson (n.p.: Macmillan, 1991), 203–11; G. B. Simpson, "Lexical Ambiguity and Its Role in Models of Word Recognition," *Psychological Bulletin* 2 (1984): 316–40; Dan Sperber and Deirdre Wilson, *Relevance: Communication and Cognition* (Cambridge, Mass.: Harvard University Press, 1986); and D. A. Swinney, "Lexical Access during Sentence Comprehension: (Re)consideration of Context Effects," *Journal of Verbal Learning and Verbal Behavior* 18 (1979): 645–59; but see Jerry Fodor, *The Modularity of Mind: An Essay on Faculty Psychology* (Cambridge, Mass.: MIT Press, 1983), 78, for an opposing view.

24. Those opposed to any definite semantics include Susanne Langer, *Philosophy in a New Key*, and Eduard Hanslick, *On the Musically Beautiful*, trans. and ed. Geoffry Payzant (Indianapolis: Hackett, 1986). Deryck Cooke's *The Language of Music* is a famous apology in favor, but he proposes far too specific a semantic for music. See chap. 3 for a more thorough discussion.

25. Leonard B. Meyer, *Style and Music: Theory, History, and Ideology*, (Philadelphia: University of Pennsylvania Press, 1989), 14.

26. Lerdahl, "Cognitive Constraints," 245.

27. Fuller, "Tendencies and Resolutions," 232.

28. I much prefer the old-fashioned "tension" and "resolution" to the currently fashionable "closure" and "non-closure" as technical terms with which to discuss syntax. One reason is that "closure" is linked with "structure." There is no closure without a structure being articulated (see Eugene Narmour, *The Analysis and Cognition of Basic Melodic Structures* [Chicago: University of Chicago Press, 1990]). I am not sure if the converse is true, that there are no structures without clo-

sure, but I can think of structures without tension, such as the drone of an Indian raga or the structure of an ostinato movement. At this point I would prefer to use "tension" as a more general quality of "requiring motion" in the music and resolution as "requiring no motion, i.e. stability or rest." The second reason is that I think of tension as a positive musical quality, and it seems inane to write that "the tremendous non-closure of this moment is perfectly timed," or anything similar.

29. Robin Lakoff, linguist, quoted in Campbell, *Grammatical Man*, 100. See chap. 7 of the present book for detailed explanations of linguistic evolution.

30. Meyer, *Style and Music*, 14.

31. See chap. 8.

32. Clarke, "Language and Music," 13.

33. Lerdahl, "Cognitive Constraints," 245.

34. Terence McLaughlin, *Music and Communication* (London: Faber and Faber, 1970).

35. One sophisticated attempt to build such a measuring scale is found in Narmour's *Analysis and Cognition of Basic Melodic Structures*. There he speaks of "closure," which may not be quite synonymous with what I mean by "tension." A more recent application of this approach to parameters of music other than melody may be found in his "Analyzing Form and Measuring Perceptual Content in Mozart's Sonata K. 282: A New Theory of Parametric Analogues," *Music Perception* 13 (1996): 265–318. The same issue presents an alternative model by Fred Lerdahl, "Calculating Tonal Tension," 319–64. Although these theories claim to measure the amount of closure or tension precisely, they rest on the great assumption that tensions from various musical sources and effects are commensurate. This is the assumption I call into question here.

36. "Recursion" is a term derived from mathematics and means that a single pattern or operation is applied over and over at successive levels of the hierarchy.

37. The variations in the minor mode, nos. 15, 21, and 25, use the pattern G minor–D minor–E-flat major–G minor (with V/iv embedded).

38. Disciples of Heinrich Schenker will argue that I have got the recursion all wrong, that the strong cadential progression vi-ii6-V-I is in the background as well as at the surface of the conclusion, and that the "modulations" count for nothing in terms of the real structure. Aside from the oft-heard complaints about the lack of external rules for making such a claim—is the recursion pattern sought out to justify itself or is there some objective criterion to support it?—I would reply that the view does not blunt my question. Is the tension on the high or background level qualitatively different from that on the low level?

39. See chap. 1.

40. Eric Bentley, *The Life of the Drama* (New York: Atheneum, 1964), 154.

41. Meyer, *Style and Music*, 103.

42. The idea of musical community is treated at length in Swain, "Musical Communities and Music Perception," *Music Perception* 11 (1994): 307–20.

43. Donald Francis Tovey, *Essays in Musical Analysis: Chamber Music* (London: Oxford University Press, 1944), 56.

44. Diane Raffman, in *Language, Music, and Mind* (Cambridge, Mass.: MIT Press, 1993), 25, says that these first two aspects alone are enough for most philosophers to recognize a syntax. In that case, the rest serve to distinguish a purely musical syntax.

CHAPTER 3

1. David A. Cruse, "Language, Meaning, and Sense: Semantics," in *An Encyclopaedia of Language*, ed. N. E. Collinge (London: Routledge, 1990), 140.

2. Marianna Pinchot Kastner and Robert G. Crowder, "Perception of the Major/Minor Distinction: IV. Emotional Connotations in Young Children," *Music Perception* 8 (Winter 1990): 189–202.

3. A summary of this kind of problem is in Aaron Ridley, "Musical Sympathies: The Experience of Expressive Music," *Journal of Aesthetics and Art Criticism* 53 (Winter 1995): 49–59.

4. David Osmond-Smith, "Between Music and Language: A View from the Bridge," in *Music and the Cognitive Sciences*, ed. Stephen McAdams and Irene Deliège (London: Harwood Academic Press, 1989), 95.

5. Hilary Putnam, "The Meaning of 'Meaning' " in *Language, Mind, and Knowledge*, ed. K. Gunderson (Minneapolis: University of Minnesota Press, 1975), 168.

6. Ridley, "Musical Sympathies," 49.

7. Igor Stravinsky, *An Autobiography* (New York: Simon and Schuster, 1936), 53; emphasis in original.

8. Raymond Monelle, *Linguistics and Semiotics in Music* (Chur, Switzerland: Harwood, 1992), 10.

9. Langer, *Philosophy in a New Key*, 237.

10. Kivy, *Corded Shell*, especially 39ff., 77.

11. Susanne K. Langer, *Feeling and Form* (New York: Charles Scribner's Sons, 1953), 27.

12. Cruse, *Lexical Semantics*, 9.

13. George A. Miller, "Semantic Relations among Words," in *Linguistic Theory and Psychological Reality*, ed. Morris Halle, Joan Bresnan, and George A. Miller (Cambridge, Mass.: MIT Press, 1978), 71.

14. Some hold propositions to be divorced from truth functions, and some hold pure identities of the form "This is x" to be propositions. It could be argued that this more generalized view of propositions might include musical passages, but that position does not affect the argument that follows. In addition, Jerrold Levinson, in *Music, Art, and Metaphysics: Essays in Philosophical Aesthetics* (Ithaca: Cornell University Press, 1990), 275–76, suggests that the expressive content of music can be propositional by matching up with analogs in the world, but he assumes that everyone will generally agree on how to identify that content. That, of course, is one of the chief problems of a musical semantics. Roger Scruton, on the other hand, seems to regard truth functional propositions as essential for semantic content; see his *Aesthetic Understanding*, 59.

15. See Foley and Van Valin, Jr., *Functional Syntax and Universal Grammar*, 8; Richard E. Grandy, "In Defense of Semantic Fields," in *New Directions in Semantics*, ed. Ernest Lepore (London: Academic Press, 1987), 260; and Ruwet, *Syntax and Human Experience*, 100–101.

16. Langer, *Philosophy in a New Key*, 282.

17. Wye Jamieson Allanbrook, *Rhythmic Gesture in Mozart:* Le Nozze di Figaro *and* Don Giovanni (Chicago: University of Chicago Press, 1983), 2–3.

18. Kofi Agawu, *Playing with Signs: A Semiotic Interpretation of Classic Music* (Princeton: Princeton University Press, 1991), 32.

19. Cruse, "Language, Meaning, and Sense," 141.

20. Allanbrook, *Rhythmic Gestures in Mozart*, 2.

21. Langer, *Philosophy in a New Key*, 232.

22. Walther Dürr concurs in his *Sprache und Musik*, 26, but does not pursue the implications that follow here.

23. Ludwig Wittgenstein discusses what he calls the "haze" of word meaning at great length at the beginning of his *Philosophical Investigations*, trans. G. E. M. Anscombe (Oxford: Basil Blackwell, 1953), beginning p. 4.

24. Cruse, *Lexical Semantics*, 51; see also Susumu Kuno, *Functional Syntax: Anaphora, Discourse, and Empathy* (Chicago: University of Chicago Press, 1987), 2.

25. As many writers have pointed out, a metaphorical context might make sense even of "misspelled floor" and other combinations that in normal speech would be nonsensical. What follows does allow for this possibility.

26. Mary Haas, "Semantic Value," in *Proceedings of the Ninth International Congress of Linguists* (The Hague: Mouton, 1964), 1066–72; see also Cruse, *Lexical Semantics*, 121. This idea also has something in common with Ludwig Wittgenstein's notion of "logical space," first outlined in the *Tractatus Logico-Philosophicus*, trans. D. F. Pears and B. F. McGuinness (1961; reprint Lon-

don: Routledge and Kegan Paul, 1974). I thank Prof. Jerry Balmuth of the Philosophy and Religion Department at Colgate University for showing me this similarity.

27. The idea of semantic range leaves intact the traditional lexical properties of prototypicality, arbitrariness, and discreteness. Prototypical meanings, or core meanings of words, lie at the center of a semantic range, less common or exotic ones at the periphery. (In the case of categories whose members are not so well defined, for instance, "game" vs. "sport," we can suppose the boundaries to overlap.) The arbitrary character of the relationship between the sound of a word and what it means is quite irrelevant, as is the discrete sounds of different words. The semantic ranges of "deck" and "floor" may indeed overlap in the community of English speakers, but there will never be any question about which is being spoken. In addition, the semantic range can include the grammatical function of a word as one of the constraints on appropriate contexts, as at least one important syntactic theory has done. See Joan Bresnan and Ronald M. Kaplan, *The Mental Representation of Grammatical Relations* (Cambridge, Mass.: MIT Press, 1982), xvii–lii.

28. One of the important empirical discoveries of linguists and psycholinguists is the fuzzy boundary in real speech between the theoretical notions of "semantics" and "syntax." It has become clear that syntactic manipulations must take the meaning of words into account, that any change in syntax, such as the change from active to passive voice, affects the meaning of the utterance, and that our memories for lexical items have syntactic "tags"; see, for example, Bresnan and Kaplan, *Mental Representation*, xvii–lii. These interactions need not disturb the traditional connotations of the two terms, namely that "semantics" refers to properties of meaning in language and "syntax" refers to the abstract relations between the things uttered. They indicate only that these two aspects of language are not functionally independent.

Although Peter Kivy denies that music can have a true semantic aspect in *Music Alone* (Ithaca: Cornell University Press, 1990), 100, the notion of musical "expression," perhaps the chief problem in the philosophical aesthetics of music, fits easily into a passages's semantic range as one of its connotations, or perhaps as a kind of index of "primitive feelings" as Jenefer Robinson proposes in "The Expression and Arousal of Emotion in Music," *Journal of Aesthetics and Art Criticism* 52 (1994): 19. Kivy's argument that one cannot give English paraphrases of instrumental music and therefore music cannot be semantic is based on much too narrow a conception of what the semantic element of natural language entails.

29. Hanslick, *On the Musically Beautiful.*

30. Edward Dent, *Handel* (London: Duckworth, 1934), 109.

31. Roger Scruton writes in *Aesthetic Understanding*, 47, that "through the leitmotif above all the music was able to emulate the descriptive range of language."

32. Cruse, *Language, Meaning, and Sense*, 142.

33. Monelle, *Linguistics and Semiotics in Music*, 208.

34. Hanslick, *On the Musically Beautiful*, 20.

35. See chap. 2.

36. Alfred Einstein, *Mozart: His Character, His Work*, trans. Arthur Mendel and Nathan Broder (New York: Oxford University Press, 1945), 190–91.

37. John Burk, *Mozart and His Music* (New York: Random House, 1959), 368.

38. See chap. 2.

39. When Scott Burnham writes that "this is how Beethoven transforms the syntactic into the semantic: the underlying syntax is now charged with meaning and assumes the ethical heft of human significance," he makes a similar judgment to explain the "heroic value" in Beethoven's Fifth Symphony, but I believe that syntactic effect is, *in general*, the most powerful source of meaning in instrumental music. See *Beethoven Hero* (Princeton: Princeton University Press, 1995), 49.

40. Charles Rosen, *The Classical Style* (New York: Viking, 1971), 267.

41. Hanslick, *On the Musically Beautiful*, 32.

42. Levinson argues for the importance of such historical particularities in "Music, Art, and Metaphysics," 68–73.

43. The individual listener resists such simple formulations of "the meaning" such as this one and the one by Einstein in large part because it seems that by agreeing to them, one surrenders the possibility that there might be other concomitant meanings equally illuminating. No one wants to limit the semantics of instrumental music so drastically.

44. Diane Raffman, interpreting Stanley Cavell, arrives at much the same conclusion, at least regarding the "ineffable" aspects of music, via a different route. See her *Language, Music, and Mind*, chap. 3, and Stanley Cavell, "Music Discomposed," in *Art, Mind, and Religion*, ed. W. H. Capitan and D. D. Merrill (Pittsburgh: University of Pittsburgh Press, 1967).

<h3 style="text-align:center">Chapter 4</h3>

1. Stephen Handel's observation that "it takes about twice as long to recognize a word in isolation (350 msec) as in a context (200 msec)" indicates the kind of time scale involved here. See *Listening*, 362.

2. Adapted from a hypothetical example in Geoffrey Leech and Jenny Thomas, "Language, Meaning, and Context: Pragmatics," in *An Encyclopaedia of Language*, ed. N. E. Collinge (London: Routledge, 1990), 197.

3. Handel, *Listening*, 134.

4. Ibid., 154.

5. J. B. Pierrehumbert, "Music and the Phonological Principle: Remarks from the Phonetician's Bench," in *Music, Language, Speech, and Brain*, ed. Johan Sundberg, Lennart Nord, and Rolf Carlson (n.p.: Macmillan, 1991), 140.

6. Milton Babbitt, "Past and Present Concepts of the Nature and Limits of Music," in *Perspectives on Contemporary Music Theory*, ed. Benjamin Boretz and Edward T. Cone (New York: Norton, 1972), 19.

7. David Butler, "Describing the Perception of Tonality in Music: A Critique of the Tonal Hierarchy Theory and a Proposal for a Theory of Intervallic Rivalry," *Music Perception* 6 (Spring, 1989): 235.

8. For example, see Lawrence W. Barsalou, "Intraconcept Similarity and Its Implications for Interconcept Similarity," in *Similarity and Analogical Reasoning*, ed. Stella Vosniadou and Andrew Ortony (Cambridge: Cambridge University Press, 1989), 77–78; George Lakoff and Mark Johnson, *Metaphors We Live By* (Chicago: University of Chicago Press, 1980), 164; David Lewin, "Music Theory, Phenomenology, and Modes of Perception," *Music Perception* 3 (Summer 1986): 342.

9. See chap. 1.

10. Handel, *Listening*, 182, referring Floyd H. Allport, *Theories of Perception and the Concept of Structure* (New York: Wiley, 1955).

11. Lewin, "Music Theory, Phenomenology, and Modes of Perception," 330; Robert O. Gjerdingen, *A Classic Turn of Phrase: Music and the Psychology of Convention* (Philadelphia: University of Pennsylvania Press, 1988), 6.

12. Fodor, *Modularity of Mind*, 53.

13. These ideas are developed and applied to music by Ray Jackendoff in *Consciousness and the Computational Mind* and in "Musical Parsing and Musical Affect," *Music Perception* 9 (Winter 1991): 199–230.

14. Dowling and Harwood, *Music Cognition*, 180; for a review of the psychoacoustical literature, see Berz, "Working Memory in Music," 354.

15. An intriguing negative demonstration of this capacity was provided by Richard M. Warren and his colleagues in "Melodic and Nonmelodic Sequences of Tones: Effects of Duration on Perception," *Music Perception* 8 (Spring 1991): 277–90, which describes how listeners failed to identify very familiar melodies such as "Yankee Doodle" when their tempo slowed to less than one note every 1.3 seconds. Presumably, the working memory could not contain information long enough to identify the tune.

16. "Working memory" is the psychologist's term for a specific model of short-term memory that includes both storage and processors, as distinct from a simple buffer that stores information for a brief time. William Berz believes that the working memory for music is a "loop" distinct from another "loop" used for speech, but whether the mechanisms are absolutely distinct, related, or the same cognitive mechanisms does not affect the argument here. See his "Working Memory in Music."

17. Jackendoff, "Musical Parsing," 215–16.

18. Ray Jackendoff in "Musical Parsing" and Eugene Narmour in *Basic Melodic Structures* and "Musical Implications" have suggested, along the lines of Fodor's cognitive modules, that basic music processors are insulated from context and that they process musical information in the same way regardless of familiarity with the music or other contextual factors. Narmour calls these brute perceptions, assuming that they are involuntary and cannot be unlearned. In this manner a V–vi cadence, even in a work known by heart, always retains some deceptive quality because it is always processed against a standard grammar. Although ingenious, I find this unpersuasive, because musical grammar, like linguistic grammar, is not monolithic. What happens when one hears a V–vi progression in Palestrina or Dufay or Copland? For listeners experienced in these idioms there is no deceptive effect. What has turned off the brutish module? Just as we react to identical phonetics differently in different languages, so do we in music. If not, we could never learn a second language. Even Fodor admits in *Modularity of Mind* (77) that contextual information must participate to this extent.

19. Handel, *Listening*, 298.

20. Narmour, *Basic Melodic Structures*, ix.

21. Ibid., x.

22. The idea of musical community, treated more technically in Swain, "Musical Communities and Music Perception," is similar to Stanley Fish's notion of "interpretive community" in *Is There a Text in This Class? The Authority of Interpretive Communities* (Cambridge, Mass.: Harvard University Press, 1980), 13–15. The two concepts share the notion of a subset within a culture based on cultural knowledge, but I would point out two important differences: (1) musical abilities that define communities are technical, often hierarchically organized, and therefore can be ranked from "basic" to "advanced"; (2) defining a musical community can be accomplished by the measurement of some objective task that is verified externally. This provides an element of objectivity to the membership of a musical community. Fish's communities define themselves by the very interpretations they make, so there is no external verification of membership available.

23. Rosen, *Classical Style*, 387.

24. For more discussion, see Swain, "Musical Communities and Music Perception."

25. This conception of genre derives directly from Sperber and Wilson, *Relevance*, 15.

26. Rosen, *Classical Style*, 404.

27. See chap. 2 on the relation of syntax and technique.

CHAPTER 5

1. Ralph Waldo Emerson, "The Poet," in *The Complete Works of Ralph Waldo Emerson*, vol. 3 (Boston: Houghton Mifflin Company, 1876), 8.

2. William Wordsworth, Preface to *Lyrical Ballads* of 1798, ed. H. Littledale (1911; reprint, London: Oxford University Press, 1959), 246–47.

3. Ezra Pound, "Vers Libre and Arnold Dolmetsch," *The Egoist*, July 1917: 90–91.

4. That is only because these sacred texts were written in stone before musicians could have their say. When church composers could make their own pieces from scratch, poetry returned in full force in the huge repertory of metric hymns and versified psalms.

5. See Lawrence Kramer, *Music and Poetry: The Nineteenth Century and After* (Berkeley: University of California Press, 1984), 6; Monelle, *Linguistics and Semiotics in Music*, 65; Roman Jakob-

son, "Principes de versification" [1923], in *Questions de poétique*, ed. Tzvetan Todorov, 2d ed. (1923; reprint, Paris: Seuil, 1973), 42.

6. Jakobson, "Principes de versification," 45; Percy Bysshe Shelley, *A Defense of Poetry*, ed. Albert S. Cook (Boston: Ginn and Company, 1891), 8.

7. Davie, *Articulate Energy*, 86; emphasis original.

8. Langer, *Philosophy in a New Key*, 260–61; emphasis original.

9. Oscar Williams, ed., *Master Poems of the English Language*, (New York: Washington Square Press, Inc., 1966), 184.

10. William Baker, *Syntax in English Poetry, 1870–1930*, (Berkeley: University of California Press, 1967), 10.

11. Gerard Manley Hopkins quoted in Roman Jakobson, "The Speech Event and the Function of Language," in *On Language*, ed. Linda R. Waugh and Monique Monville-Burston (Cambridge, Mass.: Harvard University Press, 1990), 78.

12. Davie, *Articulate Energy*, 32.

13. Shelley, *A Defense of Poetry*, 4.

14. David Burrell, *Analogy and Philosophical Language*, (New Haven: Yale University Press, 1973), 257–58, 259.

15. Here I use "notion" as a shorthand for "cluster concept," a kind of definition wherein certain aspects or characteristics cluster together to make up a particular instance of a thing, without any single one of them being essential at all times. See chap. 8 for more discussion of the cluster concept.

16. Ray Jackendoff, "Grammar as Evidence for Conceptual Structure," in *Linguistic Theory and Psychological Reality*, ed. Morris Halle, Joan Bresnan, and George A. Miller (Cambridge, Mass.: MIT Press, 1978), 226.

17. Eva Feder Kittay, *Metaphor: Its Cognitive Force and Linguistic Structure* (Oxford: Clarendon Press, 1987), 36.

18. Grandy, "Semantic Fields," 263.

19. Mary Hesse, "The Explanatory Function of Metaphor," in *Revolutions and Reconstructions in the Philosophy of Science* (Bloomington: Indiana University Press, 1980), 114.

   Eva Feder Kittay's *Metaphor* shows that what she calls "the deviant view" must be incomplete, since perfectly good sentences such as "He is up against the wall" can be used metaphorically. This kind of example actually paves the way for a musical analog, because the absurdity here resides not in the linguistic construction itself but in its contextual usage. "He is up against the wall" could only be metaphorical in a context in which it could not be literally true.

20. Davie, *Articulate Energy*, 257–58.

21. Robert Donington, *The Opera* (New York: Harcourt Brace Jovanovich, 1978), 26.

22. Robert Donington attributes the pathos of these moments to melodic outlines of the tritone, and while that is certainly part of the effect, the harmonic juxtapositions with the E-major triad are both a more specific and more palpable effect. See *Opera*, 27.

23. Johann Philipp Kirnberger, in his 1773 treatise *Die wahren Grundsätze zum Gebrauch der Harmonie*, gives his readers a reduction of this fugue as an example of his principles. Although he does not represent the successive levels as consistent harmonic rhythms of eighths, quarters, and half notes, as I do here, his harmonic reductions do account for some of the apparent breaches of traditional rules with similar explanations. See *The True Principles for the Practice of Harmony*, trans. David A. Beach and Jurgen Thym, *Journal of Music Theory* 23 (Fall 1979): 163–227, especially 210–11.

24. Detailed discussion in chap. 4.

25. Rosen, *Classical Style*, 117.

26. Williams, ed., *Master Poems*, 832.

27. For Shelley this stretching is one of the vital signs of a language: "if no new poets should arise to create afresh the associations which have been thus disorganized, language will be dead to all the nobler purposes of human intercourse." See *In Defense of Poetry*, 4–5.

28. See Bonds, *Wordless Rhetoric*, and Leonard G. Ratner, *Classic Music: Expression, Form, and Style* (New York: Schirmer, 1980).

29. Or B-flat major and D minor, depending on whether one considers the gestures in m. 28 as a VI in D minor or another temporary key through which Beethoven passes.

30. See chap. 1.

31. Rosen, *Classical Style*, 51.

32. The furious melody traded between the violins is an interesting example of the Sperber-Wilson relevance thesis applied on the syntactic level. The melody remains unaltered even though the harmony oscillates between i^{6-4} (or I^{6-4}) and V. The ear searches for the greatest possible relevance, using the harmonic context to process A and C (or C♯) as chord tones in the tonic instances, B and D as chord tones in the dominant instances. Thus this Necker Cube–like melody is able to participate in the ostinato while the harmonic rhythm moves relentlessly.

33. All the details would make a treatise, as I said before, but just as an indication of the depth involved here, consider that C is the first new key in the slow introduction of the first movement; that it is put into prominent opposition with C-sharp major in the slow movement built around an A-minor/A-major alternation; that D minor is the last coherent key in the first-movement development, which is turned to a "vague" A minor by the deft introduction of C♯; that the onset of the recapitulation is made clear by the C♯s in the winds, not the resolution of the diminished seventh; that D is used as a subsidiary key, in Neapolitan fashion, in the C-sharp key area in the exposition of the finale, but that in the parallel spot in the recapitulation Beethoven recomposes the relation so the subsidiary key is now C♯ to the principal A major, etc.

34. Scott Burnham asks, "Who . . . is Beethoven's hero? Is he really an Atlas, marked most signally by the presence of strain?" (*Beethoven Hero*, xiv). The syntactic metaphor is the most direct source of this sense.

CHAPTER 6

1. The actual design and execution of artificial languages was of course preceded by a great deal of interest in the problem on the part of various intellectuals and academic societies in the seventeenth and eighteenth centuries. See Albert Léon Guérard, *A Short History of the International Language Movement* (London: T. Fisher Unwin, 1922).

2. For corroborating views, see Carl Dahlhaus, *Analysis and Value Judgment*, trans. Siegmund Levarie (Stuyvesant, N.Y.: Pendragon Press, 1983), 17, and Rose Rosengard Subotnik, "Toward a Deconstruction of Structural Listening: A Critique of Schoenberg, Adorno, and Stravinsky," in *Explorations in Music, the Arts, and Ideas: Essays in Honor of Leonard B. Meyer*, ed. Eugene Narmour and Ruth A. Solie (Stuyvesant, N.Y.: Pendragon Press, 1988), 89.

3. The principal exceptions—early Stravinsky, Bartók, Shostakovitch, Britten, Copland—achieved the same effect by the less conscious, less artificial means of amalgamating their strong individualist tendencies (see main text below) with nationalist tendencies already developed in the nineteenth century. All had strong interest in their musical traditions of their homelands and developed those traits radically in their own compositions. Perhaps they should be known as radical nationalists. It is worth noting in the context of artificial languages that their work, with the possible exception of Bartók, was for all intents and purposes ignored in the composition schools and programs of the mid-twentieth century onward.

4. The aesthetician Theodor Adorno sees many of these systems as the abnegation of music's linguistic aspects: "Composers fell into a state of what Hegel would have termed abstract negation, a technique of consciously induced primitivism, of mere omission. Through an ascetic taboo against everything that was linguistic in music, they hoped to be able to grasp pure musicality in itself—a musical ontology, so to speak—as the residue, as if whatever was left over was then the truth. Or looked at it in a different way, they repressed the nineteenth century instead of transcending it." "Music, Language, and Composition," trans. S. Gillespie, *Musical Quarterly* 77 (1993): 408.

5. Subotnick, "Deconstruction," 89–90.

6. Milton Babbitt, "Who Cares If You Listen?" in *High Fidelity's Silver Anniversary Treasury* (Great Barrington, Mass.: Wyeth Press, 1976), 83.

7. Pieter C. van den Toorn, "What Price Analysis?" *Journal of Music Theory* 33 (Spring 1989): 169.

8. See chap. 2.

9. Rosen, *Classical Style*, 32.

10. Guérard, *International Language Movement*, 82.

11. Bryan Higman, *A Comparative Study of Programming Languages* (New York: American Elsevier, 1967), 8.

12. Lazar Ludwig Zamenhof, quoted in Pierre Janton, *Esperanto: Language, Literature, and Community*, ed. Humphrey Tonkin, trans. by Humphrey Tonkin, Jane Edwards, and Karen Johnson-Weiner (Albany: State University of New York Press, 1993), 24.

13. Zamenhof, quoted in Janton, *Esperanto*, 24–25.

14. Neville J. Ford, *Computer Programming Languages: A Comparative Introduction* (New York: Ellis Horwood, 1990), 3–5.

15. COBOL was designed by an executive committee, headed by Jean Sammet and known as the Short-Range Language Committee in 1959. See Howard Levine and Howard Rheingold, *The Cognitive Connection: Thought and Language in Man and Machine* (New York: Prentice Hall Press, 1987), 156.

16. Levine and Rheingold, *Cognitive Connection*, 153.

17. Previous to this time, in the music known today as the Ars antiqua, duration was expressed by a note's position in a sequential pattern known as a rhythmic mode.

18. Janton, *Esperanto*, 43, 44.

19. Nicholas Cook, *A Guide to Musical Analysis* (New York: George Braziller, 1987), chap. 2.

20. The perspective of music as idea avoids one conundrum that has always plagued the perspective of music as process: the problem of familiarity. If musical effects are dependent upon expectation, surprise, anything that involves the novelty of processing the musical information, then those effects should disappear as one becomes familiar with a composition. Leonard Meyer and his followers have struggled with this problem without as yet any resounding success (for a recent attempt see Jackendoff, "Musical Parsing"). But the idea of a piece, like a sculpture, is open to admiration time after time wihout loss of effect.

21. Richard H. Hoppin, *Medieval Music* (New York: Norton, 1978), 473.

22. Jeremy Yudkin, *Music in Medieval Europe* (Englewood Cliffs, N.J.: Prentice Hall, 1989), 562.

23. Christopher Page, *Discarding Images: Reflections on Music and Culture in Medieval France* (Oxford: Clarendon Press, 1993), 138.

24. Yudkin, *Music in Medieval Europe*, 575.

25. I use the terms "polyphony" and "polyphonic" simply to denote any music that consistently presents more than one pitch at a time, as an antonym to "monophony," "one sound." Thus, harmonic content is implied, but without any specific quality to it.

26. Sarah Fuller has described a phrase-ending syntax in Machaut's music of imperfect consonances, which she calls tendency sonorities, moving to perfect consonances. In particular "In its pronounced implication for resolution, a tendency sonority placed at the inception or the very end of a phrase generates ongoing impetus in and of itself and is the more striking for contradicting conventional expectations for a perfect sonority at such points. Transformation of an expected resolution sonority (R) into a tendency element (T), or substitution of another resolution for the one expected, can deflect the music from an expected tonal orientation toward some new center of pitch reference." See "Tendencies and Resolutions," 256. But since the syntax provides for progression *either* to another tendency sonority or to a resolution, the expectation she describes is weak and certainly does not provide a phrase syntax or govern dissonance treatment in the Ars nova.

Yolanda Plumley argues that "tonal relations play a crucial role in regulating the musical flow in the middleground" but only by such modernist abstraction, and by emphasizing the cadence points, can she articulate the details of the "contrapuntal structures." See *The Grammar of 14th*

Century Melody: Tonal Organization and Compositional Process in the Chansons of Guillaume de Machaut and the Ars Subtilior (New York: Garland, 1996), p. 263.

27. Yudkin, *Music in Medieval Europe*, 574.

28. See chap. 2.

29. Hoppin, *Medieval Music*, 522.

30. One imprecision in the serial system is, ironically, the construction of harmonies, for although the pitch-class content of any vertical simultaneity is fully determined by the series, the order of those pitch-classes in the chord structure from high to low is not specified.

31. van den Toorn, "What Price Analysis?" 177.

32. Lerdahl, "Cognitive Constraints," 251–52.

33. Ibid., 253.

32. Strictly speaking, of course, serialism was not the first music to abandon organization around a tonal center. But Arnold Schoenberg believed his earlier atonal experiments to be limited in scope (see *Style and Idea*, ed. Leonard Stein, trans. Leo Black, [Berkeley: University of California Press, 1975], 252), and serialism certainly became the flagship for atonal composition, as well as the target of all discussion of atonality, after he invented it.

35. Ibid., 86.

36. See chap. 2.

37. Boretz, "Nelson Goodman's *Languages of Art*," 43.

38. Carol L. Krumhansl, *Cognitive Foundations of Musical Pitch* (New York: Oxford University Press, 1990), 270–74.

39. Gustav Mahler, quoted in Samuel Lipman, *Music after Modernism* (New York: Basic Books, 1979), 34.

40. Dahlhaus, *Analysis and Value Judgment*, 54; Cook, *Guide*, 215–16; Jean-Jacques Nattiez, *Music and Discourse: Toward a Semiology of Music*, trans. Carolyn Abbate (Princeton: Princeton University Press, 1990), 154.

41. Cook, *Guide*, 215–16.

42. Schoenberg, *Style and Idea*, 215.

43. Babbitt, "Who Cares?" 83.

44. George Perle, *The Listening Composer* (Berkeley: University of California Press, 1990), 24.

45. van den Toorn, "What Price Analysis?" 169–70.

46. Babbitt, "Who Cares?" 87. It is also possible that composers who use artificial languages such as serialism never believed in the communal aspect of their syntaxes at all, an attitude much more in the line of secret acrostics and symbolisms of Renaissance and Baroque composers, but as amusements for themselves. Aside from dismissing the writing of Schoenberg, Babbitt, and all the others who have explained their systems, the position begs an enormous question: if modernist music is not to be perceived and understood in real time on the basis of their compositional systems, and there is no traditional syntax to organize the sound stream, on what basis are we to understand it? Where is the intuition or rationale that guides a composer's choices, and alerts our hearing to performers' errors, that is analogous to every other musical language of the West from the Middle Ages to the turn of this century? If no candidate can be found, then we must conclude that the sounds are, for all practical purposes, random. There are no wrong notes. That is Cage's position, of course, and all that there is to admire in his music is his philosophy.

47. Schoenberg, *Style and Idea*, 223.

48. See chap. 5.

49. Schoenberg, *Style and Idea*, 87.

CHAPTER 7

1. I use "evolution" not in any strict Darwinian sense, and certainly with no implication of progress, but as linguists use it: to mean gradual changes in a language taken as a whole.

2. Jean Aitchison, *Language Change: Progress or Decay?* 2d ed. (Cambridge: Cambridge University Press, 1991), 32.

3. Ibid., 154–56.

4. Ibid., 125–26.

5. The phonetic/phonemic distinction is discussed in chap. 1.

6. The example here is an Italian madrigal, a vocal genre. In the sixteenth century, however, vocal pieces were routinely adapted and transcribed for instrumental performance, so that the tuning problem described here is real and practical.

7. See chap. 3.

8. It is true that certain medieval theorists ascribed particular qualities to each of the modes, but these seem to exist for the theorists only in a metaphysical sense. At least, there is no correlation between song texts and these qualities, or, if there is, it has been utterly lost to modern listeners.

9. Steven Pinker, *The Language Instinct* (New York: William Morrow, 1994), 250.

10. Aitchinson, *Language Change*, 100.

11. See chap. 2.

12. Analysis of this passage is in chap. 5.

13. Pinker, *Language Instinct*, 222–27.

14. See chap. 2.

15. In a provocative essay, Stephen Pinker elicits a number of examples of rapidly developing creoles and concludes that they arise so quickly because the children, hearing the pidgin during their "critical period" of language learning, actually create a grammar by virtue of innate cognitive design. See *Language Instinct*, chap. 2.

16. Aitchison, *Language Change*, chap. 14.

17. Ibid., 115.

18. Ibid., 59–60.

19. Pinker, *Language Instinct*, 250.

20. Aitchison, *Language Change*, 136.

21. See chap. 6.

22. Aitchison, *Language Change*, 131.

23. Evidently, the sharp symbol, indicating a raised note, was extremely rare in the fourteenth, fifteenth, and early sixteenth centuries. However, the rules indicating the *subsemitonium modi* trace back to the writing of Jehan de Murs in the fourteenth century. Nevertheless, agreement about whether to raise the penultimate cadential note in a case such as this was as difficult in the Renaissance community as it is today. See "Musica ficta," *The New Grove Dictionary of Music and Musicians*, vol. 12 (London: Macmillan, 1980), 805, 807–8.

24. Carl Dahlhaus, *Studies on the Origin of Harmonic Tonality*, trans. Robert O. Gjerdingen (Princeton: Princeton University Press, 1990), 119.

25. Meyer, *Style and Music*, 134; 99–100.

26. See chap. 6.

27. The poetic genres offer analogs, of course, but since poetry is largely a written medium, its perception is fundamentally different from that of music, whose genres must be immediately negotiable.

28. See chap. 8.

29. See chap. 4.

30. See chap. 3.

31. See chap. 2.

32. See Handel, *Listening*, chap. 4, and Swain, "The Need for Limits in Hierarchical Theories of Music."

33. Lass, *On Explaining Language Change*, 119–20.

34. This is a somewhat less formal version of the definition established in my article "Music Perception and Musical Communities," where it reads: "Formally defined, a musical community is

that group of listeners for whom a perceptual object of music is real and has practical value" (311). Note that I also include composers in the term "listeners," because composers are simply community members who happen to produce music as well as perceive it.

Robert Kraut begins an essay with a similar argument: "attributions of musical significance and musical understanding depend upon the specification of a relevant community. To understand a musical event just is to *experience it the way members of the relevant community experience it*" (emphasis in original). However, he does not take the indeterminacy of musical passages to be similar in kind to the indeterminacy of semantic units in language, as I do, and does not seem to account for the various competencies in such communities, so that his analogy does not proceed in the same way. See "Perceiving the Music Correctly," in *The Interpretation of Music: Philosophical Essays*, ed. Michael Krausz (Oxford: Clarendon Press, 1993), 108.

35. Aitchison, *Language Change*, 10.
36. Ibid., 176.
37. Nicholas Cook, "The Perception of Large-Scale Tonal Closure," *Music Perception* 5 (Winter 1987): 197–206.
38. The major exceptions to the principle in practice are operas and oratorios, which substitute for the unifying principle a coherent plot, and certain "loose" genres such as rags and marches in which the second, quite discrete, section is often in the key subdominant to the opening one.
39. J. N. Hattiangadi, *How Is Language Possible? Philosophical Reflections on the Evolution of Language and Knowledge* (La Salle, Ill.: Open Court, 1987), 172

CHAPTER 8

1. There is some evidence that music and speech may share "circuitry" in the physical brain. See Dowling and Harwood, *Music Cognition*, and Oscar S. M. Marin, "Neuropsychology, Mental Cognitive Models, and Music Processing," in *Music and the Cognitive Sciences*, ed. Stephen McAdams and Irene Deliège (London: Harwood Academic, 1989), 255–63.
2. The aesthetician Theodor Adorno also adopts the view, from a completely different rationale, that music is languagelike with essential differences. See "Music, Language, and Composition," 401–14.
3. Wittgenstein says that instead of clear definitions, "we see a complicated network of similarities overlapping and criss-crossing: sometimes overall similarities, sometimes similarities of detail" that he prefers to call a "family resemblance." See *Philosophical Investigations*, 31.
4. Some would disagree. See, for example, Jackendoff, *Consciousness and the Computational Mind*, chap. 8. For a summary of the evidence in favor of prototypes in perception, see Lakoff and Johnson, *Metaphors We Live By*.
5. Lerdahl, "Cognitive Constraints," 245–46.
6. See chap. 1.
7. Shelley, *Defense of Poetry*, 8; Robert Frost, attribution in *The Oxford Dictionary of Quotations*, 3d ed. (Oxford: Oxford University Press, 1979), 219.
8. Nicholas Cook, "Perception: A Perspective from Music Theory," *Musical Perceptions*, ed. Rita Aiello with John Sloboda (New York: Oxford University Press, 1994), 77.
9. See Stephen Pinker's analysis of the pragmatics of the Watergate tapes in *Language Instinct*, 222–27.
10. Powers, "Language Models and Music Analysis," 37–38.
11. A more technical discussion of objectivity, musical discourse, and musical communities may be found in Swain, "Music Perception and Musical Communities."
12. Heidi Dulay, Marina Burt, and Stephen Krashen, *Language Two* (New York: Oxford University Press, 1982), 13–14.
13. Ibid., 14.
14. Pinker, *Language Instinct*, chap. 3.

15. Jamshed Barucha, "Tonality and Expectation," in *Musical Perceptions*, ed. Rita Aiello with John Sloboda (New York: Oxford University Press, 1994), 213–39.
16. Meyer, *Style and Music*, 3.
17. See Joseph P. Swain, "Leonard Meyer's New Theory of Style," *Music Analysis* 11 (July-October 1992): 335–54.
18. Meyer, *Style and Music*, 39, 43.
19. I use "rules" here in the general sense of grammatical rule that obtains throughout this book. Be warned that Meyer has a very specific usage for that word in his book.
20. Meyer, *Style and Music*, 44–48.
21. Ibid., 21. Meyer has held this position for a long time. As a point of departure in *Explaining Music* (Chicago: University of Chicago Press, 1973) he writes on page 7: "Style analysis . . . is normative. It is concerned with discovering and describing those attributes of a composition which are common to a group of works—usually ones which are similar in style, form, or genre. . . . Style analysis, in its pure form, ignores the idiosyncratic in favor of generalization and typology."
22. See chap. 4.
23. Meyer, *Explaining Music*, 6. This position is essentially unchanged in *Style and Music*, 26: "Though criticism depends on the generalizations of style analysis, it uses these to illuminate what is unique about particular compositions."
24. Joseph Kerman, "A Profile for American Musicology," *Journal of the American Musicological Society* 18 (Spring 1965): 65. A form of Meyer's view of criticism as concerned with the exceptional is attributed by aesthetician Patricia Herzog to the aesthetics of Peter Kivy. Kivy describes criticism as a kind of puzzle-solving. See Herzog, "Music Criticism and Musical Meaning," *Journal of Aesthetics and Art Criticism* 53 (Summer 1995): 309.
25. Meyer, *Style and Music*, 60.
26. Rosen, *Classical Style*, 20. Donald Mitchell makes the distinction between style and musical language in his book *The Language of Modern Music* (1963; reprint, London: Faber and Faber, 1993), 73, but never explains it.
27. The technical aspect is consonant with Arnold Schoenberg's notion of style, which is the means by which musical ideas are brought into the world. See his essay "New Music, Outmoded Music, Style and Idea" in *Style and Idea* and Murray Dineen's discussion of it in "Adorno and Schoenberg's Unanswered Question," *Musical Quarterly* 77 (1993): 415–27.
28. Jerome Roche put the matter rather pessimistically: "One might almost say that it is easier to describe Palestrina's motets by what they did not do rather than by what they did." *Palestrina* (London: Oxford University Press, 1971), 35.
29. The source of this tension is the gestalt law of good continuation, which states that a pattern established over time tends to be continued over time. If we have heard eight entrances at intervals of about four beats, we expect that pattern to continue and experience tension when it does not. This is an application of Leonard B. Meyer's classic account of expectation and delay, first proposed in his *Emotion and Meaning in Music* (Chicago: University of Chicago Press, 1956).
30. Rosen, *Classical Style*, 20.
31. In her essay on music criticism Patricia Herzog admits the indispensability of technique ("Music Criticism," 310) but by apparently separating it from music's semantic qualities sells it short as a source of greatness. But it seems inescapable that what can be "expressed" depends on the techniques that create the modes of expression. If Palestrina cannot handle the counterpoint, then that particular effect of his motet is doomed, regardless of the depth of his human personality or his intentions. In music, particularly, how it is said is often the lion's share of what is said.

Herzog's view is not untypical of those who believe strongly in an essential emotional component to musical experience, for whom technical mastery is distracting, even inimical, to the composer's most important goals. In earlier decades this attitude toward technique was so strong that Tovey was moved to write, somewhat ironically that "At the present day, the crudities of those elementary technical makeshifts which are sometimes falsely called 'academic principles' have provoked an equally crude reaction against everything that happens to interest those artists who know the technique of their art. It sometimes seems as if the surest way to damage the reputation of a work is to show that its structure is ingenious beyond the reach of amateurish plodding" (*Essays in Musical Analysis: Chamber Music*, 29).

32. Rosen, *Classical Style*, 22.

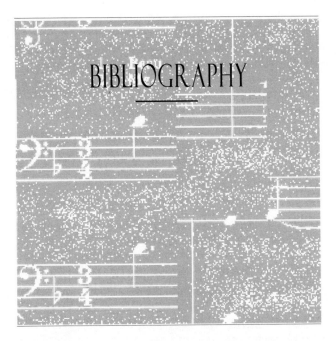

BIBLIOGRAPHY

Adorno, Theodor W. "Music, Language, and Composition." Trans. S. Gillespie. *Musical Quarterly* 77 (1993): 401–14. Originally published as "Musik, Sprache, und ihr Verhältnis im gegenwärtigen Komponieren," in *Semantica*, ed. Archivo di Filosofia (Rome: F. Boca, 1955).

Agawu, Kofi. *Playing with Signs: A Semiotic Interpretation of Classic Music*. Princeton: Princeton University Press, 1991.

Aiello, Rita, and John A. Sloboda, ed. *Musical Perceptions*. New York: Oxford University Press, 1994.

Aitchison, Jean. *Language Change: Progress or Decay?* 2d ed. Cambridge Approaches to Linguistics, ed. Jean Aitchison. Cambridge: Cambridge University Press, 1991.

Allanbrook, Wye Jamieson. *Rhythmic Gesture in Mozart:* Le Nozze di Figaro *and* Don Giovanni. Chicago: University of Chicago Press, 1983.

Allerton, D. J. "Language as Form and Pattern: Grammar and Its Categories." In *An Encyclopaedia of Language*, ed. N. E. Collinge. London: Routledge, 1990.

Allport, Floyd H. *Theories of Perception and the Concept of Structure*. New York: John Wiley and Sons, 1955.

Babbitt, Milton. "Past and Present Concepts of the Nature and Limits of Music." In *Perspectives on Contemporary Music Theory*, ed. Benjamin Boretz and Edward T. Cone. New York: Norton, 1972.

Babbitt, Milton. "Who Cares If You Listen?" In *High Fidelity's Silver Anniversary Treasury*. Great Barrington, Mass.: Wyeth Press, 1976. First published in *High Fidelity*, February 1958.

Baker, William. *Syntax in English Poetry, 1870–1930*. Berkeley: University of California Press, 1967.

Barsalou, Lawrence W. "Intraconcept Similarity and Its Implications for Interconcept Similarity." In *Similarity and Analogical Reasoning*, ed. Stella Vosniadou and Andrew Ortony. Cambridge: Cambridge University Press, 1989.

Bharucha, Jamshed. "Tonality and Expectation." In *Musical Perceptions*, ed. Rita Aiello with John Sloboda. New York: Oxford University Press, 1994.

Batteux, Charles. *Les Beaux arts reduits á un même principe*. Paris: Durand, 1746.

Bentley, Eric. *The Life of the Drama*. New York: Atheneum, 1964.

Bernstein, Leonard. *The Unanswered Question: Six Talks at Harvard*. Cambridge, Mass.: Harvard University Press, 1976.

Berz, William L. "Working Memory in Music: A Theoretical Model." *Music Perception* 12 (Spring 1995): 353–64.

Bever, Thomas G. "Language and Perception." In *Communication, Language, and Meaning: Psychological Perspectives*, ed. George A. Miller. New York: Basic Books, 1973.

Beyer, Esther. *Musikalische und sprachliche Entwicklung in der frühen Kindheit*. Hamburg: R. Krämer, 1994.

Bonds, Mark Evan. *Wordless Rhetoric: Musical Form and the Metaphor of the Oration*. Cambridge, Mass.: Harvard University Press, 1991.

Boretz, Benjamin. "The Construction of a Musical Syntax." Parts 1 and 2. *Perspectives of New Music* 9, no. 1 (1970): 23–42; 9, no. 2–10, no. 1 (1971): 232–70.

———. "Nelson Goodman's *Languages of Art* from a Musical Point of View." In *Perspectives of Contemporary Music Theory*, ed. Benjamin Boretz and Edward T. Cone. New York: Norton, 1972.

Breig, Werner. "Zur musikalischen Syntax in Schütz 'Geistlicher Chormusik.'" In *Alte Musik als aesthetische Gegenwart: Bach, Händel, Schütz; Bericht über den Internationalen musikwissenschaftlichen Kongress, Stuttgart 1985*. Kassel: Bärenreiter, 1987.

Bresnan, Joan, and Ronald M. Kaplan. *The Mental Representation of Grammatical Relations*. Cambridge, Mass.: MIT Press, 1982.

Brown, Roger. "The Development of Language in Children." In *Communication, Language, and Meaning: Psychological Perspectives*, ed. George A. Miller. New York: Basic Books, 1973.

Burk, John. *Mozart and His Music*. New York: Random House, 1959.

Burnham, Scott. *Beethoven Hero*. Princeton: Princeton University Press, 1995.

Burrell, David. *Analogy and Philsophical Language*. New Haven: Yale University Press, 1973.

Bussman, Hadumod. "Syntax." In *Lexikon der Sprachwissenschaft*. Stuttgart: Alfred Kröner, 1983.

Butler, David. "Describing the Perception of Tonality in Music: A Critique of the Tonal Hierarchy Theory and a Proposal for a Theory of Intervallic Rivalry." *Music Perception* 6 (Spring 1989): 219–42.

Campbell, Jeremy. *Grammatical Man: Information, Entropy, Language, and Life*. New York: Simon and Schuster, 1982.

Carroll, David W. *Psychology of Language*. Monterey, Calif: Brooks/Cole, 1986.

Cavell, Stanley. "Music Discomposed." In *Art, Mind, and Religion*, ed. W. H. Capitan and D. D. Merrill. Pittsburgh: University of Pittsburgh Press, 1967.

Clarke, Eric F. "Issues in Language and Music." In *Music and the Cognitive Sciences*, ed. Stephen McAdams and Irene Deliège. London: Harwood Academic, 1989.

Cone, Edward T. "On Derivation: Syntax and Rhetoric." *Music Analysis* 6 (1987): 237–55.

Cook, Nicholas. *A Guide to Musical Analysis*. New York: George Braziller, 1987.

———. "Perception: A Perspective from Music Theory." *Musical Perceptions*, ed. Rita Aiello with John Sloboda. New York: Oxford University Press, 1994.

———. "The Perception of Large-Scale Tonal Closure." *Music Perception* 5 (Winter 1987): 197–206.

Cooke, Deryck. *The Language of Music*. New York: Oxford University Press, 1959.

Cruse, David A. "Language, Meaning, and Sense: Semantics." In *An Encyclopaedia of Language*, ed. N. E. Collinge. London: Routledge, 1990.

———. *Lexical Semantics*. Cambridge: Cambridge University Press, 1986.

Crystal, David. *The Cambridge Encyclopedia of Language*. Cambridge: Cambridge University Press, 1987.

Dahlhaus, Carl. *Analysis and Value Judgment*. Trans. Siegmund Levarie. Stuyvesant, N.Y.: Pendragon Press, 1983.

———. *Studies on the Origin of Harmonic Tonality*. Trans. Robert O. Gjerdingen. Princeton: Princeton University Press, 1990.

Davie, Donald. *Articulate Energy: An Inquiry into the Syntax of English Poetry*. London: Routledge and Kegan Paul, 1955.

Dent, Edward. *Handel*. London: Duckworth, 1934.

Dineen, Murray. "Adorno and Schoenberg's Unanswered Question." *Musical Quarterly* 77 (1993): 415–27.

Donington, Robert. *The Opera*. New York: Harcourt Brace Jovanovich, 1978.

Dowling, W. Jay, and Dane L. Harwood. *Music Cognition*. New York: Academic, 1986.

Downing, Thomas A. *Music and the Origins of Language: Theories from the French Enlightenment*. Cambridge: Cambridge University Press, 1995.

Dulay, Heidi, Marina Burt, and Stephen Krashen. *Language Two*. New York: Oxford University Press, 1982.

Dürr, Walther. *Sprache und Musik: Geschichte, Gattungen, Analysemodelle*. Kassel: Bärenreiter, 1994.

Einstein, Alfred. *Mozart: His Character, His Work*. Trans. Arthur Mendel and Nathan Broder. New York: Oxford University Press, 1945.

Emerson, Ralph Waldo. "The Poet." In *The Complete Works of Ralph Waldo Emerson*. Vol. 3. Boston: Houghton Mifflin Company, 1876.

Faltin, Peter. *Phänomenologie der musikalischen Form: Eine experimentalpsychologische Unter-suchung zur Wahrnehmung des musikalischen Materials und der musikalischen Syntax*. Wiesbaden: Franz Steiner, 1979.

Feld, Steven, and Aaron A. Fox. "Music and Language." *Annual Review of Anthropology* 23 (1994): 25–53.

Fish, Stanley. *Is There a Text in This Class? The Authority of Interpretive Communities*. Cambridge, Mass.: Harvard University Press, 1980.

Fodor, Jerry. *The Modularity of Mind: An Essay on Faculty Psychology*. Cambridge, Mass.: MIT Press, 1983.

Foley, William A., and Robert D. Van Valin, Jr. *Functional Syntax and Universal Grammar*. Cambridge Studies in Linguistics, ed. B. Comrie, vol. 38. Cambridge: Cambridge University Press, 1984.

Ford, Neville J. *Computer Programming Languages: A Comparative Introduction*. New York: Ellis Horwood, 1990.

Fuller, Sarah. "Tendencies and Resolutions: The Directed Progression in *Ars Nova* Music." *Journal of Music Theory* 36 (1992): 229–58.

Gjerdingen, Robert O. *A Classic Turn of Phrase: Music and the Psychology of Convention*. Philadelphia: University of Pennsylvania Press, 1988.

Godwin, Joscelyn. *The Mystery of the Seven Vowels: In Theory and Practice*. Grand Rapids, Mich.: Phanes Press, 1991.

Goodman, Nelson. *Languages of Art: An Approach to a Theory of Symbols*. 2d ed. Indianapolis: Hackett, 1976.

Grandy, Richard E. "In Defense of Semantic Fields." In *New Directions in Semantics*, ed. Ernest Lepore. London: Academic, 1987.

Guérard, Albert Léon. *A Short History of the International Language Movement*. London: T. Fisher Unwin, 1922.

Haas, Mary. "Semantic Value." In *Proceedings of the Ninth International Congress of Linguists*. The Hague: Mouton, 1964.

Handel, Stephen. *Listening: An Introduction to the Perception of Auditory Events*. Cambridge, Mass.: MIT Press, 1989.

Hanslick, Eduard. *On the Musically Beautiful: A Contribution towards the Revision of the Aesthetics of Music*. Trans. and ed. Geoffry Payzant. Indianapolis: Hackett, 1986.

Hattiangadi, J. N. *How Is Language Possible? Philosophical Reflections on the Evolution of Language and Knowledge*. La Salle, Ill.: Open Court, 1987.

Herzog, Patricia. "Music Criticism and Musical Meaning." *Journal of Aesthetics and Art Criticism* 53 (Summer 1995): 299–312.

Hesse, Mary. "The Explanatory Function of Metaphor." In *Revolutions and Reconstructions in the Philosophy of Science*. Bloomington: Indiana University Press, 1980. First published in *Logic, Methodology, and Philosophy of Science*, ed. Y. Bar-Hillel. Amsterdam: n.p., 1965.

Higman, Bryan. *A Comparative Study of Programming Languages*. New York: American Elsevier, 1967.

Hoffmann, E. T. A. *The Poet and the Composer*. 1816.

Hoppin, Richard H. *Medieval Music*. New York: Norton, 1978.

Jackendoff, Ray. *Consciousness and the Computational Mind*. Cambridge, Mass: MIT Press, 1987.

———. "Grammar as Evidence for Conceptual Structure." In *Linguistic Theory and Psychological Reality*, ed. Morris Halle, Joan Bresnan, and George A. Miller. Cambridge, Mass.: MIT Press, 1978.

———. "Musical Parsing and Musical Affect." *Music Perception* 9 (Winter 1991): 199–230.

———. "Rhythmic Structures in Music and Language." In *Phonetics and Phonology: Rhythm and Meter*, ed. Paul Kiparsky and Gilbert Youmans. New York: Academic, 1989.

Jakobson, Roman. "Principes de versification." 1923. Reprint in *Questions de poétique*, ed. Tzvetan Todorov, 2d ed. Paris: Seuil, 1973.

———. "The Speech Event and the Function of Language." In *On Language*, ed. Linda R. Waugh and Monique Monville-Burston. Cambridge, Mass.: Harvard University Press, 1990.

Janton, Pierre. *Esperanto: Language, Literature, and Community*. Ed. Humphrey Tonkin. Trans. Humphrey Tonkin, Jane Edwards, and Karen Johnson-Weiner. Albany: State University of New York Press, 1993.

Kastner, Marianna Pinchot, and Robert G. Crowder. "Perception of the Major/Minor Distinction: IV. Emotional Connotations in Young Children." *Music Perception* 8 (Winter 1990): 189–202.

Kerman, Joseph. "A Profile for American Musicology." *Journal of the American Musicological Society* 18 (Spring 1965): 61–69.

Kirnberger, Johann Philipp. *The True Principles for the Practice of Harmony*. Trans. David A. Beach and Jurgen Thym. *Journal of Music Theory* 23 (Fall 1979): 163–227.

Kittay, Eva Feder. *Metaphor: Its Cognitive Force and Linguistic Structure*. Oxford: Clarendon Press, 1987.

Kivy, Peter. *The Corded Shell: Reflections of Musical Expression*. Princeton: Princeton University Press, 1980.

———. *Music Alone*. Ithaca: Cornell University Press, 1990.

Klima, Edward S., and Ursula Bellugi. *The Signs of Language*. Cambridge, Mass.: Harvard University Press, 1979.

Kramer, Lawrence. *Music and Poetry: The Nineteenth Century and After*. Berkeley: University of California Press, 1984.

Kraut, Robert. "Perceiving the Music Correctly." In *The Interpretation of Music: Philosophical Essays*, ed. Michael Krausz. Oxford: Clarendon Press, 1993.

Krumhansl, Carol L. *Cognitive Foundations of Musical Pitch*. Oxford Psychology Series, no. 17. New York: Oxford University Press, 1990.

Kuno, Susumu. *Functional Syntax: Anaphora, Discourse, and Empathy*. Chicago: University of Chicago Press, 1987.

Lakoff, George, and Mark Johnson. *Metaphors We Live By*. Chicago: University of Chicago Press, 1980.

Langer, Susanne K. *Feeling and Form*. New York: Charles Scribner's Sons, 1953.

———. *Philosophy in a New Key: A Study in the Symbolism of Reason, Rite, and Art*. 3d ed. Cambridge, Mass.: Harvard University Press, 1956.

Lass, Roger. *On Explaining Language Change*. Cambridge Studies in Linguistics, ed. B. Comrie, no. 27. Cambridge: Cambridge University Press, 1980.

Leech, Geoffrey, and Jenny Thomas. "Language, Meaning, and Context: Pragmatics." In *An Encyclopaedia of Language*, ed. N. E. Collinge. London: Routledge, 1990.

Lerdahl, Fred. "Calculating Tonal Tension." *Music Perception* 13 (1996): 319–64.

———. "Cognitive Constraints on Compositional Systems." In *Generative Processes in Music: The Psychology of Performance, Improvisation, and Composition*, ed. John A. Sloboda. Oxford: Clarendon Press, 1988.

Lerdahl, Fred, and Ray Jackendoff. *A Generative Theory of Tonal Music*. Cambridge, Mass.: MIT Press, 1983.

Levine, Howard, and Howard Rheingold. *The Cognitive Connection: Thought and Language in Man and Machine*. New York: Prentice Hall, 1987.

Levinson, Jerrold. *Music, Art, and Metaphysics: Essays in Philosophical Aesthetics*. Ithaca: Cornell University Press, 1990.

Levman, Bryan G. "The Genesis of Music and Language." *Ethnomusicology* 36 (Spring 1992): 147–70.

Lewin, David. "Music Theory, Phenomenology, and Modes of Perception." *Music Perception* 3 (Summer 1986): 327–92.

Liberman, Alvin, and Alan Prince. "On Stress and Linguistic Rhythm." *Linguistic Inquiry* 8 (1977): 249–336.

Lipman, Samuel. *Music after Modernism*. New York: Basic Books, 1979.

Marin, Oscar S. M. "Neuropsychology, Mental Cognitive Models, and Music Processing." In *Music and the Cognitive Sciences*, ed. Stephen McAdams and Irene Deliège. London: Harwood Academic, 1989.

McAdams, Stephen, and Irene Deliège, eds. *Music and the Cognitive Sciences*. London: Harwood Academic, 1989.

McLaughlin, Terence. *Music and Communication*. London: Faber and Faber, 1970.

Meyer, Leonard B. *Emotion and Meaning in Music*. Chicago: University of Chicago Press, 1956.

———. *Explaining Music: Essays and Explorations*. Chicago: University of Chicago Press, 1973.

———. *Style and Music: Theory, History, and Ideology*. Studies in the Criticism and Theory of Music, ed. Leonard B. Meyer. Philadelphia: University of Pennsylvania Press, 1989.

Miller, George A. 1978. "Semantic Relations among Words." In *Linguistic Theory and Psychological Reality*, ed. Morris Halle, Joan Bresnan, and George A. Miller. Cambridge, Mass.: MIT Press, 1978.

Mitchell, Donald. *The Language of Modern Music*. 1963. Reprint, London: Faber and Faber, 1993.

Monelle, Raymond. *Linguistics and Semiotics in Music*. Chur, Switzerland: Harwood, 1992.

"Musica Ficta." In *The New Grove Dictionary of Music and Musicians*, ed. Stanley Sadie. London: Macmillan, 1980.

Narmour, Eugene. *The Analysis and Cognition of Basic Melodic Structures: The Implication-Realization Model*. Chicago: University of Chicago Press, 1990.

———. "Analyzing Form and Measuring Perceptual Content in Mozart's Sonata K. 282: A New Theory of Parametric Analogues." *Music Perception* 13 (1996): 265–318.

———. "The Top-Down and Bottom-Up Systems of Musical Implication: Building on Meyer's Theory of Emotional Syntax." *Music Perception* 9 (Fall 1991): 1–26.

Nattiez, Jean-Jacques. *Music and Discourse: Toward a Semiology of Music*. Trans. Carolyn Abbate. Princeton: Princeton University Press, 1990.

Osmond-Smith, David. "Between Music and Language: A View from the Bridge." In *Music and the Cognitive Sciences*, ed. Stephen McAdams and Irene Deliège. London: Harwood Academic, 1989.

Page, Christopher. *Discarding Images: Reflections on Music and Culture in Medieval France*. Oxford: Clarendon Press, 1993.

Perle, George. *The Listening Composer*. Berkeley: University of California Press, 1990.

Pierrehumbert, J. B. "Music and the Phonological Principle: Remarks from the Phonetician's Bench." In *Music, Language, Speech, and Brain*, ed. Johan Sundberg, Lennart Nord, and Rolf Carlson. Wenner-Gren Center International Symposium Series, no. 59. N.p.: Macmillan, 1991.

Pinker, Steven. *The Language Instinct*. New York: William Morrow, 1994.

Plumley, Yolanda. *The Grammar of 14th Century Melody: Tonal Organization and Compositional Process in the Chansons of Guillaume de Machaut and the Ars Subtilior*. New York: Garland, 1996.

Pound, Ezra. "Vers Libre and Arnold Dolmetsch." *Egoist*, July 1917: 90–91.

Powers, Harold. "Language Models and Music Analysis." *Ethnomusicology* 25 (1980): 1–60.

Putnam, Hilary. "The Meaning of 'Meaning.'" In *Language, Mind, and Knowledge*, ed. K. Gunderson. Minnesota Studies in the Philosophy of Science, no. 7. Minneapolis: University of Minnesota Press, 1975.

Raffman, Diane. *Music, Language, and Mind*. Cambridge, Mass.: MIT Press, 1993.

Rakowski, A. 1991. "Context-dependent Intonation Variants of Melodic Intervals." In *Music, Language, Speech, and Brain*, ed. Johan Sundberg, Lennart Nord, and Rolf Carlson. Wenner-Gren Center International Symposium Series, no. 59. N.p.: Macmillan, 1991.

Ratner, Leonard G. *Classic Music: Expression, Form, and Style*. New York: Schirmer, 1980.

Ridley, Aaron. "Musical Sympathies: The Experience of Expressive Music." *Journal of Aesthetics and Art Criticism* 53 (1995): 49–59.

Riemann, Hugo. *Musikalische Syntaxis: Grundriss einer harmonischen Satzbildungslehre*. Leipzig: Breitkopf und Härtel, 1877.

Roads, Curtis. "Grammars as Representations for Music." In *Foundations of Computer Music*, ed. Curtis Roads and John Strawn. Cambridge, Mass.: MIT Press, 1985.

Robinson, Jenefer. "The Expression and Arousal of Emotion in Music." *Journal of Aesthetics and Art Criticism* 52 (Winter 1994): 13–22.

Roche, Jerome. *Palestrina*. London: Oxford University Press, 1971.

Rosen, Charles. *The Classical Style: Haydn, Mozart, Beethoven*. Expanded ed. New York: Norton, 1997.

———. *The Romantic Generation*. Cambridge, Mass.: Harvard University Press, 1995.

Rousseau, Jean-Jacques. "Essai sur l'origine des langues." 1781. Reprint in *Écrits sur la musique*. Vol. 5 of *Oeuvres complètes*, ed. Bernard Gagnebin and Marcel Raymond. Paris: Gallimard, 1995.

Ruwet, Nicholas. *Syntax and Human Experience*. Ed. and trans. John Goldsmith. Chicago: University of Chicago Press, 1991.

Schoenberg, Arnold. *Style and Idea*. Ed. Leonard Stein. Trans. Leo Black. Berkeley: University of California Press, 1975.

Scruton, Roger. *Aesthetic Understanding*. London: Methuen, 1983.

Shelley, Percy Bysshe. *A Defense of Poetry*. Ed. Albert S. Cook. Boston: Ginn, 1891.

Simpson, G. B. "Lexical Ambiguity and Its Role in Models of Word Recognition." *Psychological Bulletin* 2 (1984): 316–40.

Smoliar, Stephen. Review of *The Language of Music* by Deryck Cooke. *Computer Music Journal* 18 (1994): 101–5.

Sperber, Dan, and Deirdre Wilson. *Relevance: Communication and Cognition*. Cambridge, Mass.: Harvard University Press, 1986.

Stravinsky, Igor. *An Autobiography*. New York: Simon and Schuster, 1936.

Subotnik, Rose Rosengard. "Toward a Deconstruction of Structural Listening: A Critique of Schoenberg, Adorno, and Stravinksy." In *Explorations in Music, the Arts, and Ideas: Essays in Honor of Leonard B. Meyer*, ed. Eugene Narmour and Ruth A. Solie. Stuyvesant, N.Y.: Pendragon Press, 1988.

Swain, Joseph P. "The Concept of Musical Syntax." *Musical Quarterly* 79 (Summer 1995): 281–308.

———. "Leonard Meyer's New Theory of Style." *Music Analysis* 11 (July-October 1992): 335–54.

———. "Musical Communities and Music Perception." *Music Perception* 11 (Spring 1994): 307–20.

———. "The Need for Limits in Hierarchical Theories of Music." *Music Perception* 4 (Fall 1986): 121–48.

———. "The Range of Musical Semantics." *Journal of Aesthetics and Art Criticism* 54 (Spring 1996): 135–52.

———. "What Is Meant by 'Musical Structure'?" *Criticus Musicus* 2 (1994): 20–44.

Swinney, D. A. "Lexical Access during Sentence Comprehension: (Re)consideration of Context Effects." Journal of Verbal Learning and Verbal Behavior 18 (1979): 645–59.

Tovey, Donald Francis. *Essays in Musical Analysis: Chamber Music*. London: Oxford University Press, 1944.

van den Toorn, Pieter C. "What Price Analysis?" *Journal of Music Theory* 33 (Spring 1989): 165–89.

Warren, Richard M. "Melodic and Nonmelodic Sequences of Tones: Effects of Duration on Perception." *Music Perception* 8 (Spring 1991): 277–90.

Wehnert, Martin. "Zur syntaktischen-semantischen Korrelation in den Streichquartetten Leoš Janáčeks." *Deutsches Jarhbuch der Musikwissenschaft* 18 (1973–1977): 185–94.

Williams, Oscar, ed. *Master Poems of the English Language*. New York: Washington Square Press, 1966.

Winograd, Terry. *Language as a Cognitive Process*. Vol. 1, *Syntax*. Reading, Mass.: Addison-Wesley, 1983.

Wittgenstein, Ludwig. *Philosophical Investigations*. Trans. G. E. M. Anscombe. Oxford: Basil Blackwell, 1953.

Wordsworth, William. Preface to *Lyrical Ballads* of 1798. 1911. Reprint ed. H. Littledale, London: Oxford University Press, 1959.

Yudkin, Jeremy. *Music in Medieval Europe*. Englewood Cliffs, N.J.: Prentice Hall, 1989.

GLOSSARY

artificial language a language whose components, including fundamental elements, their proper syntactic relations, and their semantic content, are invented by a single person or small group. Examples include Esperanto and BASIC.

binary opposition phonological model specifying phonetic features in pairs of opposite traits, e.g., voiced vs. unvoiced, rounded vs. unrounded, high vowels vs. low vowels.

bottom-up perceptual processing by which the information contained in incoming stimuli is integrated to construct the percept.

cadence harmonic-melodic event in music that conveys the end of a phrase or larger articulation.

canon passage of strict imitation, as in a round.

cantus firmus repeating melody, often borrowed from the chant repertory and presented in slow rhythms, around which a motet or Mass movement is composed.

categorical perception mode of perception that instantly classifies a stimulus as an example of a type, such as the phoneme /t/ as opposed to /d/, disregarding fine differences among particular instances.

chant vocal music, often associated with religion and religious ritual, whose chief characteristic is the lack of a consistent meter. In the Western tradition, chant is monophonic, that is, unharmonized.

co-articulation altered pronounciation of a particular phoneme caused by the requirements of surrounding phonemes in speech. This deformation is normally not noticed by listeners or controlled by speakers.

complementarity principle of serial composition that specifies the relation of a subset of the twelve possible pitch classes to another mutually exclusive subset.

connotation the set of all concepts that may be associated with a word or concept; the broad meaning, often distinguished from denotation.

consonance, acoustic or sensory the criterion of consonance deriving from the Pythagorean harmonic ratios, not from the preferences or uses of a particular musical community.

context-free language an artificial language or system of symbols that claims no dependence on externals of any kind, including background information about the outside world or immediate contextual information.

denotation set of things or concepts to which a word or concept applies; similar to extension of a term; a restricted kind of meaning, often contrasted with connotation.

diphthong a vowel that varies in quality within the syllable (e.g., English "house").

discreteness property of lexical items in a language (words, mostly) providing a kind of categorical relation between the sound tokens representing those items and their meanings, so that mispronunciation or purposeful alteration of sounds does not change attached meanings in any kind of gradual way.

dominant fifth note of a traditional Western major or minor scale; also, a chord constructed on such a note, characterized by high harmonic tension that is resolved by motion to the tonic triad; also, the key related to the "home" or central tonic of a composition by the interval of a fifth.

embedding syntactic principle by which particular units in a pattern may each be elaborated by lower-level structural patterns made up of similar units. Example: the object in "He doesn't know *what he is doing*" contains within itself all the constitutents of a sentence.

features characteristics that specify a particular sound, e.g., voiced, bilabial, stop (/b/).

frequency formants concentrations of energy in sound output, appearing on spectrographs as spots at particular frequencies.

fugue a composition that highlights imitation.

functional harmony progressions of chords ordered by specific syntactic relations that produce effects of tension and resolution, typical of Western music after ca. 1600.

generative grammar theory of grammar providing a finite set of rules capable of producing all the possible legitimate sentences in a natural language.

gestalt laws fundamental principles of perception that account for intuitive integration of parts into wholes. Proximity (the relative closeness of components in space or time), similarity (the degree to which components resemble one another), and good continuation (the progress of a predictable trend) are the three most often cited.

harmonic progression sequence of chords.

harmonic rhythm rate of chord change.

harmonics higher pitches that accompany the production of a fundamental pitch at certain intervals; strong ones usually occur at the perfect octave, twelfth (perfect fifth), and seventeenth (major third) above the fundamental.

icon one of Charles Peirce's three types of meaning in which the referent has a physical resemblence with the signifier, as in onomatopoeia.

imitation a contrapuntal texture based on a single theme, as when one voice (leader) overlaps another (follower) that enters with the same theme first heard in the leader.

index one of Charles Peirce's three types of meaning in which the referent has some causal or necessary relation with the signifier, e.g., smoke is an index of fire.

interlingual transfer the appearance of habits and forms of one's native language in a second language where they may or may not be appropriate.

interval vector a description of the interval content of a pitch-class set.

intonation in linguistics, the pattern of stresses and tones in speech; in music, the art of playing the required pitches precisely in tune.

inversion occurs when the successive intervals between the notes of a melody are reversed in direction. An upward leap of a fifth is converted into a downward leap of a fifth, etc. Also, any chord in which its root is not the lowest sounding pitch.

isorhythm organizational technique associated with the music of the Ars nova of the fourteenth century that provides a repeated melody of relatively slow durations. The specific pattern of relative durations and pitches does not change during the composition. Over this structural melody, other faster moving and more freely composed melodies are added.

leitmotif a theme or motive in an opera that comes to represent some object in the opera: character, emotion, physical object, relation, etc.

lexicon part of linguistic memory that stores semantic information, or word meanings; also, the store of word meanings in any given language.

libretto text for an opera

linguistic community group that shares tacit knowledge of a natural language.

long-term memory apparently limitless store of comparatively durable information that is consciously recalled. This information, particularly when learned through language, is stored in forms unlike the original percepts, which is why we can recall what a recent speech was about without recalling the exact words used. Many believe it to be stored in networks, whereby the predicates and connotations of one bit of information may be connected to those of related bits in complex arrays.

meter consistent pattern of accented and unaccented beats.

motet medieval composition using a melodic fragment of chant in its tenor voice and combining it with faster-moving voices above, which often have different texts. Also, a Renaissance piece of polyphony, ususally setting one of the psalms or some other single sacred text.

motive short but characteristic melodic-rhythmic pattern, e.g., the first four notes of Beethoven's famous Fifth Symphony; a musical thought.

musical community a group of listeners for whom a perceptual object of music is real and has practical value.

natural language a language whose components, including fundamental elements, their proper syntactic relations, their semantic content, and their pragmatic conventions, are taught by communities defined by that language (e.g., English, Japanese, Hindi, etc.).

Neapolitan musical relation deriving from the chromatically lowered second step of the scale. The Neapolitan relation in D major would be signified by the pitch E♭.

onset transients the acoustic information corresponding to the initial excitation of a musical note or, in speech, of a consonant; typically, this information will differ markedly from the steady state of a note and will often carry important acoustic cues that help the hearer identify the instrument or the consonant itself.

ostinato composition that repeats a bass melody without change while continuously inventing accompanying melodies above it.

period in some theories of musical phrasing, a pair of phrases based on the same melodic-harmonic material, the first of which makes an incomplete cadence and the second of which makes a complete one.

pitch class group of pitches that share the same letter designation (e.g., all B♭s) and thus share octave relations with one another.

phone sound unit of speech, defined in universal terms.

phoneme mentally conceived sound unit of a particular natural language.

phonetics aspect of linguistics concerned with the production and acoustics of sounds in languages.

phonology aspect of a language concerning the available sounds and their interrelationships.

polyphony music in which more than one melody at a time is heard simultaneously; any harmonized melody

pragmatics aspect of a language concerning the practical applications of phonology, syntax, and semantics and their results; the use of language in real situations.

presentational meaning meaning without predication, e.g., the meaning of a single word in isolation.

proposition an abstraction that relates a person to a particular belief or other attitude, typically expressed in language by a verb such as "think," "deny," etc. (very often implied only) followed by a "that" clause.

recursion linguistic principle by which a grammatical item (sentence, noun phrase, verb phrase, etc.) in a sentence can subsume or dominate another similar grammatical item in a hierarchical system. Example: the sentence "He doesn't know *what he is doing*" governs within itself all the constitutents of another sentence: "What is he doing?"

reference semantic aspect of language by which words or other semantic units indicate things in the world.

referent in one account of meaning, the thing pointed to by the sound token.

resolution a perception of musical stability or stopping in the apparent motion of music.

retrograde the backwards version of a melody.

row a sequence of the twelve available pitch classes, each used once, that forms the basis of a serial composition. Characteristic manipulations of this sequence include transposition, inversion, retrograde, and retrograde inversion.

scalar system of arranging sound values along a continuum such as pitch. Each individual is characterized by its position along the scale.

semantics aspect of a language that concerns meaning, including the language's power to refer, to denote, to connote, to communicate with other members of the linguistic community.

semiotics theory associated with the analysis of signs.

semitone one half step, the smallest interval in the inventory of Western major and minor scales.

sensory consonance and dissonance the criterion of consonance and dissonance deriving from the Pythagorean harmonic ratios, not from the preferences or uses of a particular musical community.

serialism twentieth-century compositional theory providing that pitch syntax is founded in a unique ordered sequence (series or tone row) of the twelve available pitch classes for each composition. Every melody or harmony of that composition is built from that sequence or one of its standard derivations: its transposition, its inversion, its retrograde, or its inverted retrograde. Other musical elements such as dynamics or duration may also be ordered for a particular composition, thus further predetermining the profile of individual musical events.

symbol one of Charles Peirce's three types of meaning in which the referent has an arbitrary relation with the signifier.

syntax aspect of a language that concerns the proper arrangement of items (usually words) in sequence.

tension a perception of instability in music, an apparent necessity to continue with further musical events.

texture the number of voices in a polyphonic composition; also, the quality of their relationship. When each voice seems significant, the texture is contrapuntal; when one predominates, the texture is homophonic.

tonic the central pitch of a tonal composition, toward which melodic and harmonic motion tend, indicated by the key of the piece; also, the triad constructed on that pitch, characterized by harmonic stability.

top-down perceptual processing that uses background knowledge and immediate context to interpret the stimuli impinging on the senses at any given moment and to make predictions about upcoming stimuli.

topic a traditional musical figure having a semantic value commonly shared among members of a musical community, e.g., "storm" music, fanfares, dirge music, etc.

transposition changing the pitches of a melody or musical pattern while maintaining the internal patterns of intervals. This preserves the original identity of the melody even though its transposed version is made up of notes different from its original version.

triad most typical chord structure of the Western tradition, consisting of the set of a note (the root), two notes superimposed at the intervals of a third and fifth, and all their octave transpositions.

truth values the evaluation of a proposition as true or false.

word painting setting of text to music in such a way that the music presents an iconic image of the meaning of the text, e.g., a descending melody for the word "falling."

working memory psychologist's term for a specific model of short-term memory that includes both storage and processors, as distinct from a simple buffer that stores information for a brief time.

INDEX

Bold type indicates a musical example.